Table of Contents

Communicating Data
with Tableau

Ben Jones

Beijing · Cambridge · Farnham · Köln · Sebastopol · Tokyo

Communicating Data with Tableau

by Ben Jones

Printed in the United States of America.

Published by O'Reilly Media, Inc., 1005 Gravenstein Highway North, Sebastopol, CA 95472.

O'Reilly books may be purchased for educational, business, or sales promotional use. Online editions are also available for most titles (*http://my.safaribooksonline.com*). For more information, contact our corporate/institutional sales department: 800-998-9938 or *corporate@oreilly.com*.

Editor: Julie Steele	**Indexer:** Lucie Haskins
Production Editor: Kristen Brown	**Cover Designer:** Karen Montgomery
Copyeditor: Jasmine Kwityn	**Interior Designer:** David Futato
Proofreader: Eliahu Sussman	**Illustrator:** Rebecca Demarest

June 2014:   First Edition

Revision History for the First Edition:

2014-06-12:   First release

See *http://oreilly.com/catalog/errata.csp?isbn=9781449372026* for release details.

ISBN: 978-1-449-37202-6

[LSI]

Preface

There is a huge opportunity to find and share the insights contained in data. This is not a new development. People from Florence Nightingale to William Playfair to Dr. John Snow and countless others have been changing the world with data for centuries.

The challenges we face today are different, and so are the tools at our disposal. But just as back then, the person who would perfect the art of communicating data in our time must be at once analytical, articulate, and creative. That is to say: the result, when done well, often involves a combination of numbers, words, and images.

More than anything, however, empathy is required. The person doing the communicating must understand the members of the audience: what will make sense to them, what motivates them, and what concerns them. The inherent challenge and the resulting satisfaction of making a meaningful impact with data are what draw me to this endeavor more than anything else.

Tableau Software has developed and created a visualization querying engine and user interface that make it easy to discover and communicate with data. Once you get the hang of it, it can be a real pleasure to use. Tableau makes it possible to quickly view data from a number of different angles, to combine it with additional data sets and conduct a more sophisticated analysis, and to craft a message that will really hit home.

But to fully unlock the power of Tableau, the communicator of data needs to appreciate what will work well in each particular situation. The software is designed to steer the user down the straight and narrow pathway of best practices, but it is up to the user to know when to adhere to rules of thumb, and when to break them. Also, there are many options to choose from, and many decisions to make when crafting a message. It's important to understand the range of alternatives, how to use each one well, and which to employ.

In my current role as Tableau Public Product Manager at Tableau, I have the privilege of interacting with a host of talented individuals who are setting data free from the confines of spreadsheets and tables and making it easy to see what the data shows about our world. On my own blog, I have been attempting to do the same thing for the past three years, and after dozens of projects and experiments, I have learned a number of techniques that work well, and some that don't work so well.

In this book, I have attempted to provide advice to the would-be communicators of data, to guide them in the proper usage of Tableau to achieve the desired effect. My hope is that this book will help others learn what I have learned, and avoid the mistakes I wasn't wise enough to dodge the first time around.

Intended Audience

This book is for anyone who has data and who wants to use it to learn something about their world, which they can then share with others around them. More particularly, it's for people who are brand new to Tableau, or who have been using it for a while but are looking to improve the outcome of their communication efforts. That applies to analysts and managers in corporations, journalists within media organizations, leaders of nonprofits, researchers, teachers, and anyone else who is passionate about a subject for which data is available.

Tableau is a software tool for programmers and nonprogrammers alike. It does not require knowledge of any computer programming languages as a prerequisite, but a basic familiarity with data types, spreadsheets, and statistics is necessary. The examples used throughout the book can be re-created by connecting to Excel spreadsheets that are available for download on *http://dataremixed.com/books/cdwt*. While Tableau Desktop allows users to connect to data in a wide variety of databases, cloud sources, and Hadoop technologies, the goal is to provide material that anyone can follow along with.

Although even experts can learn from others, I haven't particularly geared this book toward the guru-level Tableau user. Furthermore, it's not intended to be an exhaustive manual that covers every function and feature in the software.

At the time of writing of the first version of this book, Tableau Desktop 8.1 and Tableau Public 8.1 are available for purchase and download, respectively. A free trial version of Tableau Desktop 8.1 can also be downloaded and installed. Tableau is currently available for Windows only.

Assumptions This Book Makes

This book assumes that the reader has data and that it's ready to use. Example files are available in a formatted and cleaned state, but this book will not cover all of the steps necessary to get a data set into this state. While these data wrangling tasks often account for much of the time and effort involved in any project, they go beyond the scope of what's covered in this book.

This book further assumes that the reader has access to Tableau Desktop 8.1 or Tableau Public 8.1, which is currently only available to install on Windows.

Contents of This Book

Chapter 1, *Communicating Data*, discusses the basic process of encoding a data-driven message into a signal and transmitting (presenting) it to receivers (audience members), who then decode it and take some action based on their understanding of the message.

Chapter 2, *Introduction to Tableau*, deals with the different software products that Tableau offers, as well as the basics of the Tableau user interface.

Chapter 3, *How Much and How Many*, teaches how to communicate a single group of absolute numerical quantities in the form of measurements (how much) and counts (how many).

Chapter 4, *Ratios and Rates*, covers normalized comparisons of a single group of quotients that either have the same units (ratios) or different units (rates). Calculated fields and ranks are introduced, and a simple data blending example is included.

Chapter 5, *Proportions and Percentages*, covers another kind of normalized comparison: part-to-whole relationships per unit and per one hundred. We'll introduce Quick Filters, Table Calcs, and reference lines in this chapter.

Chapter 6, *Mean and Median*, deals with the important topic of measures of central tendency, featuring the new box-and-whisker plot chart type, as well as the oft-used dual-axis chart.

Chapter 7, *Variation and Uncertainty*, addresses a challenging but important topic by showing readers how to give an accurate and honest view of the real world, instead of painting an overly simplistic picture.

Chapter 8, *Multiple Quantities*, takes the analysis to a new dimension by considering how to effectively communicate more than one variable at a time. Scatterplots, tooltips, and trend lines feature prominently in this chapter.

Chapter 9, *Changes Over Time*, tackles a critical element of every data visualization: time. Simple methods like line plots are included as well as more advanced chart types like connected scatterplots, Gantt bar charts, and slopegraphs.

Chapter 10, *Maps and Location*, walks the reader through the fundamental concepts of visualizing geospatial data by creating both circle maps and filled maps.

Chapter 11, *Advanced Maps*, covers more sophisticated map types such as shape maps, maps with paths, custom background images, and mapping shape files on axes.

Chapter 12, *The Joy of Dashboards*, is a tour of different styles of dashboards: explanatory, exploratory, storytelling, and infographics. This chapter gives a sense of the different ways people combine multiple charts and objects into a single view.

Chapter 13, *Building Dashboards*, shows readers how to employ an eight-step process to build richly interactive dashboards in Tableau.

Chapter 14, *Advanced Dashboard Features*, gives readers a sense of how dashboards can be enhanced with web pages, tabs, navigation affordances, and animation.

Conventions Used in This Book

The following typographical conventions are used in this book:

Plain text
> Indicates keyboard accelerators (such as Alt and Ctrl).

Italic
> Indicates new terms, URLs, email addresses, filenames, file extensions, pathnames, directories, menu titles, menu options, and menu buttons.

`Constant width`
> Indicates commands, options, fields, types, properties, parameters, values, objects, events, event handlers, the contents of files, or the output from commands.

`Constant width bold`
> Shows commands or other text that should be typed literally by the user.

`Constant width italic`
> Shows text that should be replaced with user-supplied values.

 This element signifies a tip, suggestion, or general note.

 This element indicates a warning or caution.

Using Code Examples

Supplemental material (examples, exercises, etc.) is available for download at *http://dataremixed.com/books/cdwt*.

This book is here to help you get your job done. In general, you may use the code in this book in your programs and documentation. You do not need to contact us for permission unless you're reproducing a significant portion of the code. For example, writing a program that uses several chunks of code from this book does not require permission. Selling or distributing a CD-ROM of examples from O'Reilly books does require permission. Answering a question by citing this book and quoting example code does not require permission. Incorporating a significant amount of example code from this book into your product's documentation does require permission.

We appreciate, but do not require, attribution. An attribution usually includes the title, author, publisher, and ISBN. For example: "*Communicating Data with Tableau* by Ben Jones. Copyright 2014 Ben Jones, 978-1-449-37202-6."

If you feel your use of code examples falls outside fair use or the permission given above, feel free to contact us at *permissions@oreilly.com*.

Safari® Books Online

 Safari Books Online (*www.safaribooksonline.com*) is an on-demand digital library that delivers expert content in both book and video form from the world's leading authors in technology and business.

Technology professionals, software developers, web designers, and business and creative professionals use Safari Books Online as their primary resource for research, problem solving, learning, and certification training.

Safari Books Online offers a range of product mixes and pricing programs for organizations, government agencies, and individuals. Subscribers have access to thousands of books, training videos, and prepublication manuscripts in one fully searchable database from publishers like O'Reilly Media, Prentice Hall Professional, Addison-Wesley Professional, Microsoft Press, Sams, Que, Peachpit Press, Focal Press, Cisco Press, John Wiley & Sons, Syngress, Morgan Kaufmann, IBM Redbooks, Packt, Adobe Press, FT Press, Apress, Manning, New Riders, McGraw-Hill, Jones & Bartlett, Course Technology, and dozens more. For more information about Safari Books Online, please visit us online.

How to Contact Us

Please address comments and questions concerning this book to the publisher:

O'Reilly Media, Inc.
1005 Gravenstein Highway North
Sebastopol, CA 95472
800-998-9938 (in the United States or Canada)
707-829-0515 (international or local)
707-829-0104 (fax)

We have a web page for this book, where we list errata, examples, and any additional information. You can access this page at *http://bit.ly/comm-data-tableau*.

To comment or ask technical questions about this book, send email to *bookquestions@oreilly.com*.

For more information about our books, courses, conferences, and news, see our website at *http://www.oreilly.com*.

Find us on Facebook: *http://facebook.com/oreilly*

Follow us on Twitter: *http://twitter.com/oreillymedia*

Watch us on YouTube: *http://www.youtube.com/oreillymedia*

Acknowledgments

I'd like to thank the founders and developers of Tableau Software for making the product that makes this book possible, and for being bold enough to make such a highly functional version of the product, Tableau Public, entirely free. I wouldn't have gotten started without it.

I'd like to thank O'Reilly Media for agreeing to work with this first-time author, and my editor, Julie Steele, for helping me navigate what turned out to be a much more challenging and time-consuming endeavor than I expected.

I'd also like to thank all the people who have taught me what I know over the years: the gracious and welcoming community of data visualization enthusiasts and professionals like Andy Kirk, Alberto Cairo, and Santiago Ortiz; the incredibly talented community of Tableau Public authors like Joe Mako, Andy Kriebel, Peter Gilks, Jonathan Drummey, Ramon Martinez, Kelly Martin, Anya A'Hearn, Robb Tufts, Ryan Sleeper, and countless others; and my colleagues within Tableau who share my passion for data, like Ellie Fields, Andy Cotgreave, Mike Klaczynski, Jewel Loree, Daniel Hom, and Dustin Smith, to name just a few.

Lastly, and most importantly, I'd like to thank my wife, Sarah, and our two wonderful sons, Aaron and Simon, who supported me in so many ways throughout the writing of this book, which was also our first year in the Seattle area. You three mean everything to me.

Sarah, I dedicate this book to you.

CHAPTER 1

Communicating Data

*"As the cathedral is to its foundation
so is an effective presentation of facts
to the data."*

—Willard Cope Brinton

There's something breathtaking about witnessing data communicated well—it's a lot like encountering an architectural wonder. Think of the first time you saw the video of Hans Rosling interacting with global development data on stage, or when you first viewed a well-designed *New York Times* visualization online. When data is communicated well, it's easy to appreciate both the data itself and the delivery of that data at the same time. Those two elements can be fashioned together into an overall experience that makes you feel that you understand the world better, and that you want to do something with your newfound understanding.

On the other hand, think of a time when you suffered through a presentation at work that included poorly designed charts and graphs containing extraneous information, or all those infographics you wish you never laid eyes on that skewed the figures horribly and left you feeling dumber. Either the foundation was hopelessly cracked or the building itself was inexcusably shabby, or both. Not every building is a cathedral.

What's the difference between these two types of experiences? It's a question of whether those who designed and delivered the message were adept at communicating data.

This is a book about just that. Communicating data is simply a special case of communicating in general (more about that in a minute)—one that incorporates quantitative statements about the universe. In this context, we aren't using the word "data" in the general sense of factual information, but in the more specific sense of "information in numerical form that can be digitally transmitted or processed" (*http://bit.ly/mw-dic*)—ones and zeros in databases, spreadsheets, and tables.

This is also a book about using Tableau. This book will show you how to use Tableau to communicate data well, though you can apply the principles and methods covered in this book to using other tools. It's not intended to be an exhaustive Tableau manual, nor is it intended to guide you in the actual acquiring and storing of your data. While those are necessary steps, the goal of this book is to help you take all that data you have and convey its message with efficiency and impact.

A Step in the Process

How is "communicating data" distinct from the other steps in the overall process that begins with a question and ends with a shared insight? Figure 1-1 presents the overall data discovery process, and shows where communicating data fits in that process.

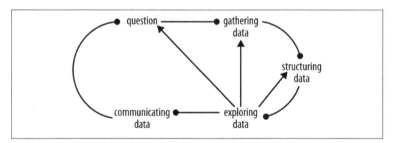

Figure 1-1. The data discovery process

The highly iterative process often begins with a *question*, which can be specific ("which combination of products occurs the most often?") or general ("what can we learn about historical sales of our products?"). The next step is *gathering data* if it's available (e.g., historical sales). Then comes the often arduous process of *structuring data*, also called "data munging" or "data wrangling." In this step, data is formatted, shaped, merged, converted, and otherwise manipulated into a form that is amenable to the next step, *exploring data*. In this step, the data is viewed and analyzed from a number of angles until one or more insights are gleaned. These insights form the message involved in *communicating data*, the step at which quantitative statements are shared with others. While this book primarily concerns this final step, it will also touch on the other steps in the process, as they contribute to the formation of the message to be communicated.

In order to examine the idea of communicating data in greater detail, let's return to the birthplace of information theory: Bell Laboratories.

A Model of Communication

The year was 1949, and two employees at Bell Laboratories—Claude Elwood Shannon and his coauthor Warren Weaver—published a seminal article in the University of Illinois Press called *The Mathematical Theory of Communication (http://bit.ly/shannon-weaver)*. In it, they introduced a model of communication systems in which an "information source" selects a message and then a "transmitter" changes this message into the signal which is actually sent over the communication channel from the transmitter to the receiver" (see Figure 1-2).

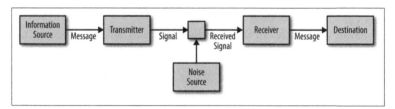

Figure 1-2. A model of communication systems

To illustrate the model, consider oral speech: the information source is the brain of a certain person; the transmitter is this person's vocal system; the channel is the sound waves that travel as particles in the air collide; the receiver is the auditory system of a second person; and the destination is this second person's brain. The noise source includes other sounds present at the time the first person speaks.

Shannon and Weaver describe how this model can apply to a wide variety of cases, including those in which the symbols are "written letters or words, or musical notes, or spoken words, or symphonic music, or pictures." Put simply, the model describes the process of one mind attempting to affect another, and it's the very essence of the human experience.

In this book, we're dealing with the case in which the symbols communicated are abstract graphic representations of data in the form of charts, graphs, and maps: data visualizations. Viewing the communication of data in this conceptual framework is helpful because it reminds us of what we should be taking into account. Knowing how the system can fail is a key first step.

Three Types of Communication Problems

In order to begin to understand how we can communicate data well, it's helpful to consider the types of communication problems that Shannon and Weaver identified:

The technical problem
> How accurately can the symbols of communication be transmitted?

The semantic problem
> How precisely do the transmitted symbols convey the desired meaning?

The effectiveness problem
> How effectively does the received meaning affect conduct in the desired way?

As far as technology has advanced since these problems were outlined, we still often suffer from *technical problems*—inadequate screen resolution, broken audio, grainy video, poor print quality—anything that results in the receiver receiving something different than what was originally crafted. Considering all the different devices, operating systems, and software the person on the receiving end could be using, it can be challenging to make sure the message itself is intact.

The *semantic problem* occurs when we encode the message using inappropriate visualization types, or when the symbols chosen won't be understood by the person on the receiving end. For example, encoding a value using a circle's diameter rather than its area will skew the perceived proportions (see Figure 1-3).

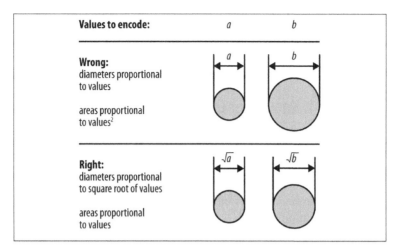

Figure 1-3. Sizing proportional to area rather than diameter

Another example of the semantic problem occurs when symbols are used that are only understood by a subset of all the audience members, such as the donkey and elephant icons that represent the Democratic and Republican parties of the American political system.

The *effectiveness problem* is the "so what?" problem, and it might be the most important. If everything falls into place, and the message is perfectly encoded, transmitted, decoded, and understood, but the recipient doesn't care, or doesn't take the desired action, then the communication ultimately failed.

Six Principles of Communicating Data

In order to address these three types of communication problems, I'd like to propose six principles to consider when communicating data. They are numbered in the general order that they transpire, though it's fully recognized that this process is highly iterative and rarely proceeds in a straight line. Communicating is a creative process—one that involves crafting and refining a message—and as such it will necessarily involve many loops:

1. Know your goal
2. Use the right data
3. Select suitable visualizations
4. Design for aesthetics

5. Choose an effective medium and channel

6. Check the results

Let's look at these principles in detail.

Principle #1: Know Your Goal

It's important to note that "information" and the "message" are not synonymous. Information is the set of all possible messages that can be selected by the information source. The message is what was selected from this set to be communicated. Why does this matter? In a world where information is increasing exponentially, choosing your message is an important first step.

Before you choose your message, however, it's critical to know your goal, which you can articulate by answering a few key questions up front (see Figure 1-4):

- Who are you trying to communicate with? (target audience)
- What do you want them to know? (intended meaning)
- Why? What do you want them to do about it? (desired effect)

Figure 1-4. Elements of the goal

The answers to these questions may be very different for different disciplines. A data journalist working on a breaking story doesn't have the same goal as a business intelligence analyst working in a corporation. That they would communicate data differently shouldn't be surprising, and may be entirely appropriate.

The important part is articulating your goal—actually writing out the answers to the three questions just listed. If you're not certain about the answer to any one of these questions, don't go any further until you're sure. (And it's OK if your sole purpose is to make someone laugh. You don't have to be trying to achieve world peace with every data message.)

Principle #2: Use the Right Data

As the saying goes, sometimes less is more. One of the most impactful examples of communicating data that I've ever seen involved the presentation of a single number: 14. That was the single data point shared with a group of managers assembled to discuss customer service within an organization. The group of managers came to learn that this number represented the number of times a particular customer had been transferred between departments during a single call to a helpline. It motivated an entire organization to revamp the customer experience.

Sometimes less is really less, though. While driving in the car, I heard a report on the radio in which a number of cities were compared based on the percentage of fish packages that were mislabeled. Digging into the data myself later that day, I found that the sample sizes were too small to infer much of anything about the relative mislabeling rates in the cities. A whole host of listeners were misled by the story at least as much as by the fish labels.

And more is often less. It's possible, and actually quite typical, to overwhelm the audience with data. It's easy to see why this happens: you worked hard to gather the data, and it feels like that data increases the weight of your message and lends additional credibility. But all that extra data only serves to drown out the message. Shannon and Weaver identified this problem: "if you overcrowd the capacity of the audience, you force a general and inescapable error and confusion." In other words, if a data point doesn't add to your message, then it detracts from it.

The last and most important point about selecting data is that your message must be both ethical and based on sound epistemology. In other words: don't lie with statistics—we have enough of that to contend with already. Don't fall prey to the many and various forms of statistical and logical fallacies, such as mistaking correlation for causation, taking unreasonable inductive leaps, applying the Gaussian when it doesn't apply, inferring more than the sample size allows, and so on. These are just a few of the many icebergs to avoid (in this book, I hope to show you how to avoid some of them when you use Tableau).

Principle #3: Select Suitable Visualizations

Once you've identified the data that you'll need to make your point, the next step is deciding how to encode the message. Encoding the data means converting the data values themselves into abstract graphical representations, like size or color or shape.

Knowing how the human mind makes use of different graphical displays of information to perform specific tasks is the key to avoiding the semantic problem (wherein the symbols don't convey the intended meaning precisely). Luckily for us, the last half-century has produced pioneers in the field of information visualization who have shed considerable light on this topic.

What type of data do you have?

Tableau's own Jock Mackinlay has produced a helpful framework for identifying the order of effectiveness of different encoding variables based on the type of data being used. First, let's start with a description of the different types of data: quantitative, ordinal, and nominal (see Figure 1-5).

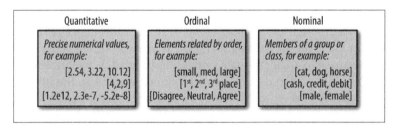

Figure 1-5. Different types of data

What are the most effective types of visualizations for your data type?

Once you've identified what data type or types you will need to get your point across, you need to decide what variables you will use (*http://bit.ly/great-vis*) to encode the data (see Figure 1-6).

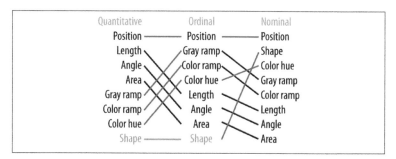

Figure 1-6. Effectiveness of data encoding

A few points are immediately obvious:

- Position is the most effective form of encoding for all data types.
- Length, angle, and area decrease in effectiveness from quantitative to ordinal to nominal.
- Color hue increases in effectiveness from quantitative to ordinal to nominal.

Keeping this ranking in mind as you select your visualization type will help ensure you are crafting a message that will be easily decoded and understood by your audience.

If the overall quality of the communication were only affected by the ease of decoding, we would not need any more principles. In actuality, we also need to consider aesthetics, media and channel, and the actual impact.

Principle #4: Design for Aesthetics

Let me play devil's advocate: Why consider aesthetics at all? Isn't any attempt to make a visualization "look better" just chart junk or design fluff? Won't graphic elements that aren't data just get it the way? Shouldn't the data itself be beautiful enough for readers?

I understand this viewpoint, I really do. I've seen plenty of attempts to beautify data visualizations that either distract the audience or, worse, distort the data so as to completely mislead the audience. We all agree that this result must be avoided. One way to avoid it is to banish all aesthetic elements forevermore. And yet, that's not a world I'd want to live in, because there is a clear value to elegant design and what Willard

Cope Brinton called "judicious embellishment of charts" (*http://bit.ly/ brinton-charts*).

The value? Aesthetic elements can arouse interest and enhance memory. So long as they do so without overly hampering cognition, they can be used to achieve the goal.

There are a number of aesthetic elements of every data visualization, and a handful of common mistakes people make when creating them:

- Poor color schemes
- Distracting fonts
- Many different fonts
- Sloppy alignment
- Vertical or angled labels
- Dark background colors
- Thick borders or grid lines
- Useless images and clip art
- Lazily accepting most software defaults

Consider Figure 1-7, which shows two charts that illustrate the growth of the number of possible moves in a chess game as the game progresses. The default Excel chart is on the left and a redesigned version is on the right.

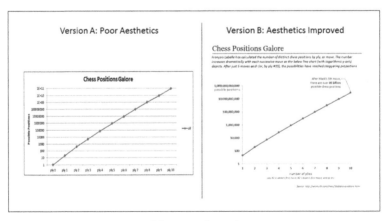

Figure 1-7. Two versions of the same line plot

In both cases, it's just a line on a log-linear scale, but which are you more likely to pay attention to? Aesthetics matters.

Figure 1-8 shows another example of poor design and improved design, this time showing the growth of employment at Apple after the return of Steve Jobs in 1997.

A little design goes a long way. If you know a good graphic artist, take her out for coffee and get her input. Design is a whole separate discipline that you could spend a lifetime learning about and perfecting, but paying even a small amount of attention to how your data visualizations look can mean the difference between being ignored and arousing interest, or between being quickly forgotten and being remembered for a while to come.

In this book, we'll cover how to address the aesthetics of visualizations created in Tableau.

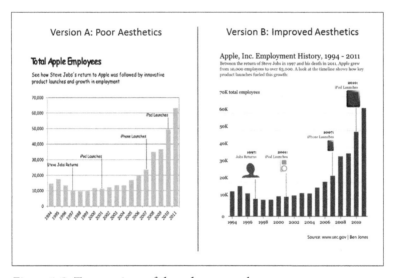

Figure 1-8. Two versions of the column graph

Principle #5: Choose an Effective Medium and Channel

What form the message takes (medium) and how it gets delivered to the audience (channel) are critical elements of any data communication effort. Care needs to be taken in selecting the "how," the "when," and the "where" to improve the chances that your audience is reached and your goals are met.

Earlier, I referred to Hans Rosling's famous presentation at TED in February of 2006: the animation of the GapMinder scatterplot, along with the narration and the pointing and arm waving, are key features of the communication effort. The data set he was presenting was complex, and the communication effort was also complex. He pulled it off, and the impact has been incredibly deep.

When you communicate data, there are a few choices to make about how you will do it:

- Standalone graphics or narrated?
- Static, interactive, animated, or combined graphics?
- If narrated: recorded, live, or both?
- If live: remote, in person, or both?
- In all cases: broadcast, directed, or both?

The framework in Figure 1-9 shows how these choices typically relate in terms of effort, reach, and likely impact.

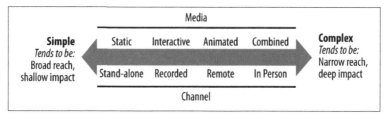

Figure 1-9. A spectrum of data communication types

On the one hand, it's obviously very simple and easy to create a static chart and send an email to a group of colleagues or publish it to the Web as a standalone graphic. This approach to communicating data could have a very deep impact on your target audience, but it most likely will not. It's also important to note that the cost in time and effort is very low.

On the other hand, narrating a combined set of static and dynamic graphics in person to a live audience is a very complex endeavor. A limited number of people will be present, but if you pull it off like Hans Rosling has, the impact could be enormous. The effort is high (and don't forget to rehearse).

These are both extreme examples of communicating data. The area in between these two extremes includes publishing blog posts that combine interactive data visualizations and detailed commentary—something Tableau Public makes very easy to do.

As with anything, there is a trade-off between cost and impact at play here. If your target audience is a small firm in South Africa and the stakes are high, for example, getting on an airplane to walk them through the data may be a good investment. On the other hand, if you'd like as many people as possible in the general public to receive a data message, you'll have to find an effective way to broadcast the message. Knowing your goal, and knowing who makes up your target audience, informs these decisions.

Principle #6: Check the Results

It is a good habit in general to incorporate into your efforts feedback loops and checkpoints that help you gauge whether you've achieved your intended results or not. This allows for course correction in the case of woefully unmet goals, or fine-tuning in the case of slight miscues.

There are a few questions to ask when you check the results. We'll call this the "RUI":

Reach
> Did the audience even receive your message at all? Who did and who didn't?

Understanding
> Did the audience interpret the data message in the way you intended?

Impact
> Did the audience react in the way you wanted them to react?

Asking these questions will help you hone your message and communicate data better, and it also will show an appropriate degree of respect to your audience.

Summary

In this chapter, we considered the act of communicating data as an integral step in a larger data discovery process, and an important type of communication in general. We also considered three problems that can get in the way of communicating data well—the technical problem, the semantic problem, and the effectiveness problem. Lastly, we considered six principles to overcome these problems and achieve our goals. These six principles can be applied regardless of the tool or software used.

In the next chapter, we'll provide a general overview of one particular software tool for communicating data: Tableau.

CHAPTER 2

Introduction to Tableau

"We help people see and understand data."

—Tableau Software mission statement

Tableau software helps people communicate data through an innovation called VizQL, a visual query language that converts drag-and-drop actions into data queries, allowing users to quickly find and share insights in their data. The version of Tableau available at the time of writing is Tableau 8.

The goal of this chapter is to help you understand the different types of Tableau software, the basic user interface, how Tableau deals with data, and how data can be visualized in a variety of different ways. If you are already an intermediate Tableau user, you may want to skip this chapter and move on to Chapter 3.

Using Tableau

With Tableau, "data workers" first connect to data stored in files, cubes, databases, warehouses, Hadoop technologies, and even some cloud sources like Google Analytics. They then interact with the Tableau user interface to simultaneously query the data and view the results in charts, graphs, and maps that can be arranged together on dashboards. When it's time to communicate key insights, there are a variety of options depending on the product being used, from sending files to embedding interactive visualizations online to sharing via social media.

Tableau facilitates the data discovery process (finding insights in data) as well as the data communication process (creating explanatory graphics, exploratory dashboards, and data storytelling) with no programming required.

My Tableau Story

The first time I encountered Tableau, I was researching data visualization tools and methods because I recognized a huge gap between what I could do with the tools at my disposal and what I wanted to do. It was 2011, and I had come to accept that sharing richly interactive data dashboards on the Web would require me to learn a programming language like D3 or Processing. Having done just enough programming in engineering school (if Fortran still counts as programming) and beyond to feel up for the challenge, I set about to see what I could do.

In the early stages of learning to code, a contact of mine recommended that I download Tableau Public, the freely available version of the data visualization PC software, and experiment with the user interface. I did, and after watching a few online training videos, I was amazed at what I could do in my very first session. I began creating data visualizations and embedding them in a WordPress site, and connecting with an online community of enthusiasts and experts.

Tableau Products

Chances are you bought this book because you already have one or more Tableau products and you'd like to learn how to use them better. For those who aren't already familiar with the different data visualization software products Tableau offers (*http://bit.ly/tableau-prod*), there are four main types:

Tableau Desktop
A Windows application that comes in two editions (Personal and Professional), and is most useful for analysts and business users. Personal allows connection to files and local saving only, while Professional also allows individuals to connect to a wider variety of data sources and save to your own server, Tableau Online servers, or Tableau Public servers.

Tableau Server
> Best suited for enterprise-wide deployments, this is a business in-
> telligence system for secure access to enterprise data and user in-
> teraction via web portals on a company intranet (requires Desktop
> Professional).

Tableau Online
> A new hosted solution for storing and accessing data dashboards
> in the cloud (requires Desktop Professional), this is geared toward
> consultants and companies.

Tableau Public
> The best option for journalists and bloggers, Tableau Public is a
> free application and visualization hosting service for sharing of
> publicly available data on the Web (exists as a standalone Win-
> dows application, or can be published to via Desktop Professio-
> nal).

All four of these products incorporate essentially the same data visualization user interface and VizQL engine. As you can see from this
list, Tableau Desktop Professional is the cornerstone product that allows users to access the other products. The products differ in the types
of data sources users can connect to and how visualizations can be
shared with others.

There are two other minor products that round out the offerings:

Tableau Public Premium
> An annual subscription service that allows customers to prevent
> viewers of visualizations hosted on Tableau Public from down-
> loading the workbook and accessing the underlying data (also re-
> quires purchase of Desktop Professional).

Tableau Reader
> A free Windows application that allows users to open saved Ta-
> bleau workbook files (*.twbx*) and to view and interact with visu-
> alizations that have been created and saved locally with Tableau
> Desktop or downloaded from the Web via Tableau Public. Users
> of Tableau Reader cannot create new visualizations or change the
> design of existing ones.

Figure 2-1 illustrates how these products interact to allow the user to
convert data stored in various formats into visualizations and then
share them with others.

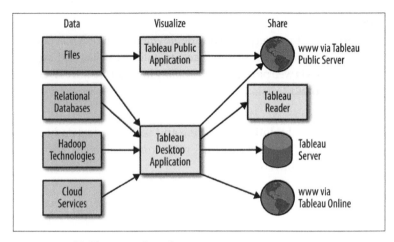

Figure 2-1. Tableau product diagram

Connecting to Data

Tableau Desktop Professional allows users to connect to an unlimited amount of data stored in the following types of data sources:

- Files such as Excel, Access, comma-delimited files, and Tableau Data Extracts
- Traditional relational databases such as MySQL and Oracle
- Hadoop technologies such as Hortonworks Hadoop Hive and Cloudera Hadoop
- Cloud sources such as Google Analytics and Salesforce

For a complete list, see the online Tableau Product technical specification sheet (*http://bit.ly/tableau-specs*).

Tableau Desktop Personal and Tableau Public only allow users to connect to Excel, Access, comma-delimited files, and OData sources. Tableau Reader only opens packaged Tableau workbooks (*.txbx*), and as previously mentioned, is "read-only."

The Tableau User Interface

Every Tableau workbook contains both sheets and dashboards. Sheets are for creating individual visualizations, and dashboards are for combining sheets and other objects like images, text, and web pages on the same canvas, and adding interactions between them such as filtering and highlighting. Let's consider these elements separately.

Sheets

After connecting to a data source in Tableau, the user will be presented with the Tableau user interface for a Sheet (Figure 2-2 shows it connected to the sample data set "World Bank Indicators" that comes with Tableau Desktop).

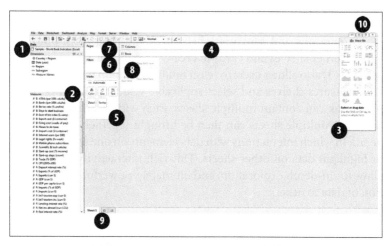

Figure 2-2. The Tableau user interface for a new Sheet

The following are the major components of the Sheet view, as indicated in the screen shot in Figure 2-2:

1. The list of data sources (can be more than one)

2. Dimensions and Measures: fields available to visualize in the selected data source

3. The "Show Me" card (shown opened): view applicable visualization types for selected fields

4. The Columns and Rows shelves: controls grouping headers (Dimensions) and axes (Measures)

5. The Marks card: control visualization encoding of color, size, label text, tooltip text, and shape

6. The Filters shelf: filters visualizations by Dimensions or Measures

7. The Pages shelf: filters the visualization by stepping or animating based on a particular field

8. The view itself: this is the "canvas" where the data visualizations will appear

9. Sheets and Dashboard tabs: show what has been created or create new Sheets or Dashboards

10. The session tabs: connect to data, show all tabs in a workbook, or see all workbooks for a user

The drag-and-drop user interface allows users to click on the fields in the Dimensions and Measures shelves (2) and drag them onto the various other shelves and cards to create views of the data. The Show Me card (3) also allows users to select multiple fields in the Dimensions and Measures shelves and select applicable visualization types. Each workbook can contain multiple sheets, each with a different view of the data. Multiple sheets can then be brought together onto a dashboard, in which interactions with data elements on one sheet can filter or highlight data on other sheets. This rich interactivity is what can allow for in-depth exploration, and ultimately, powerful communication of data to others.

Dashboards

If the user clicks on the *New Dashboard* icon, or selects *Dashboard →
New Dashboard*, a new user interface will appear, as shown in
Figure 2-3.

The following are the major components of the Dashboard view:

1. The list of Sheets created in the current workbook

2. Dashboard objects to add (images, text, etc.)

3. Tiled versus Floating object control: affects the object being dragged onto the dashboard

4. Dashboard Layout outline: shows all sheets and objects included on a dashboard

5. Dashboard size control: allows the users to specify the width and height of the dashboard

6. Sheets and Dashboard tabs: show what has been created or create new Sheets or Dashboards

7. The Dashboard itself

8. The session tabs: connect to data, show all tabs in a workbook, or see all workbooks for a user

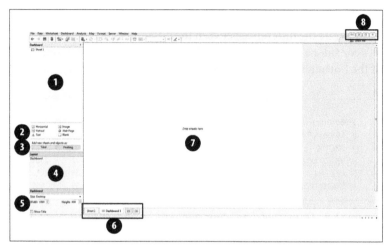

Figure 2-3. The Tableau user interface for a new Dashboard

In this book, we will make extensive use of the dashboard view, combining multiple visualizations on one canvas to allow for rich interactivity.

The toolbar

In addition to the components just listed, both the Sheet view and the Dashboard view include a toolbar and menu items at the top, by default. The toolbar includes the all-important *Undo* (left arrow) and *Redo* (right arrow) controls in the upper left, which allow users to step backward and forward in the current session from the time the workbook was opened to the most recent step taken. Also included in the toolbar are controls to *Save, Connect to Data, Sort, Group, Show Labels, Toggle to Presentation Mode*, and change the *Fit* of the sheets, among a few other icons.

Data types

When a user connects to a data source, Tableau automatically classifies each field as either a *Dimension* or a *Measure*. It's helpful to think of Dimensions as fields you can use to group or categorize your data; Measures are fields you can do math with, like summing or averaging.

Dimensions can be further grouped into strings, dates, and geographic fields (which generate latitude and longitude Measures based on internal lookup tables native to Tableau). Measures can be either discrete or continuous (more about this later).

To illustrate the difference between the different data types in Tableau, let's consider a very simple data table: the population and surface area of the boroughs of New York, as shown in Figure 2-4.

	A	B	C	D	E	F
1	Borough	County	State	Population	Area sq-mi	Year
2	MANHATTAN	New York	New York	1,619,090	23	2011
3	BRONX	Bronx	New York	1,408,473	42	2011
4	BROOKLYN	Kings	New York	2,565,635	71	2011
5	QUEENS	Queens	New York	2,272,771	109	2011
6	STATEN ISLAND	Richmond	New York	470,728	58	2011

Figure 2-4. Data table showing population and area in New York boroughs

In this simple data set, Tableau interprets each column as a distinct field, and uses the column headers (the values in the first row) as the field names. Figure 2-5 shows how these different fields appear in Tableau.

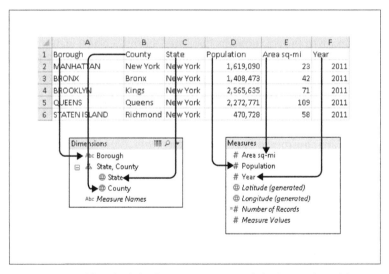

Figure 2-5. Tableau's default interpretation of the boroughs table

By default, Tableau interprets Borough as a string (as indicated by the blue Abc to the left of the field name); County and State as geographic data types (as indicated by the blue globes next to these field names); and Population, Area sq-mi, and Year as continuous measures (as indicated by the green # to the left of these field names).

Notice that a few other fields appear in italics in the Dimensions and Measures areas. These fields aren't included in the originial table, but are rather generated by Tableau. The generated dimensions include:

Measure Names
> This field is a string type that provides a list of all of the names of the fields in the Measures section (in this case, Area sq-mi, Population, Year, and Number of Records).

The generated measures include:

Measure Values
> This continuous numeric field contains all of the numerical values of the Measures: every number included in the table, whether population, area, or year.

Number of Records
> This numeric field is a count of the entries in the data source. This field is useful for showing how many of each dimension exists in the data set. Figure 2-6 shows how the Number of Records for each borough is 1 (there is 1 row for each borough) and the Number of Records for the state of New York is 5 (there are 5 rows that all have the string value "New York" in the State field).

Latitude (generated) *and* Longitude (generated)
> These fields are the coordinates that correspond to the fields recognized as geographic data types (County and State). Tableau automatically recognizes a number of geographic fields and generates latitidue and longitude coordinates. For example, as shown in Figures 2-7 and 2-8, double-clicking on County creates a symbol map with a single circle in the center of each county, and double-clicking State creates a symbol map with a single circle in the center of the state of New York.

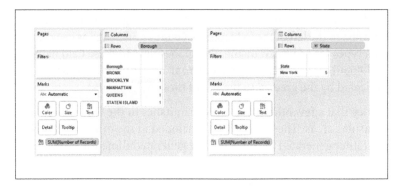

Figure 2-6. Illustration of the Number of Records field

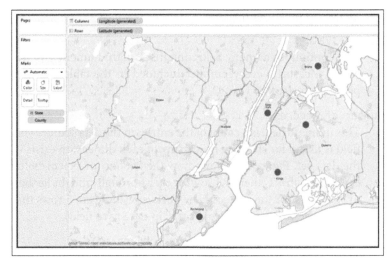

Figure 2-7. Symbol map for the geographic field "County"

Figure 2-8. Symbol map for the geographic field "State"

Changing data types

Tableau allows you to convert Dimensions to Measures and vice versa. Simply drag a field from one area of the screen to another, as shown in Figure 2-9.

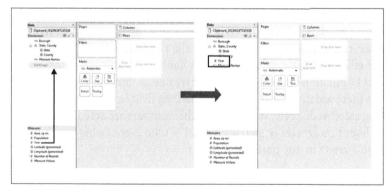

Figure 2-9. Changing a field from a Measure to a Dimension

Notice how the color of the # symbol next to the field name changes from green (for continuous) to blue (for discrete). This is another important distinction between data types. Tableau draws axes when continuous data types are used in visualizations (resulting in lines and scatterplots), and it creates headers when discrete data types are used (resulting in bars, columns, and tables).

For example, consider the two visualizations in Figure 2-10, which show Area on the Columns shelf (the horizontal or x-axis) and Population on the Rows shelf (the vertical or y-axis).

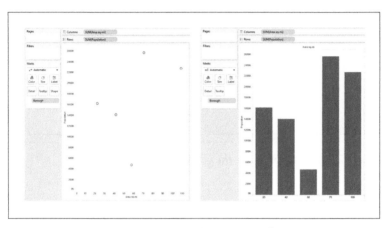

Figure 2-10. Area as a continuous data type (left); area as a discrete data type (right)

On the left, Area is plotted as a continuous axis (the Area "pill" on the left is green), while on the right, each value for Area is given its own discrete column (the Area "pill" on the right is blue). This illustrates the effect of changing data types in Tableau. In this case, both Area and Population should probably be treated as continuous data types, but there are times when a numerical data field (a dimension) should be treated as discrete, such as when the numbers are actually codes for different categories (e.g., 0 = type 1, 1 = type 2, etc., where type 1 and type 2 aren't in any particular order).

Calculated fields

The ability to create calculated fields from the fields in your workbook is a very useful feature of Tableau. For instance, what if you wanted to figure out which borough in our example data table had the highest population density? The workbook already includes both population and area, so all you need to do is divide them to answer your question. With calculated fields, you can do just that. Right-click anywhere in the Dimensions or Measures area and select Create Calculated Field. Then, complete the Calculated Field dialog, as shown in Figure 2-11.

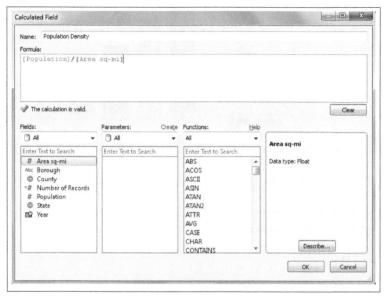

Figure 2-11. Creating a calculated field

After clicking OK, you will notice that a new continuous field called Population Density appears in the Measures area with an = to the left of it, indicating a calculated field.

Creating visualizations

Tableau features a simple drag-and-drop interface that allows the user to quickly explore different data visualization types. For example, dragging Borough onto the Columns shelf, Population onto the Rows shelf, and Population Density onto the Color shelf results in the column chart shown in Figure 2-12.

This chart shows that while Brooklyn has the largest population as indicated by the tallest column, Manhattan has the highest population density as indicated by the darkest green shade.

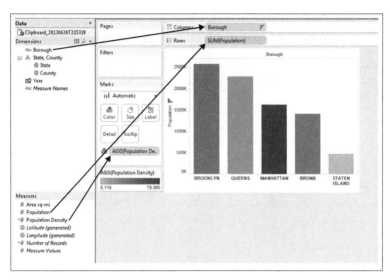

Figure 2-12. Creating a simple column chart in Tableau

Show Me

Another way to create a visualization in Tableau is to use the Show Me card. Show Me indicates which chart types are applicable based on the fields selected. Select multiple fields by holding the Control key. For example, if you select County, hold the Control key, and then select Population Density, the Show Me card will show a number of possible visualizations. Selecting the filled map icon in the top right results in the choropleth map of New York counties shown in Figure 2-13.

This simple user interface allows for fast visual analytics. Users can explore their data in a visual way, creating various chart types and encoding variables like size and color based on the different data fields themselves.

In Chapter 1, I made the point that in an age of increasing information, it's critical to choose a message from the information set that is both meaningful and impactful. Finding a compelling message is the critical first step in communicating data well. By facilitating the data exploration and discovery process, Tableau allows users to quickly find the most compelling message to share.

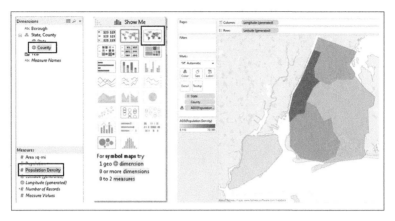

Figure 2-13. Creating a filled map in Tableau using Show Me

Summary

In this chapter, we were introduced to the different Tableau product offerings. We then covered the Tableau user interface, starting with an introduction to Sheets and Dashboards, and then moving on to a discussion of different data types. Finally, we created a simple visualization on a Sheet by both dragging and dropping fields onto the Rows and Columns shelves, and using the Show Me card.

In the next chapter, we'll cover in more detail how to discover relationships within our data.

CHAPTER 3

How Much and How Many

*"Numerical quantities focus on expected values,
graphical summaries on unexpected values."*

—John Tukey

Communicating data is sharing comparisons, and comparisons are examinations of relative amounts. We make comparisons all day long, without consciously deciding to do so. We love to explore how things are similar or how they are different. Whether we discover something unexpected or confirm a long-held belief, we walk away with a satisfying feeling of knowing.

But we can be highly skeptical of comparisons that others communicate to us. "Our product is better than our competitor's." "The economy has gotten worse since my opponent took office." We're exposed to comparisons such as these constantly, so it's natural for us to be wary of them. Some comparisons are definitely odious.

What does this mean when it comes to communicating data? The onus is on the communicator to convey the message accurately and effectively, in order to earn the trust and attention of the target audience. It starts with understanding the nature of the comparison to be made.

Comparisons can include multiple layers, but at their core they always reduce to either *how much* or *how many*.

How much involves noncountable nouns like revenue or measurements:

- "How much money did we earn this past quarter?"
- "How much carbon dioxide is in the atmosphere?"

How many involves countable nouns like people or distinct events:

- "How many customers do we have?"
- "How many goals did players score this season?"

Often, these two types of comparisons are visualized using the same chart types, but the way they are created in Tableau can differ depending on how your data is arranged (more on that soon).

In this chapter, we'll cover the simplest of quantitative comparisons: single variables as either measurements (how much) or counts (how many). In later chapters, we'll focus on elements such as time and location, and then we'll explore how to best apply these techniques to fields such as statistics, finance, and data journalism.

Communicating "How Much"

To start with, let's consider comparisons involving quantities that are measured rather than counted. This includes fields such as revenue, weight, distance, and time, among countless others. Most likely, your data source doesn't include a record for each dollar, pound, mile, or hour. Rather, a single record could be a transaction like a sale or a shipment, each having a measurement associated with it:

- A sales order resulting in revenue of $95
- An overnight shipment weighing 5.2 lbs.
- A flight covering 2,408 miles in 5 hours and 28 minutes

Additionally, your data source could be a summary table, such as total monthly revenue for a number of months, or shipping weight for all packages. In this format, each row in the data set is an aggregation of a number of individual records. It's important to understand the level of aggregation of your underlying data set.

You already know from Chapter 1 that these measurements form quantitative data types, as opposed to ordinal or nominal. And you know from Chapter 2 that Tableau sees them as continuous Measures (green pills), like the `Area sq-mi` field for each of New York's boroughs.

An Example of How Much

Staying with the New York theme in our example data, let's consider garbage. How much garbage does the City of New York Department of Sanitation (DSNY) collect from each borough? Well, each borough is further divided into community districts. A summary table of the total tonnage collected from each of the 59 community districts during September 2011 is available on the NYC Open Data site (*http://bit.ly/nyc-tonnage*).

Figure 3-1 shows a portion of the data table.

	A	B	C	D	E	F	G
1	Month	Borough	CommunityDistrict	RefuseTonsCollected	PaperTonsCollected	MGPTonsCollected	
2	2011 / 09	Manhattan	1	1241.24	420.95	216.91	
3	2011 / 09	Manhattan	2	2245.23	500.94	269.77	
4	2011 / 09	Manhattan	3	3178.24	388.52	257.06	
5	2011 / 09	Manhattan	4	2279.71	517.98	335.69	
6	2011 / 09	Manhattan	5	1348.82	278.28	152.43	
7	2011 / 09	Manhattan	6	3117.88	628.98	385.61	
8	2011 / 09	Manhattan	7	5461.86	1232.56	617.15	
9	2011 / 09	Manhattan	8	5904.28	1225.57	643.79	
10	2011 / 09	Manhattan	9	2717.01	291.66	190.29	
11	2011 / 09	Manhattan	10	2962.33	224.69	156.22	
12	2011 / 09	Manhattan	11	2329.99	180.59	110.67	
13	2011 / 09	Manhattan	12	5281.14	434.96	380.6	
14	2011 / 09	Bronx	1	2052.58	91.27	76.03	
15	2011 / 09	Bronx	2	1664.38	82.04	97.48	
16	2011 / 09	Bronx	3	1917.67	80.88	78.65	
17	2011 / 09	Bronx	4	4588.12	169.44	167.9	
18	2011 / 09	Bronx	5	3735.12	164.09	207.24	
19	2011 / 09	Bronx	6	2328.64	95.04	112.25	
20	2011 / 09	Bronx	7	3926.07	237.94	244.82	
21	2011 / 09	Bronx	8	2651.04	351.2	237.54	
22	2011 / 09	Bronx	9	4510.36	200.64	235.91	
23	2011 / 09	Bronx	10	2860.96	378.97	274.43	
24	2011 / 09	Bronx	11	3307.65	333.6	251.35	
25	2011 / 09	Bronx	12	4185.39	390.3	404.84	
26	2011 / 09	Brooklyn	1	4819.68	535.61	372.21	
27	2011 / 09	Brooklyn	2	2356.85	472.87	288.6	

Figure 3-1. DSNY Collection Tonnages data table

The first question to ask of the data set is a rather simple one, but let's state it as precisely as possible:

> "How does the amount of refuse (in tons) that DSNY reportedly collected from each borough during September 2011 compare?"

To find the answer, we'll start by connecting Tableau to the data set by clicking Connect to Data and browsing to the file. Once you have Tableau connected to the DSNY Collection Tonnages data set, you will see Sheet 1 as a blank canvas with the data fields arranged, as shown in Figure 3-2.

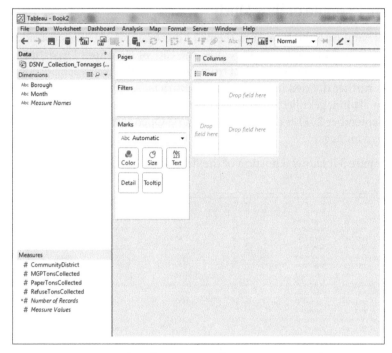

Figure 3-2. Connected to the DSNY Collection Tonnages data set

Notice that Tableau has decided that Borough and Month are discrete (blue) string Dimensions, and that CommunityDistrict and the three forms of garbage (MGP stands for "Metal, Glass, and Plastic") collected are continuous (green) numerical Measures.

To begin, click Borough, hold down the Control key, click RefuseTon sCollected, and then click Show Me in the upper-right corner of the screen. Notice that a number of options are highlighted, and that there is a blue box around the *horizontal bars* option. This is Tableau's way of suggesting you use that chart type, based on the principles of data encoding effectiveness outlined in Figure 1-6.

Comparing Comparisons

Before blindly accepting any recommendation, let's consider all the different ways we could show the comparison of refuse collected in the boroughs. Figure 3-3 shows 11 different options (we'll consider maps in Chapter 10).

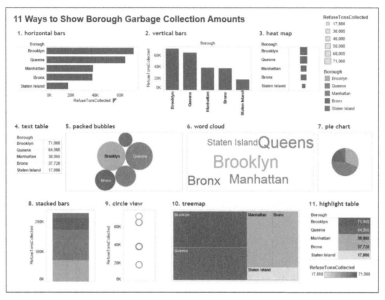

Figure 3-3. Eleven ways to show a simple quantitative (noncounting noun) comparison

All 11 chart types were created by Ctrl-selecting both `Borough` and `RefuseTonsCollected`, selecting a view from the Show Me panel, and sorting in descending order (except the vertical bars and the word cloud, which were made from slight modifications to the horizontal bars and packed bubbles charts, respectively). No additional chart components were added, such as labels. The defaults were accepted.

Which view gives the best sense of the relative amounts collected? Most likely you'd agree that it's the horizontal bar chart (chart 1). Its advantage over the vertical bar chart (chart 2) is that the bar labels are easier to read. Both make use of length to encode the amounts. As it turns out, we're pretty good at comparing lengths.

In which other view can you tell, for example, that Manhattan produced *slightly* more refuse than the Bronx, and that both yielded about twice as much as Staten Island? Not in the pie chart (chart 7), where it's even difficult to discern which slice is the biggest. Refer again to Figure 1-6 for a reminder of why this is the case.

But in which views can you speak to the *precise* amounts collected? If you needed to know, for example, exactly how much more than 70,000 tons were collected in Brooklyn, which would you use? Without adding data labels to the other views, the only ones that can help with this task are the text table (chart 4), and the highlight table (chart 11).

When precision is required, tables work best, which is why finance departments make such wide use of them. The highlight table adds some comparative value with the "color ramp" encoding. At a glance, the color gradient gives a very general sense of which yielded the most, and whether the amount collected was slightly more (Manhattan over the Bronx) or a great deal more (Brooklyn over Staten Island).

The point here is that your choice of view type should depend largely on the message to be communicated, which in turn depends on the task to be accomplished. Who are you communicating with, and how does the presentation of the data relate to the tasks at hand? These are critical questions to answer.

Fine-Tuning the Default

If we decide to go with the recommended horizontal bar chart, we will get a view that is sorted in alphabetical order, as shown in Figure 3-4.

Notice that Tableau has placed a green pill on the Columns shelf and a blue pill on the Rows shelf. The Rows shelf contains the Dimension (or nominal field) Borough, and you can see that there is a different row for each borough. The Columns shelf contains SUM(RefuseTon sCollected), which indicates that Tableau has added the amounts in the RefuseTonsCollected field for all of the community districts in each borough, and is displaying the total (we'll explore other measures such as averages and medians later).

Rather than using the Show Me drawer, you could have manually dragged both fields from the Dimensions and Measures sections on the left side onto the Rows and Columns shelf, respectively. Click the left Undo button and try it out.

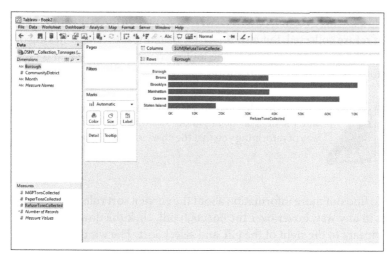

Figure 3-4. Horizontal bar chart of refuse tons collected

Unless another more compelling sort presents itself, it's standard convention for horizontal and vertical bar charts to be sorted in descending order (i.e., with the longest bars at the top for horizontal bar charts and the tallest bars at the left for vertical bar charts.) How do we do that in Tableau?

Sorting

To sort the bars by length, simply click the Sort icons in the toolbar above the canvas, as shown in Figure 3-5.

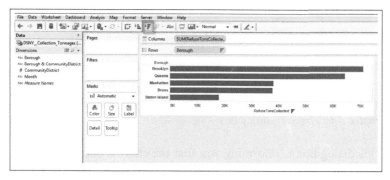

Figure 3-5. Sorting using the toolbar icons

Now it's more organized and easier to see not only the relative amounts of refuse collected, but also the order from most to least. Clicking on the "Sort ascending" icon in the toolbar reverses the order and positions the smallest bar at the top.

 Also notice the appearance of the small sorted bar icon inside the blue Borough pill on the Rows shelf. This is Tableau's way of informing you that the chart is sorted based on borough.

To find out more information about the current sort rule, or to modify it in any way, hover over the Borough pill, click the down arrow that appears to the right of the pill, and select Sort. The window shown in Figure 3-6 appears.

Figure 3-6. The Sort dialog box

This dialog box is informing you that the chart is currently sorting Borough in descending order based on the sum of the RefuseTonsCollected field. Go ahead and try some different options and see how the chart changes. You can even create your own manual sort by using the section at the bottom. After playing around with some different sorts, use the Undo button to return to the sort shown in Figure 3-5.

We've seen a number of different ways to show the refuse collection amounts by borough, but is there an even more effective way to communicate this data? In the next section, we'll explore a chart type called the *dot chart*, the use of which is advocated by Naomi Robbins.[1]

The Dot Chart

Going back to Figure 1-6 yet again, we see that the most effective way of encoding quantitative information is to use position. Which of the chart types in Figure 3-4 utilizes position to encode the amount of refuse collected? Only the circle view (chart 9). And yet its effectiveness is limited by the fact that all of the circles are in the same column, meaning the green circle for Manhattan and the blue circle for the Bronx are overlapping, and making it virtually impossible to tell them apart.

One way to resolve this is to drag the blue Borough pill from the Color shelf to the Column shelf, as shown in Figure 3-7.

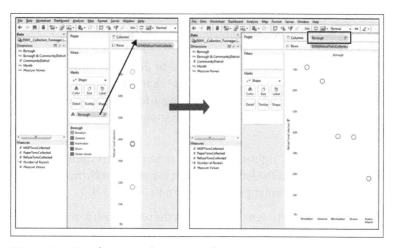

Figure 3-7. Resolving overlapping circles

The resulting chart is almost identical to the vertical bar chart, except that instead of using bars as the Mark type, it makes use of rings, or circles. Each borough has its own column, so there is no need to use color to differentiate them from one another.

---

1. Naomi B. Robbins, *Creating More Effective Graphs* (Chart House, 2013).

Before, we decided that the horizontal bar layout was superior to the vertical bar layout, so a further improvement to this layout would be to flip the chart 90 degrees by using the Swap function, as shown in Figure 3-8.

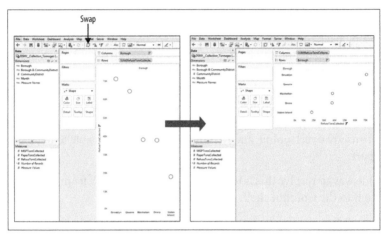

Figure 3-8. Using the Swap function to rotate view

To complete the dot chart, all we need to do is add horizontal lines extending across each row. Typically, dot charts include on-center grid lines that pass through each dot. Adding grid lines that pass between each dot involves using the built-in Format function, so we'll start there.

To edit the format, right-click anywhere in the chart itself and select Format. Notice that the lefthand panel changes from Dimensions and Measures to the Format panel, as shown in Figure 3-9.

To add grid lines between the dots, click the paintbrush icon, then click the Rows tab, and choose a line type from the Grid Lines drop-down selector. Choosing the straight line yields the chart shown in Figure 3-10.

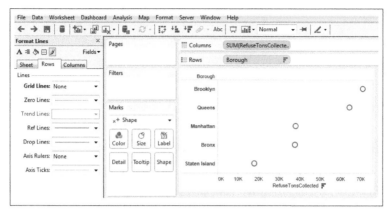

Figure 3-9. The Format panel

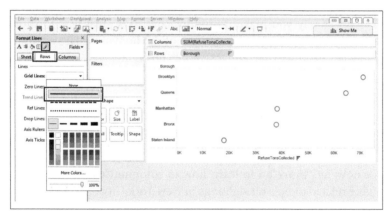

Figure 3-10. Adding grid lines to form the dot chart

With some extra formatting that we'll discuss later when we cover dual-axis charts, Figure 3-11 shows the final dot chart, complete with on-center grid lines and closed gray dots.

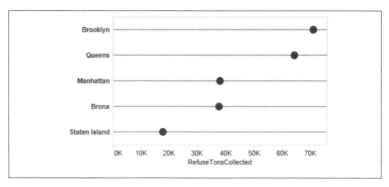

Figure 3-11. The formatted dot chart

The dot chart could have also been created by starting with the horizontal bar chart and changing the *Marks* type from *Automatic* or *Bars* to *Circle* (for closed dots) or *Shape* (for open dots or other shapes). Whichever way you make it, the dot chart is a great way to show quantities as it leverages the strength of the human visual system to compare quantities based on a symbol's position.

We've considered a very basic case of communicating *how much* involving collection of garbage in New York boroughs. We'll come back to this data set in later chapters as we seek to answer more interesting questions, like which borough yields the most garbage per person, and which recycles the most.

For now, let's move on to learn how to communicate counts with a highly related topic—rat sightings in New York City.

Communicating "How Many"

Recall that communicating "how many" is pertinent to *countable* nouns like people and events. The previous example used a very simple and highly summarized data set—garbage tons per community district and borough for a whole month. But data sets don't start that way very often, at least not in today's world. Data is captured at the transaction level in business (e.g., sales orders) or at the incident level in government (e.g., arrests).

Communicating "how many" is very common and useful for data at the most granular possible level. For example, perhaps you want to show how many sales orders involved customers who are retired, or maybe you're interested in presenting how many arrests were DUIs.

Customers and arrests are not things you *measure*, like tons of refuse in the previous section, they're things you *count*. While the visualization types are the same, the method to create them in Tableau can be different.

A Tale of Two Formats

Let's consider an example of the same data structured two ways. Figure 3-12 shows the raw data for rat sightings as captured by the 311 call center in New York on the lefthand side, and a pivot table of this data set by borough on the righthand side.

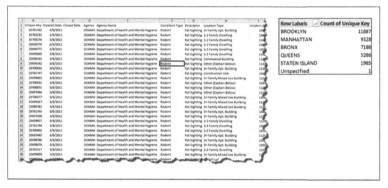

Figure 3-12. Data at the incident level and aggregate level

If your data is at the aggregate level (like the Excel pivot table on the righthand side of Figure 3-12), you will deal with it in Tableau similar to the garbage collection data. Tableau will recognize Count of Unique Key (which you will probably rename something like Rat Sightings) as a continuous Measure, exactly like RefuseTonsCollected in the previous example.

But if your data looks like the raw data table on the left, which is far more common, how can you communicate how many rat sightings were reported in each borough? There are two ways: Number of Records and Count.

Counting Dimensions

We introduced the concept of the Number of Records in the previous chapter. To review, Number of Records is a Measure field that Tableau generates when you connect to a data source, and it tells you how many individual records, or rows, are present for each Dimension (or nominal data type).

To see how it works, connect to the rat sighting data set, and drag the `Number of Records` field onto the Text shelf within the *Marks* card. You will see that there are 35,655 total records in the rat sightings data set. If you then drag `Borough` onto the Rows shelf, you will reproduce the pivot table shown in Figure 3-13.

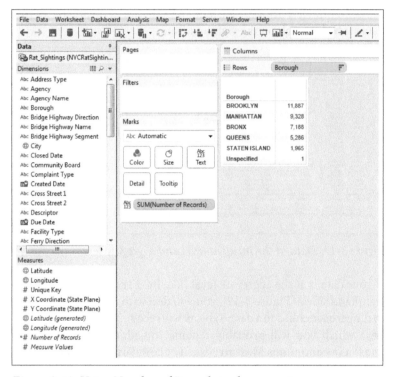

Figure 3-13. Using Number of Records to show counts

Notice how the `Number of Records` pill is a summation. To understand how `Number of Records` behaves, imagine a field in the data set of 1s. Summing this field for Brooklyn, for example, shows that there are 11,887 times that "Brooklyn" appears in the `Borough` field. This can be a very helpful way to find anomalies or errors in the data set. For example, if you replace `Borough` in the Rows shelf with `City`, you will see the table shown in Figure 3-14. Notice anything wrong with the highlighted city name?

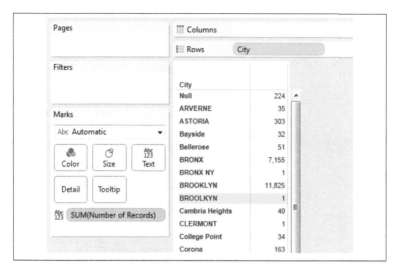

Figure 3-14. Using Number of Records to check for errors

Evidently, there was one record in which the city name was incorrectly recorded as BROOLKYN. These types of errors are ubiquitous, especially in human-recorded data sets. Checking for them is an important part of the "exploring data" step outlined in Figure 1-1.

Returning to the boroughs analysis, you can see how the Number of Records field can now be used just like the RefuseTonsCollected field in our previous example. In fact, Ctrl-selecting Borough and Number of Records and then clicking the *Show Me* panel allows for creation of all of the same chart types shown in Figure 3-4.

In this way, you can follow the same steps as in the previous example to create the dot chart of rat sightings by borough shown in Figure 3-15.

Alternatively, you can create identical views to the ones shown by replacing SUM(Number of Records) with CNT(Unique Key). Each record has a unique identification key, and counting how many unique keys are associated with each borough is identical to summing the number of records.

To do this, right-click on Unique Key and drag it over the pill in the Columns shelf. When you drop the field by releasing the right mouse button, a menu will appear that allows you to specify how Tableau should deal with the Unique Key field. Choose *CNT(Unique Key)* and notice that the only thing that changes is the green pill in the Columns shelf.

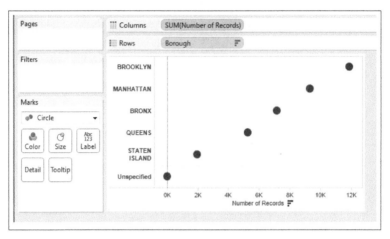

Figure 3-15. Dot chart of count of rat sightings by borough

Histograms: How Many of How Much?

In both of the previous examples—garbage collection and rat sightings —the independent variable in the category was borough, which is a nominal variable. It was fairly easy to sum measurements or count instances for each borough.

But what if the independent variable is ordinal or quantitative? For example, returning to the garbage collection example, what if I wanted to show how many community districts yielded certain amounts of refuse?

One way to show counts of quantitative variables is the histogram, which was first introduced by the father of mathematical statistics, Karl Pearson (*http://bit.ly/rsta-pearson*), in 1895. The histogram is very straightforward to build in Tableau using the *Show Me* panel. In the DSNY workbook, click the `RefuseTonsCollected` field in the Measures panel, click to open the *Show Me* panel in the upper right, and then select *histogram* in the bottom row of options.

Tableau creates the histogram shown in Figure 3-16.

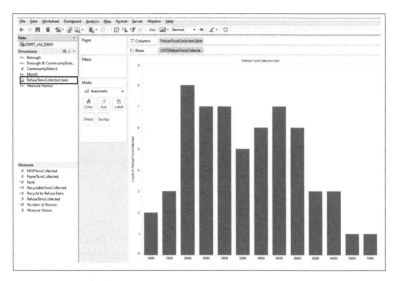

Figure 3-16. The histogram

Notice that Tableau has automatically created a new field in the Dimensions area called `RefuseTonsCollected (bin)`. This data field type is used to determine the discrete intervals into which the individual records are bucketed. The Rows shelf, which in this case determines the height of each bar, includes `CNT(RefuseTonsCollected)`. This field gives a value according to the number of records in each bin.

How can we read this chart? The first bar of the chart shows that there were two records (community districts, in this case) that produced between 1,000 and 1,500 tons of refuse (technically $1,000 \leq x < 1,500$). The second bar, with a height of three, is for community districts producing between 1,500 and 2,000 tons of refuse, and so on. The bin size is therefore 500 tons. You can easily see that the most common amount of refuse to be collected during the month of September 2011 was between 2,000 and 2,500 tons (eight community districts fell in that range).

If you would prefer to show more or fewer bars in the histogram, you can modify the bin size by right-clicking on the newly created `Refu seTonsCollected (bin)` field in the Dimensions area and then selecting *Edit*. The dialog box shown in Figure 3-17 opens, allowing you to change the size of the bins.

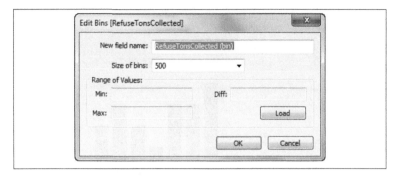

Figure 3-17. The Edit dialog box for the histogram bin field

Play with some different bin sizes and see if you can create a better histogram than the default view. Figure 3-18 shows two different histograms: one with more bins (bin size = 100) and the other with fewer bins (bin size = 1,000).

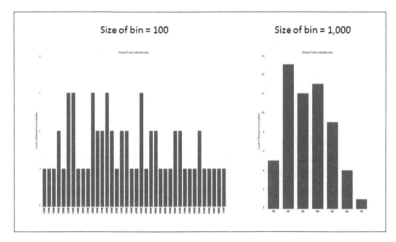

Figure 3-18. Histograms with different bin sizes

It's a case of Goldilocks and the three bears, wouldn't you say?

There's one thing to watch out for with histograms made in Tableau. If you look closely at the histogram with bins sized at 100 tons, you'll notice that some intervals are missing. The first bar is for 1,200–1,300 tons and the second is for 1,300–1,400 tons. You'd expect the third bar to be for 1,400–1,500 tons, but it isn't. It's for 1,600–1,700 tons. Why is this? It's because there aren't any community districts that produced between 1,400 and 1,500 tons of refuse. There should still be a column there, but with a bar height of zero. How can we make this adjustment? Right-click in the bar labels and check the *Show Missing Values* box, as shown in Figure 3-19.

Figure 3-19. The Show Missing Values box for histograms

What results is a version of the smaller bin size histogram that I still wouldn't recommend using, but at least it's accurate. Figure 3-20 now shows the intervals of refuse tonnage that have no community districts falling into them.

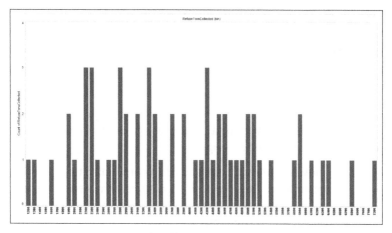

Figure 3-20. Histograms should be shown with missing values

Lastly, I prefer to edit the bar sizes and colors to look more like a histogram made in a standard statistical graphics tool. Clicking on the *Size* card and moving the slider all the way to the right, changing the color from blue to gray, and adding a dark gray border color yields the version shown in Figure 3-21.

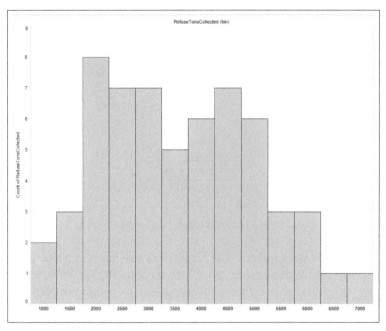

Figure 3-21. A histogram with improved formatting

Summary

How much and *how many* are foundational types of comparisons that we make every day. Whenever data is communicated, one of these two comparisons (or both) is being made. Knowing your options, and evaluating which will work best for the task at hand, is an important first step in encoding the message.

We've seen how to work with Tableau when communicating the most basic of comparisons: those in which only one variable is involved. Now, let's move on to explore how to communicate data when more than one comparison is being made.

CHAPTER 4

Ratios and Rates

*"We are the safest large city in America,
but any crime rate is too high."*

—Michael Bloomberg, former mayor
of New York City

Until now, we've considered absolute amounts of countable and measurable nouns, like population, tons of garbage collected, and number of rat sightings by borough. Pleasant, I know.

But not all boroughs are created equal. As we saw in Chapter 1, they have different surface areas and different numbers of people living in them. The fact that they produce different amounts of garbage isn't surprising, and probably doesn't make for a very interesting message to communicate to an audience.

These absolute comparisons, while helpful for showing the big picture, aren't generally considered "apples-to-apples" comparisons. There are apples, and, well, there are Big Apples.

A helpful way to "normalize" comparisons is using ratios, rates, proportions, and percentages. What's the difference between these four?

- A *ratio* is a comparison of two terms expressed as a quotient. For example, Manhattan produced 0.264 tons of recycle for every ton of refuse. Ratios can be expressed as "x to y," "x:y," "x/y," or as a decimal.

- A *rate* is a ratio in which the two terms have different units. For example, the population density of Brooklyn is 36,136 residents per square mile. Rates are often predictive because time can be used as the denominator (crime rates, population growth rates, etc.).

- A *proportion* is a ratio in which the numerator is a partial amount and the denominator is the total amount (expressed as a number between 0 and 1). For example, the proportion of the NYC population living in the Bronx is 0.169. A proportion is expressed as a number between 0 and 1.

- A *percentage* is a ratio comparing a number to 100. For example, 16.9% of NYC residents live in the Bronx. A percentage is generally a number between 0 and 100, but can be larger than 100 (e.g., "sales have increased by 150% year-over-year").

These types of normalized comparisons can make for much more interesting messages to communicate. Luckily, they are quite easy to create in Tableau. We'll explore the first two in this chapter, and the last two in the next.

Ratios

The data source itself may include a field that is a ratio, but most often the raw data includes terms that an analyst needs to combine to create a ratio. Tableau can handle these types of computations with Calculated Fields, in which new fields can be created by combining existing fields using a variety of operations. We introduced the concept in Chapter 2, and now we'll build on it.

Let's return to the DSNY data set to illustrate the technique, and we'll see if the ratio comparison is any more interesting than the absolute figures.

The data reported by DSNY includes three continuous Measures (quantitative fields) for each community district:

RefuseTonsCollected
Amount of nonrecyclable garbage

PaperTonsCollected
Amount of recyclable paper

MGPTonsCollected
Amount of recyclable metal, glass, and plastic

The second two data types (paper and MGP) are both recyclable, and so can be summed to create a new variable for each community district that we will call `RecyclableTonsCollected` to stay consistent with the provided nomenclature.

A comparison of the ratio of recyclable material to refuse would be interesting to consider, as it would indicate which communities in New York City are doing a better job recycling.

First, we'll need to create a new calculated field that sums the two recyclable fields. Right-click anywhere in the lefthand Dimensions or Measures panels, and select *Create Calculated Field*. Then, fill out the resulting dialog box, as shown in Figure 4-1.

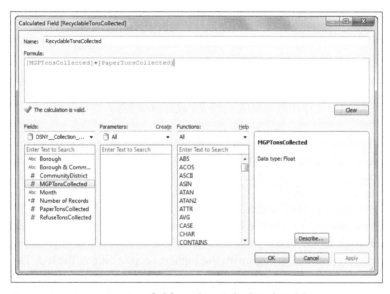

Figure 4-1. Summing two fields with a Calculated Field

Next, let's create a second calculated field that creates the ratio of recyclable material to refuse. Right-click in the Dimensions or Measures area again and fill out the dialog box as shown in Figure 4-2.

Notice that we put the numerator and denominator in brackets, preceded by SUM. This is critical, because as we move up a level of from community district to borough, we don't want to *add* the individual ratios of each community district; we want to create a new ratio that represents the quotient of the aggregate amounts. The first approach would create a larger ratio that is misleading.

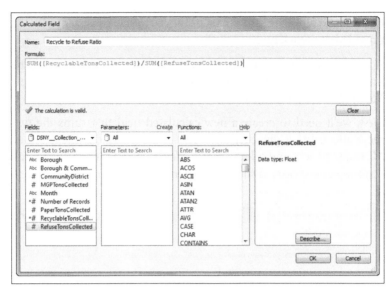

Figure 4-2. Creating a ratio with a Calculated Field

Now that we've created the ratios, how can we best visualize them? Let's start with a simple bar chart of the aggregate ratios of each of the boroughs. To create one, we'll drag the Borough field from the Dimensions area on the left to the Rows shelf, and we'll drag the Recycle to Refuse Ratio calculated field to the Columns shelf. Color wouldn't strictly be needed, but we'll add it anyway for aesthetics by dragging Borough to the Color shelf. Lastly, we'll sort the bars in descending order to put the borough with the highest recycle ratio at the top. The screen shot in Figure 4-3 shows the resulting view.

We can easily see from this simple bar chart that Manhattan has the highest ratio of recycle to refuse, but that it still only recycles about one ton of material for every four tons of trash. The ratio for Manhattan is about twice as great as the ratio for the Bronx.

Does this mean each community district in Manhattan had a higher recycle ratio than each community district in the Bronx? Not necessarily, as we're dealing with the terms in the aggregate.

How would we communicate the results at a community district level? If we just replace Borough with CommunityDistrict in the Rows shelf, then we'll get a bar chart where all the community district #1s will be aggregated, and all the community district #2s will be aggregated, and so on. Aggregating community districts in this way isn't very meaningful. Instead, we'd like to see community district ratios for each borough.

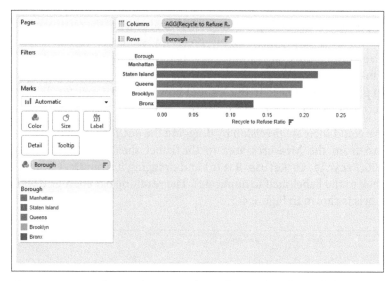

Figure 4-3. Visualizing the ratio of recycle to refuse for each borough

To make this comparison, let's click and drag the `Borough` pill from the Rows shelf up to the Columns shelf, and add the `CommunityDistrict` field from the Measures panel to the Rows shelf to create a grid of bar charts, as shown in Figure 4-4.

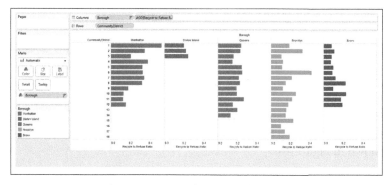

Figure 4-4. Ratios by community district and borough

From this view, we can now see that even within boroughs, not all community districts are created equal. Manhattan community district

#1 has the highest ratio overall, but it's clear that some community districts in the Bronx have higher ratios than some in Manhattan.

But what if we wanted to know the exact ratios? The bar charts in Figure 4-4 make it fairly easy to get a general sense of the relative ratios for the community districts, but precision isn't easily obtained, is it? Can you tell the exact ratio for Manhattan community district #1? I can't. If knowing the precise amounts is a task our audience will want to perform, we'll need to think about how to make it easy for them to accomplish that task.

We could increase precision by dragging the `Recycle to Refuse Ra tio` from the Measures area to the Label shelf (or Ctrl-selecting `AGG(Recycle to Refuse Ratio)` and dragging it from the Columns shelf to the Label shelf to duplicate). The resulting bar chart grid with labels is shown in Figure 4-5.

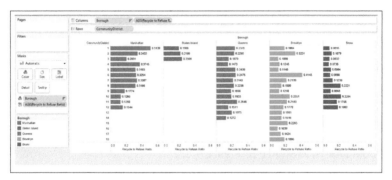

Figure 4-5. Adding labels to the bar chart grid

That's a lot of decimal places, isn't it? Our audience probably doesn't need to know the ratio to the fourth decimal place (ten-thousandths). We can change the number of digits shown by right-clicking the `Recycle to Refuse Ratio` in the Measures panel, selecting *Default Properties*, then *Number Format*, and choosing *Number (Custom)*. In the resulting dialog box, we'll change the decimal places to three, as shown in Figure 4-6.

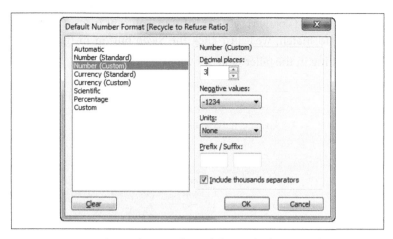

Figure 4-6. Specifying the number of decimal places in the Measures panel

Notice that the labels in the bar chart grid change accordingly.

What we really have here is a table that has been augmented by adding bars with lengths proportional to the values in each cell. Another way to show this precise comparison is by getting rid of the bars and instead coloring each cell by the ratio—a highlight table.

Let's make a highlight table by starting with a new sheet. Ctrl-click Borough, CommunityDistrict, and Recycle to Refuse Ratio, and then open the *Show Me* panel and select *highlight table.* Tableau creates the view shown in Figure 4-7.

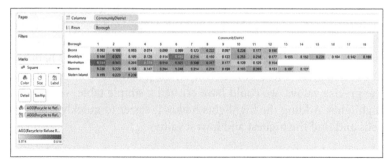

Figure 4-7. The default highlight table for Recycle to Refuse Ratio

Notice that Tableau created a highlight table that's "flipped" compared to our bar chart grid shown in Figure 4-5 (Borough is in Rows instead

of Columns, and `CommunityDistrict` is in Columns instead of Rows).
To flip it to match, we'll just click the *Swap* button in the toolbar,
, resulting in the taller table shown in Figure 4-8.

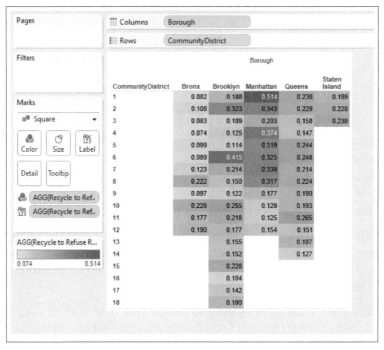

Figure 4-8. The highlight table with Rows and Columns swapped

Tableau has defaulted to a sequential green color palette, meaning the
gradient increases proportionally with increasing `Recycle to Re`
`fuse Ratio`. Our eyes can easily pick out the darkest cell, and we also
find the lightest rather easily. Most people can distinguish between
about six different levels of intensity. If the goal were to communicate
the precise values, we could have created a simple table without the
highlights. Adding the highlights makes it easier to quickly compare
cells and find the highest and lowest values.

It's still not immediately obvious which community district has the
second-highest ratio, though. Our eyes have to dart around to all the
dark cells and read and memorize the values. Eventually we settle on
Brooklyn community district #6 as having the second-highest ratio,
but the task gets harder as we move along. Which has the third highest?
The fourth? Is there an easier way to facilitate this assessment of rank?

What we'd like is a simple list of community districts in descending order of the ratio. To make this list, let's first create a new field that combines the `Borough` and `CommunityDistrict` fields into a single Dimension.

Ctrl-click `Borough` and `CommunityDistrict` so they are both selected, then right-click on one of the two selected fields (either will do fine) and select *Combine Fields*. A new string field will appear in the Dimensions area called `Borough & CommunityDistrict (Combined)`.

Create the list shown in Figure 4-9 by dragging `Borough & Communi tyDistrict` to the Rows shelf, `Recycle to Refuse Ratio` to the Columns shelf, and `Borough` to the Color shelf, sorting in descending order.

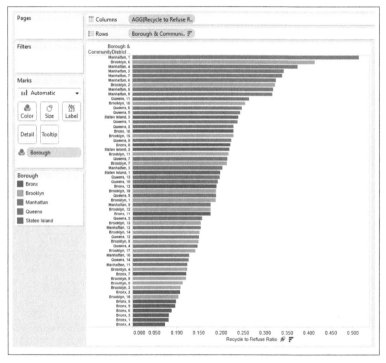

Figure 4-9. Bar chart of community districts

Now we can quickly tell which are the top four or five districts, and which are the bottom four or five. Using the colored bars, we also can see some patterns, like that the districts with the lowest ratio are all in the Bronx (blue), and most of the top ten are in Manhattan (green).

But if I asked you to pick out the tenth or the fifteenth districts, you'd have to count down from the top, right? Not the easiest task to perform. How can we add rank to this list to easily pick out the order from 1 to 59?

Two Ways of Adding Rank

Let's create a Rank field. To do so, right-click anywhere in the Dimensions or Measures panel on the left and select *Create a Calculated Field* once again. This time, name the field Rank and enter INDEX(). As soon as the message appears in the bottom left indicating "the calculation is valid," blue text will also appear in the top right that says "Default Table Calculation." Click on this blue text and change the *Compute using* drop-down to *Borough & CommunityDistrict (Combined)*, as shown in Figure 4-10.

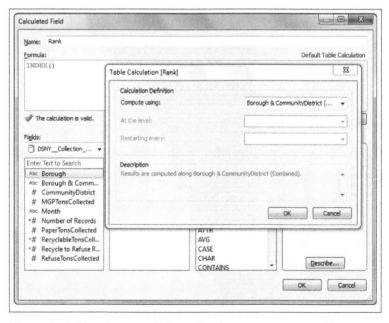

Figure 4-10. Creating a rank for each of the 59 community districts

This tells Tableau that the rank should apply to the combination of Borough and CommunityDistrict.

After clicking *OK* twice, we now see a new field in the Measures panel called Rank. Notice that this field is continuous (the # symbol is green), but we can consider the rankings to be discrete integers, because there is no rank between any two successive ranks. To change the Rank data field type, right-click on it in the Measures panel and select *Convert to Discrete*. The # symbol next to Rank will turn blue, indicating that it's discrete. We're now ready to add Rank to the chart.

To add the Rank field to the bar chart, simply drag it to the left of Borough & CommunityDistrict (Combined) on the Rows shelf. After removing the row dividers, we have the colored, sorted, and now ranked bar chart shown in Figure 4-11.

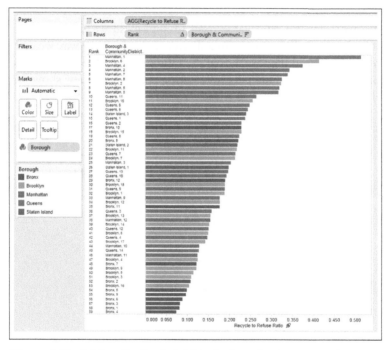

Figure 4-11. Adding the Rank field to the bar chart

Alternatively, since the launch of Version 8.1, users can create a similar Rank field by making use of the new Rank Table Calculation. To do so, drag another instance of Recycle to Refuse Ratio to the columns shelf, click in the down arrow of the new pill, and change it to *Discrete*, and then click the down arrow again and select *Quick Table Calculation* and then *Rank*. Finally, click the down arrow once more and select *Compute using*, then choose *Borough CommunityDistrict (combined).* (This calcuated field also lets you handle ties in different ways.)

Now the only task this chart doesn't facilitate is gleaning precise values. We could add the labels to the right of the bars as we did in Figure 4-5 by simply dragging the `Ratio` field to the Label shelf, but perhaps a better approach would be to add the labels to the left of the bars so as not to interfere with the perception of the bars' lengths.

Because `Recycle to Refuse Ratio` is a continuous data field (the # symbol is green), if we just drag it out onto the Rows shelf to the right of `Borough & CommunityDistrict`, Tableau will create 59 y-axes for each of the bars. Try it and see what I mean.

We just want the ratio value itself to appear, so we'll first convert `Recycle to Refuse Ratio` to a discrete field the same way we converted `Rank`, and then we'll drag the ratio onto the Rows shelf to the far right, leaving a blue pill and creating the updated view shown in Figure 4-12.

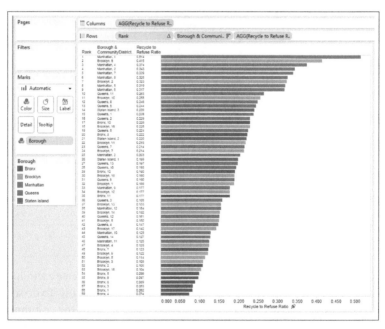

Figure 4-12. Precise values added to the left of the bars

We've now visualized the ratio in a way that makes it easy for our audience to perform a number of different tasks very quickly:

- Get a general sense of how the 59 community districts compare relative to one another
- Determine which districts have the highest ratios, and which have the lowest
- Get a general sense of which boroughs have districts at the top of the list, and which have districts at the bottom
- Know the precise ratio for any district
- Pick out any district in rank order (e.g., the 12th or the 28th)

This view is a very versatile and useful way to communicate the ratio of recycle to refuse. But it doesn't tell us which community districts produced more trash overall *per person*. For all we know, the districts at the top may be recycling a lot, but they may also be producing a much higher amount per person. That's where rates come into play.

Rates

Recall that a rate is just a special type of ratio in which the numerator and the denominator have different units. In the previous example, the ratio of recycle to refuse involved terms with the same units—namely, tons. When we consider the trash production rate per person, our numerator is still tons, but now our denominator is the number of people.

But the data set we have been working with so far doesn't include community district population. In order to determine trash production per person, we'll need to find a way to include population data in our analysis.

Going back to the data discovery process in Figure 1-1, we've gone all the way around the horse track, and now we have a brand-new question that involves gathering new data.

Ideally, we would find population by community district for September 2011, which is when the DSNY collection data was taken. We can't find that, but we came come close: 2010 census data (*http://bit.ly/nyc-census-2010*) puts us within a year's time of the trash collection data, and is probably suitable to get a reasonable approximation of the trash production rate.

Now that we found population data, how can we create rates with it? Luckily, Tableau allows us to connect our current workbook to this new data set and "blend" it with the existing data in the workbook.

Blending Data Sources

From the *Data* menu of our current workbook, select *Connect to Data* and then *Microsoft Excel,* and browse to the population data file, connecting to the correct sheet in the file and importing the data as an extract. We now see the new data source appear in the Data area along with the DSNY data, as shown in Figure 4-13.

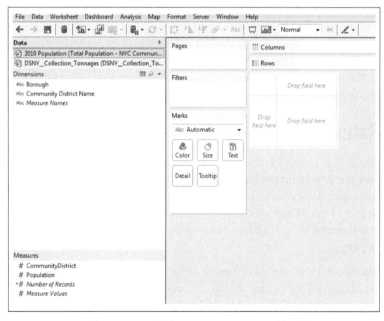

Figure 4-13. Adding a second data source to a workbook

The newly imported data set is highlighted in the Data area, and the fields for that data set are shown in the Dimensions and Measures panels below. If we click on the DSNY data set, the data fields for that data set will show below.

Notice that CommunityDistrict is in the Dimensions panel of the DSNY set, but it's in the Measures area of the new population data source. Let's match them up by dragging CommunityDistrict from the Measures panel of the population table into the Dimensions area.

Because both data sources now have a Dimension called `Borough` and a Dimension called `CommunityDistrict`, Tableau will link them together for us. If the fields to link had different names, we would have to manually link them using *Data → Edit Relationships*.

Visualizing Rates

Now that we have linked these two data sources, our updated Tableau workbook contains both terms of the refuse per person ratio: the measurement of the amount of refuse in tons (the numerator) and the count of the number of people in each community district (the denominator). We'll create the rate the same way we created the ratio in the previous section, but now we need to create a calculated field that includes fields from two different sources, as shown in Figure 4-14.

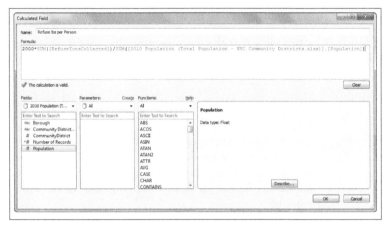

Figure 4-14. Creating a rate using fields from two data sources

Using the `SUM` aggregation type for both terms in the rate means that we can get meaningful rates for boroughs as well as community districts. Also, notice we are converting from short tons (US) to pounds (lbs.) by multiplying the numerator by 2,000—which is how many pounds are in each ton. On a per person basis, it's much easier for us to think in terms of pounds, so this is a better unit to use for this comparison.

Now that we have created the rate, we can visualize it. We'll follow the same steps that we used to create the ratio bar chart in Figure 4-12 to create the rate comparison bar chart shown in Figure 4-15.

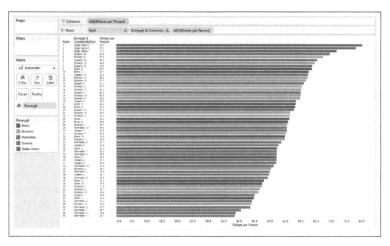

Figure 4-15. Comparing rates in a bar chart

It's clear from this view that the three community districts in Staten Island produced the most refuse per person in September 2011, at a rate of more than 70 pounds per person.

 A word of caution about these results: often, data visualization and data analysis are best used to propose new questions to ask. Data is great at helping us make comparisons, but it doesn't always answer "why?" and "how?" It can be easy for us to jump to conclusions based on what the data shows, but some further qualitative investigation is frequently required.

Why are the Staten Island community districts at the top of this chart? The chart itself doesn't tell us. It helps us formulate the next question. Does this mean every person who lives on Staten Island produced 70 to 80 pounds of trash that month? No, that's not what the data shows. The data just shows how much trash was collected from their communities. DSNY provided *overall* refuse collected, not just for residences, so perhaps there are industries or businesses on Staten Island that produced a lot of trash.

The point is to be careful with what we communicate, and not to communicate more than the data gives us license to say.

Summary

In this chapter, we learned how to use Calculated Fields and blended data sources to create ratios (quotients) and rates (quotients with mixed units). We also learned the Index function as well as the Rank table calculation, and created highlight tables and bar charts to compare different dimensions—at both the borough and community district levels. This enabled us to go beyond overall amounts ("how much") and to consider relative amounts ("how much per").

In the next chapter, we'll consider another type of normalized comparison: proportions and percentages.

CHAPTER 5

Proportions and Percentages

*"Baseball is ninety percent mental and
the other half is physical."*

—Yogi Berra

Anyone who wants to master the discipline of communicating data needs to learn how to convey proportions and percentages effectively. We see these types of comparisons every day, from the quarterly sales reports to the sports page box scores to the side panels of cereal boxes. Getting them right is important (unless you're Yogi Berra).

Recall from Chapter 4 that proportions are ratios expressed as values from 0 to 1—where the numerator is a partial amount and the denominator is the total—and percentages are simply ratios expressed as an amount in each hundred. They are most often used to communicate three different types of comparisons:

- Part-to-whole
- Current-to-historical
- Actual-to-target

Let's consider each one of these types of comparisons one at a time, starting with part-to-whole.

Part-to-Whole

Just how much of baseball is physical, and how much is mental? If these two aspects of the game are mutually exclusive and collectively exhaustive, they should sum to 100%, right? Yogi's bogus math in this chapter's epigraph is funny because it's different than what we know to expect.

In honor of Yogi, let's stick with baseball as we consider proportions. In this section, we'll consider the team batting statistics for the 2012 New York Yankees (*http://bit.ly/2012-yankee-stats*).

Followers of the sport of baseball have long been fascinated with proportions of outcomes (called stats). As a boy, I would spend all of my weekly allowance on packs of baseball cards, and each player card would have a table of the player's career stats on the back: games played, hits, doubles, triples, runs, home runs, batting average. My friends and I memorized these stats for our favorite players.

Batting average was of particular importance. It was the quintessential metric for efficiency at the plate. Of all the times a batter came to bat, how often did he get a hit, not including the times he was walked or hit by a pitch?

 Batting average is one of the three stats (along with home runs and runs batted in, or RBI) that together make up the "triple crown" of Major League Baseball batting statistics.

A stat that has recently earned more focus is the "On Base Percentage," or OBP, in which the number of times a player gets a hit, walks, or is hit by a pitch is divided by the number of plate appearances (minus sacrifice hits). It's rarely expressed as a percentage, though. For example, Raul Ibanez's OBP in 2012 was 0.308, which is a proportion, not a percentage. A percentage would need to be expressed, well, in percent, like 30.8%.

Conveniently, these proportions are already included in the 2012 Yankee player stats table, so we don't need to create them with calculated fields like we did with the recycle ratios in Chapter 4. Let's go ahead and create a simple visualization of the players' batting averages.

To start, we'll drag Name onto the Rows shelf, resulting in a list of all of the players on the Yankee roster in 2012. Next, we'll drag BA (for batting average) onto the Columns shelf, and sort in descending order. We'll have a simple bar chart, as shown in Figure 5-1.

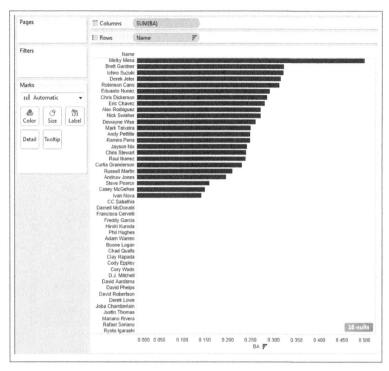

Figure 5-1. Bar chart showing BA for every Yankee with at least one at bat in 2012

Notice that almost half of the players have a batting average of 0.000, and there's a note in the lower-right corner of the view telling us there are "16 nulls," or 16 players that didn't have any at bats. The players with a batting average of 0.000 only came to the plate a few times.

Further, notice that Melky Mesa, at the top of the list, has a batting average of exactly 0.500. He only had two at bats in the 2012 season, earning a single hit and locking in his "team best" batting average for the year. Surely, including these players isn't a good way to communicate this proportion. One approach would be to filter out every player who didn't have a certain number of at bats.

Introducing Filters and Quick Filters

One of the most powerful aspects of Tableau is that charts can be filtered using the same drag-and-drop user interface that you've been learning over the past few chapters. If we want to filter out all the players who have less than 100 at bats, for instance, we would only need to drag the AB (for at bats) field into the Filters shelf above the Marks card, and then fill out the resulting dialog box, as shown in Figure 5-2.

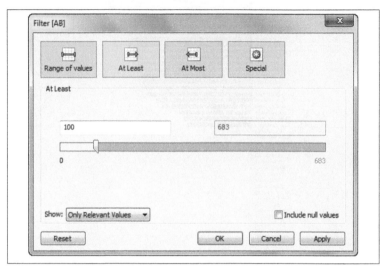

Figure 5-2. Filtering the BA bar chart to show only players with at least 100 at bats

We can drag the slider to the left or right, or enter a number into the text entry box to set the minimum number of at bats, or we can filter a number of different ways using the tiles across the top. We'll click *OK* with the setting shown in Figure 5-2, and the bar chart changes to the view shown in Figure 5-3.

Notice the green AB pill in the Filters section in the top left. We'll consider other types of filters as we go along. One other important control to learn is the *Quick Filter* control. If we hover over the green AB pill and click the small down arrow that appears within the pill, we can select *Show Quick Filter*, and Tableau will place a slider control on the canvas for us. It can be moved around, and I've moved it below the Marks card, as shown in Figure 5-4.

It becomes very easy to filter the view using Quick Filters. Drag the slider to change the minimum number of at bats required to appear in the bar chart, and see players' names come and go from the list.

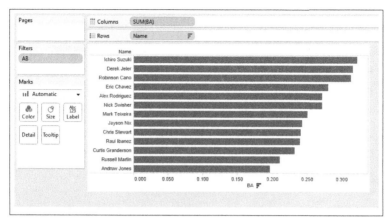

Figure 5-3. The filtered BA bar chart

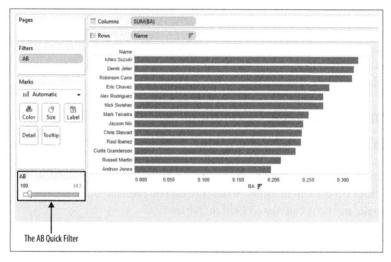

Figure 5-4. The AB Quick Filter added to the Sheet

To tidy up the view, we can change the view to the dot chart discussed in Chapter 3 and add the Rank field covered in Chapter 4. The resulting batting average dot chart is shown in Figure 5-5.

This was a fairly straightforward example, as the proportions were already computed for us and included as fields in the data set. After we learned how to filter out the players who didn't have sufficient at bats, we were able to apply some of the same techniques to create the final views.

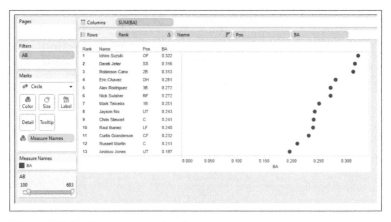

Figure 5-5. Batting average dot chart

What happens when the proportions aren't neatly calculated for us, and when it's not a simple matter of creating a ratio from two existing fields using a calculated field? For example, what if we wanted to know what percentage of the team's overall home runs were hit by each player?

Introducing Table Calculations

When I first started using Tableau, I didn't know much about table calculations. If I wanted to find out what percentage of the overall team's home run count was hit by Robinson Cano, for example, I'd either do the calculations myself outside of Tableau, or I'd struggle to make my own calculated field in Tableau.

There's no need to jump through these hoops. Let's look at the easy way to compute *percent of total*.

We'll start by placing the players' names on the Rows shelf and dragging HR (for home runs) onto the Column shelf. Just as we filtered the batting average chart, let's get rid of all players who don't have at least one home run by dragging HR to the Filter shelf and selecting *At Least* one home run. Adding the Rank field as before, we can now easily see that 18 different Yankees hit at least one home run for the team during the 2012 season, as shown in Figure 5-6.

We haven't done anything new yet; we've just applied the same techniques previously covered to the home run field. How do we easily compute percent of total?

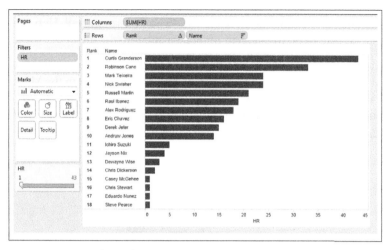

Figure 5-6. Bar chart showing Yankees in 2012 with at least one home run

First, let's visualize the players' home run tallies in comparison to the overall team number. To do so, select the *Analysis* menu from the top, and then choose *Totals → Show Column Totals*. Adding SUM(HR) to the Label shelf yields the view shown in Figure 5-7.

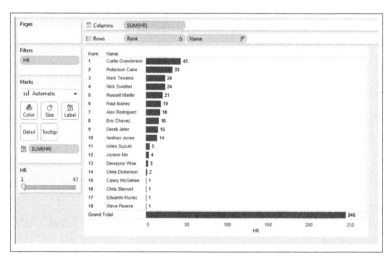

Figure 5-7. Home run bar chart with team total added

To answer my earlier question, I can now see that Robinson Cano hit 33 home runs, and that the team hit 245 home runs overall. How do I get Tableau to do the percent of total calculation for me?

To label each player bar as a percent of total rather than an absolute amount of home runs, hover over the green SUM(HR) pill in the Marks card (the one that's being used to generate the labels) and click the small down arrow that appears within the pill. Choose *Quick Table Calculation → Percent of Total*, as shown in Figure 5-8.

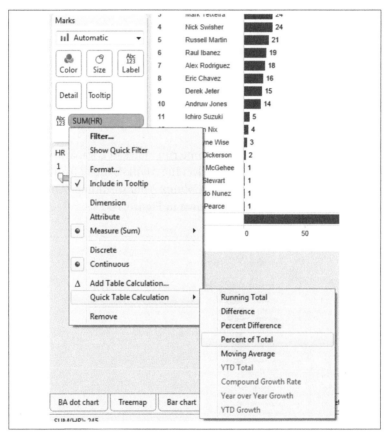

Figure 5-8. Changing the label to a "Percent of Total" table calculation

After doing so, notice that the chart changes to the view in Figure 5-9, showing the players' home run contributions as a percent of the total team amount (shown with the Column totals removed).

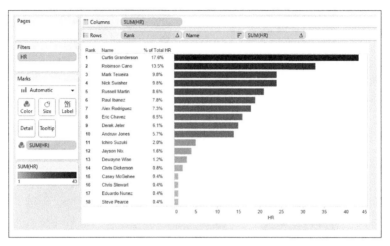

Figure 5-9. Home run tallies with labels shown as Percent of Total

This is a very simple example of a table calculation, or "table calc," as they are commonly called. (We'll revisit this topic a few more times in greater depth as we go forward.)

Now that we can easily determine the contribution of each player to the overall team home run amount, is there a better way to visualize it than the view in Figure 5-9? Figure 5-10 shows three alternatives.

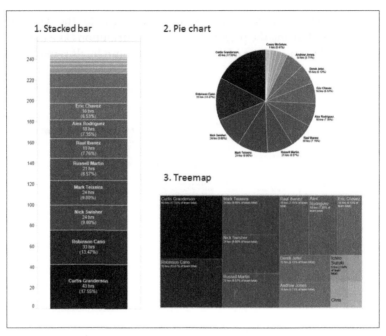

Figure 5-10. Three alternative ways to show the proportion of home runs hit by each player

Do you feel that any of the three views in Figure 5-10 is an improvement over the simple bar chart in Figure 5-9? What about the dot chart shown in Figure 5-11?

Each has its own merits, though the pie chart doesn't really have many. In the pie chart, I can't really tell any difference between the pie slices in the middle. There are just too many slices to discern among them.

I'd elect to use the dot chart shown in Figure 5-11. It lets us make quick comparisons and see the relative and absolute amounts, and it makes the rank order immediately obvious.

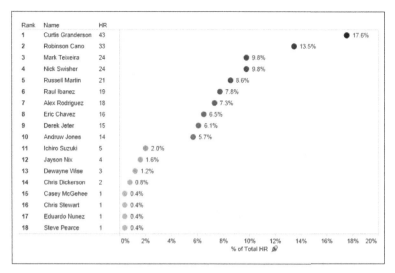

Rank	Name	HR		
1	Curtis Granderson	43		17.6%
2	Robinson Cano	33		13.5%
3	Mark Teixeira	24		9.8%
4	Nick Swisher	24		9.8%
5	Russell Martin	21		8.6%
6	Raul Ibanez	19		7.8%
7	Alex Rodriguez	18		7.3%
8	Eric Chavez	16		6.5%
9	Derek Jeter	15		6.1%
10	Andruw Jones	14		5.7%
11	Ichiro Suzuki	5	2.0%	
12	Jayson Nix	4	1.6%	
13	Dewayne Wise	3	1.2%	
14	Chris Dickerson	2	0.8%	
15	Casey McGehee	1	0.4%	
16	Chris Stewart	1	0.4%	
17	Eduardo Nunez	1	0.4%	
18	Steve Pearce	1	0.4%	

Figure 5-11. Dot chart of percentage of home runs contributed by each player

Proportions as Waterfall Charts Using Gantt

Let's look at the home run data in a slightly different way. What if we could stagger the columns of the stacked bar chart in Figure 5-10, so that each player had his own column? The resulting view would look like the chart shown in Figure 5-12, complete with pinstripes in honor of "the Bronx Bombers."

Admittedly, this chart type doesn't make the most efficient use of space, but it creates a nice stairstep effect that gives a unique sense of the part-to-whole relationship. How is this made with Tableau? It makes use of the Gantt chart type. Let's see how.

Let's start by creating a column for each player by dragging Name onto the Columns shelf, and then change the Marks type to *Gantt Bar* using the drop-down menu in the Marks card. Next, drag HR onto the Rows shelf, filter out all the players with less than one home run in the 2012 season, and sort descending. The resulting view should look like the view shown in Figure 5-13.

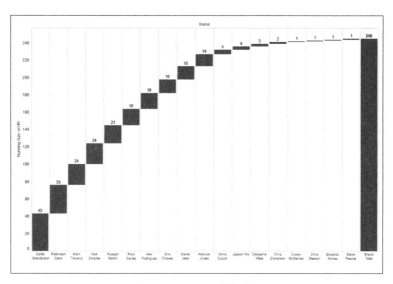

Figure 5-12. Home run data as a waterfall chart

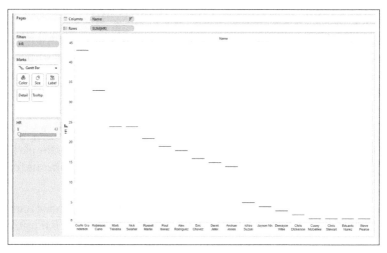

Figure 5-13. Waterfall chart in progress

The next step is to use another table calc: the running total. Hover the cursor over the green SUM(HR) pill in the Rows shelf, and when the small down arrow appears within the pill, click on it. In the menu that pops up, go to *Quick Table Calculation* and select *Running Total*. The view changes to show a cascading set of horizontal lines. Each player's home run number starts at a height that equals the sum of all of the preceding players' home runs, and grows accordingly. All we need to do now is fill in the columns and add a Grand Total column at the far right.

The trick with the waterfall chart is to create a calculated field that is the negative of the Measure you are charting. This will allow you to create columns that stretch from each horizontal line *down* to the previous level.

Right-click on HR, click *Create Calculated Field*, name it HR(rev) and enter HR*-1 in the Formula area. Drag this new field onto the *Size* mark, and the columns fill in, creating the cascading view we're looking for.

To finish the view, click *Analysis → Totals → Show Row Grand Totals*. The total column appears to the far right. To get the Yankee look and feel, change the color of the bars to dark gray and add pinstripe column dividers in the Format panel, creating the view shown in Figure 5-14, with HR labels added.

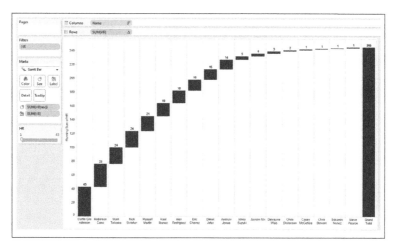

Figure 5-14. Completed waterfall chart

We've considered part-to-whole relationships in a number of different ways. Now let's consider ways to communicate current values as percentages of historical ones.

Current-to-Historical

New York hit 245 home runs in 2012; that much we know. But how did that home run tally compare with other teams in their league, and how did it compare with the amount of home runs they hit the year before? Was it the most in the league, the least, or somewhere in between? Did they improve their home run tally over 2011 or did they fail to reach the previous year's mark?

Recalling the data discovery horse race track of Figure 1-1, these are new questions that have arisen from data we have already explored and communicated. These questions send us in search of yet more data, and we find the 2011 (*http://bit.ly/2011-bat-avg*) and 2012 (*http://bit.ly/2012-bat-avg*) league team home run totals on the Web. Figure 5-15 shows the complete table.

◢	A	B	C	D	E
1	Tm	City	League	2012 HR	2011 HR
2	BAL	Baltimore	AL	214	191
3	BOS	Boston	AL	165	203
4	CHW	Chicago	AL	211	154
5	CLE	Cleveland	AL	136	154
6	DET	Detroit	AL	163	169
7	KCR	Kansas City	AL	131	95
8	LAA	Los Angeles	AL	187	129
9	MIN	Minnesota	AL	131	103
10	NYY	New York	AL	245	222
11	OAK	Oakland	AL	195	114
12	SEA	Seattle	AL	149	109
13	TBR	Tampa Bay	AL	175	172
14	TEX	Texas	AL	200	210
15	TOR	Toronto	AL	198	186

Figure 5-15. Team home run totals, 2011 and 2012

The Bullet Graph

One very efficient way to show each of these comparisons in one view is using a "bullet graph" (*http://bit.ly/wiki-bullet-graph*). Let's go ahead and connect to the data table and create a bullet graph by Ctrl-selecting City, 2011 HR, and 2012 HR, and then choosing *bullet graph* from the Show Me panel. The resulting view is shown in Figure 5-16.

In this initial view created from the *Show Me* menu, the length of the blue bars is determined by the 2011 HR totals, as evidenced by the green pill in the Columns shelf. The vertical black lines are the 2012

HR totals for each team, and the bands are at 60% and 80% of the 2012 values.

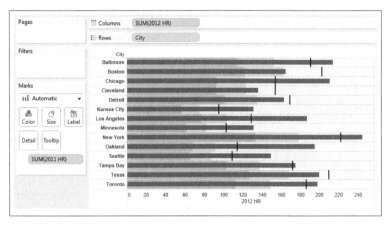

Figure 5-16. The initial bullet graph created by Show Me

Ideally, we'd prefer it to be the other way around: we want to see how the 2012 home run totals compared to the previous year. To make the switch, right-click in the x-axis and click *Swap Reference Line Fields*.

The resulting bullet graph is shown in Figure 5-17 (sorted descending and with a ratio calculated field column added).

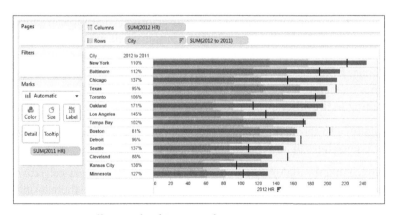

Figure 5-17. Bullet graph of AL team home runs, 2012 to 2011

What has Tableau done here? It has created a simple blue bar chart, in which the lengths of the bars are proportional to the amount of home runs hit by each team in 2012. It has also created a vertical line to each row, and color bands to facilitate easy comparison.

How do we read the bullet graph? If the blue bar goes beyond the black line, then the team hit more home runs collectively in 2012 than they did in 2011. If the blue bar falls to the left of the black line, then the team hit fewer home runs, and their 2012 tally falls into one of three bands:

- The darkest gray band is for teams that hit less than 60% of their previous year total (none fall into this leftmost band).
- The next lighter gray band is for teams that hit between 60% and 80% of their previous year total (again, none did).
- The final band is for teams that hit between 80% and 100% of their previous year total. This time, we find four teams in this region: the Rangers, the Red Sox, the Tigers, and the Indians.

Let's look at how these helpful reference lines and bands are created.

Reference Lines

Tableau has the ability to add a variety of types of reference lines and bands to charts that can be used to aid comparison. The bullet chart has built-in reference lines, but they can be added manually to any chart type.

To learn more about them, let's take a closer look at what Tableau added to the bar chart in Figure 5-14. Click in the x-axis area of the bullet graph, click *Edit Reference Line*, and notice there are two options to choose from. Tableau has created average 2011 HR lines (dark vertical lines in each row) and 60% and 80% bands for the 2011 figures (resulting in the different shaded areas in each row).

Figure 5-18 shows the dialog boxes that could be used to create these reference lines in any chart.

Notice that the dialog box on the left creates a line for every cell (row) that is equal to the average of the SUM(2011 HR). Because there is only one 2011 home run value for each team, the average is just that one value. The dialog box on the right creates distributed banding for each cell (row) that is equal to 60% and 80% of the 2011 HR average. Again, the average is just the single 2011 value for each team. The formatting controls the color of the fill, and how to fill in the regions between the boundaries.

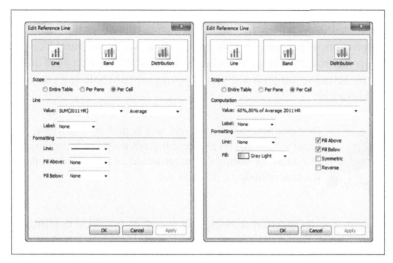

Figure 5-18. Two reference lines automatically created along with the bullet graph

Using this bullet graph, we can easily communicate a number of comparisons. It's clear that New York hit the most home runs in the league in both the 2011 and 2012 seasons, and that their 2012 tally was more than their 2011 tally. Similar questions can be answered about each team. The bullet graph is a very efficient and effective tool for comparison.

Lastly, let's briefly consider actual-to-target comparisons.

Actual-to-Target

The world is full of people and teams with goals in the form of quotas, budgets, and performance targets. These figures are tracked and monitored religiously to determine "performance to plan." Just listen to any monthly sales call. You'll hear discussions about concepts such as:

- How are we doing compared to where we want to be at the end of the year?

- How are we doing compared to where we should be right now if we want to hit our monthly goal?

These are fundamental questions in business, politics, world development, and even personal life. At their core, they are comparisons of proportion or percent, and it's fairly easy to see how charts like the ones shown in this chapter can be used to answer these types of questions. Actual-to-target is a special type of part-to-whole and current-to-historical.

 By definition, actual-to-target isn't bound by 1 or 100%, because we can always exceed our goals and targets. In the case of quotas, exceeding the target would be welcomed, while in the case of budgets, it would not.

Imagine a waterfall chart showing how spending in a fiscal year breaks down into different departments or categories. Adding a budget reference line would be an easy way to see if the expenditures were more or less than what was allocated.

Or if a sales department wanted to show how its reps were performing relative to plan, they could create a bullet graph where the blue bars represented actuals for each rep and the lines and bands represented quotas.

Summary

Proportions and percentages are ubiquitous, and in this chapter, we've seen how to communicate them well, as well as the steps involved to create effective chart types in Tableau. We've also considered table calculations in greater detail, and started using reference lines and quick filters. We introduced the bullet chart, and showed how to create the waterfall chart.

In the next chapter, we'll consider "measures of central tendency": mean and median.

CHAPTER 6

Mean and Median

"...like a statistician who drowned in a
lake of average depth six inches."

—Anonymous

Try to think of a time when you listened to a presentation about data that didn't include either an average or a median value. They're almost as common as percentages. Whether we're tracking home prices, the stock market, student test scores, or the price of gasoline, we come face to face with the notion of central tendency on a regular basis.

Why are they so commonly used? As humans, we have a hard time processing a simple list of more than a half dozen values, let alone reams and reams of raw data. The attractiveness of these measures of central tendency is that they condense a lot of data into digestible morsels that carry with them the notion of "typical."

As useful as these statistics can be to communicate data, they need to be handled with care. In this chapter, we'll see how they can be put to good use, but we'll also see how they can mislead.

The three main measures of central tendency are mean, median, and mode. Let's start with their definitions:

- The *mean* (or average) is determined by summing all of the values in a data set and dividing by the number of values. The mean is considered a "representative value," meaning if you replaced each value in the data set with the mean, the overall sum wouldn't change.

- The *median* is the middle value in a data set in which the values have been placed in order of magnitude. Thus, half the values in the data set are less than the median, and half are greater.

- The *mode* is the most commonly occurring value in a data set.

Before diving into the data, let's clarify that the goal of our discussion about mean and median isn't to recap our freshman statistics courses. This book is for practitioners, so we'll focus on the use of these statistics in communicating data.

No discussion of mean and median is complete without a healthy dose of the Gaussian distribution. We'll start there.

The Normal Distribution

The Gaussian, or normal, distribution, is something we've all been exposed to at some point. The unmistakable bell-shaped curve of the Gaussian represents a very mild style of variation, one in which the probability of a value occurring falls off dramatically the farther we move away from the mean on either side (determined by the number of standard deviations the value lies away from the mean). It's also symmetrical, and the mean, median, and mode are exactly equal. Figure 6-1 shows the characteristic shape and attributes of the normal distribution.

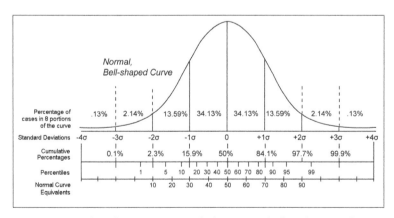

Figure 6-1. The characteristics of the normal distribution (http://bit.ly/pr-nce-links)

Distributions approximating the normal are found in nature and the physical sciences. An example that will suffice to illustrate the point is the heights (*http://bit.ly/avg-height*) of adult humans (though the distribution departs from the normal due to the medical condition known as dwarfism).

If the next flight overseas collected height measurements of 250 passengers, the heights would be more or less normally distributed. Even if the tallest person in the world happened to be on board, he would account for no more than about half a percent of the summed heights of the group (and that one person would be incredibly uncomfortable, I would imagine).

To get an empirical view of the normal distribution, let's look at another data set from baseball: runs batted in.

An Example of "Normal" Data

In baseball, a run batted in (RBI) is granted to a batter every time he enables a runner to score during his at bat. A batter can earn more than one RBI during a single at bat; a grand slam home run would result in 4 RBI—one for each of the runners on base, and one for the batter himself. A player's RBI tally is an important batting statistic; as mentioned in the previous chapter, it's part of the "triple crown" along with batting average and home runs.

Batting statistics, including RBI, for the 2012 season are available online (*http://mlb.mlb.com/stats/*), and we can download and connect to the data with Tableau. We can create a histogram as before, in order to visualize the distribution of qualifying players' RBI during the 2012 season, as shown in Figure 6-2.

At a quick glance, this distribution seems to approximate the normal curve quite well. It has a mean of 73.69 and a median of 74—measures nearly identical in magnitude. In this case, both of these measures are effective at communicating the "typical" number of RBIs earned by qualifying batters (those who have roughly 500 at bats in a season).

The histogram is a helpful way to see the overall distribution of all of the players, but what if we were interested in comparing the RBI tallies for players that play different positions on the field? Players play one of nine positions on each baseball team. Which position had the most RBI, on average? First basemen? Center fielders?

To make this comparison, we'll create a box plot.

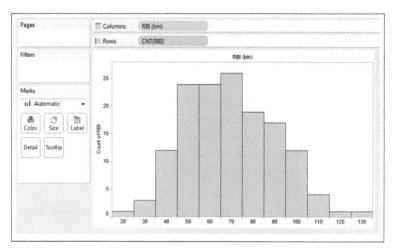

Figure 6-2. A histogram of players' RBI during the 2012 season

Box Plots

Every data set has a mean, a median, a maximum (max), and a minimum (min), among a variety of other statistics. A helpful way to visualize these statistics and to get a sense of the distribution of multiple groups in a data set is with a box plot. Figure 6-2 shows a diagram of this type of statistical chart, invented by John Tukey in the 1970s.

We can create a box plot in Tableau 8.1 and above very quickly and easily using the new box-and-whisker plot chart type in the Show Me panel. If we Ctrl-click the Player and Pos (for "Position") Dimensions, and the RBI Measure, and then open the Show Me panel and select *box-and-whisker plot*, we get the chart shown in Figure 6-4.

It's possible to create a box-and-whisker plot from scratch, and doing so will help reinforce the power of reference lines and bands like we used in the previous chapter when we created bullet graphs.

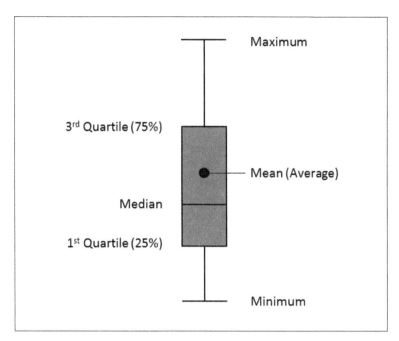

Figure 6-3. The box plot

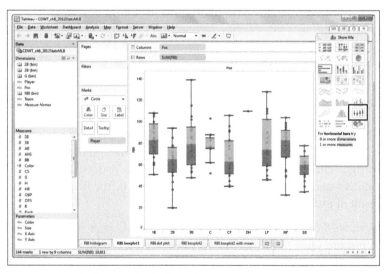

Figure 6-4. The box-and-whisker plot

Let's start by dragging Pos onto Columns and RBI onto Rows, which creates a bar chart showing the sum of all RBI for each position. Next, drag Player onto Detail and change the Marks type to *Circle*. After changing the circles to a transparent gray with a darker gray border via the Color shelf, we now have a sense of the distribution by position, as shown in Figure 6-5.

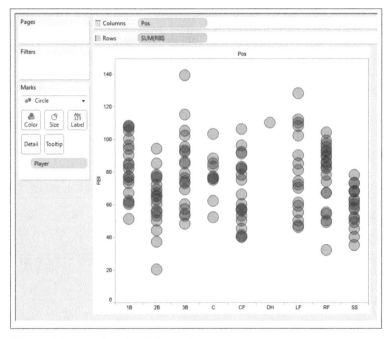

Figure 6-5. Dot plot of RBI by position

There is only one DH ("designated hitter") that completed the 2012 season with enough at bats to qualify, so we'll filter out this data point by right-clicking and selecting *Exclude*. Now we're down to eight positions—and notice the blue pill that appears in the filter shelf as a result of excluding the DH.

Next, we'll convert the dots to eight vertical lines stretching from the minimum value to the maximum value of each position by changing the Marks type from *Circle* to *Line* and then dragging Player onto the Path shelf, as shown in Figure 6-6.

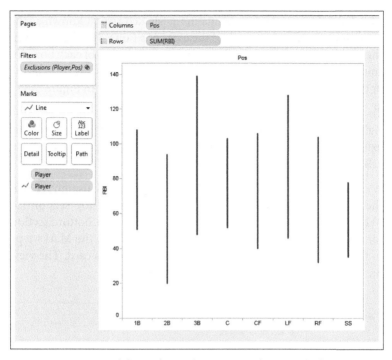

Figure 6-6. Vertical lines from the min to the max values of each position

We'll now right-click in the y-axis and select *Add Reference Line* three separate times, filling out the resulting dialog boxes one at a time, as shown in Figure 6-7.

Figure 6-7. Add Reference Line dialog boxes

The dialog box on the left results in the shaded region known as the "interquartile range" for each of the eight positions. The dialog box in the middle creates the eight horizontal lines at the top of each box plot (maximum), and the dialog box on the right creates the lines at the bottom (minimum). The resulting box plot is shown in Figure 6-8.

To add the dots for the mean, click RBI in the Measures panel with the right mouse button and drag it onto the Rows shelf to the right of the existing SUM(RBI). Select AVG(RBI) in the menu that appears when you release the right mouse button.

A second chart now appears below the box plot, and also notice that the Marks area changes to have three sections: the top section for All, or both; the middle section for SUM(RBI); and the bottom section for AVG(RBI). Click in the AVG(RBI) section, change the Marks type to *Circle*, and drag the Player field out of the Marks card. The view on the bottom changes to a dot plot of means.

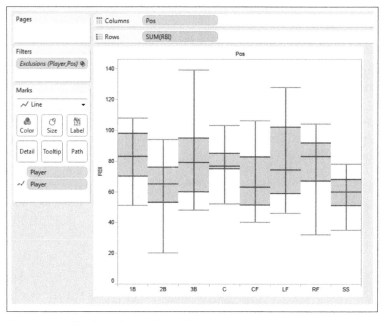

Figure 6-8. The box plot without the mean

Hover over the green AVG(RBI) pill in the Rows shelf, and when the small down arrow appears within the pill, click it and then select *Dual Axis* from the drop-down menu. The two charts in the view now overlap, and a second y-axis appears to the right. The two y-axes aren't yet synchronized (they have different maximum values). Right-click in the y-axis on the righthand side, and select *Synchronize Axis*, as shown in Figure 6-9.

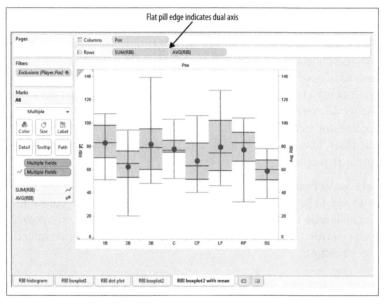

Figure 6-9. Using the synchronized dual axis to add average points to the dot plot

We can now compare the mean, median, first and third quartiles, and maximum and minimum RBI values for each of the eight positions, all in one compact view.

Just like the bullet graph, the box plot is a very dense chart type, conveying a lot of information in a visual encoding that isn't very difficult to learn. That's why it's such a popular chart type among statisticians and engineers trying to understand the central tendency and variation of multiple groups of data.

Next, let's consider how we can communicate central tendency when the distribution doesn't fit neatly into a normal distribution.

An Example of "Non-Normal" Data

The world we live in is full of non-normal data sets that are much more challenging to deal with than those that approximate the Gaussian. If the Gaussian displays a mild form of variation, then non-normal data sets display a wild form of variation: skewed to either side, multimodal, or having fat tails or distant outliers.

Distribution of wealth is notoriously non-normal. If the next flight overseas collected net worth data from each of the passengers onboard, instead of height measurements, a small number of passengers would account for a lion's share of the overall wealth. If the richest person in the world were on board (as unlikely as that may seem), he would account for virtually all of the wealth of the group. It may not be fair, but that's how it is. Very different than the distribution of height, wouldn't you say?

Let's consider an example of the distribution of money from the world of sports. Salary data for all of the 550 players in the US professional soccer league during 2012 can be found online (*http://bit.ly/2012-soccer-players*). Figure 6-10 shows a histogram of guaranteed compensation.

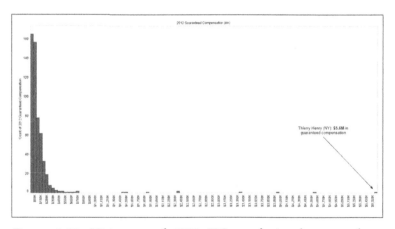

Figure 6-10. Histogram of 2012 U.S. professional soccer player salaries

Not exactly a bell-shaped curve, is it? The length of the x-axis scale isn't a mistake: those tiny bars along the baseline are the nine players that earned over $1M in guaranteed compensation in 2012. The player who earned the most in 2012 has a salary that is more than 12 standard deviations away from the mean.

Let's consider the summary statistics for this data set as tabulated in Figure 6-11.

	2012 guaranteed compensation	% earning less than
Mean	$ 163,934	76%
Standard Deviation	$ 423,846	N/A
1st Quartile	$ 44,100	25%
Median	$ 81,250	50%
3rd Quartile	$ 160,500	75%
Mode	$ 44,000	10%

Figure 6-11. Summary statistics for 2012 player compensation

Which is the best measure of central tendency? Which measure would you consider "typical" of player salaries? More than three out of four players earned less than the mean, and only 10% earned less than the mode, so neither seems very typical.

The median, by definition, has as many players above it as it has below it. This is why the median is often used as the measure of central tendency when dollars are involved: because the distribution is often quite skewed. Think about the median home price in your zip code, or the median annual salary of employees in your workplace.

Sensitivity to Outliers

To illustrate the point further, let's consider the hypothetical impact to the measures of central tendency of adding one of the world's top-paid soccer players to the league. The world's top soccer players (e.g., Lionel Messi and Cristiano Ronaldo) command about $20M in salary (not including endorsements) (*http://bit.ly/soccer-salary*). How would the summary statistics change if a new player like this were added to the mix? Consider the updated tabulation of statistics shown in Figure 6-12.

	2012 guaranteed compensation	If a player earning $20M joined MLS	% earning less than
Mean	$ 163,934	$ 199,999	84%
Standard Deviation	$ 423,846	$ 945,895	N/A
1st Quartile	$ 44,100	$ 44,100	25%
Median	$ 81,250	$ 81,332	50%
3rd Quartile	$ 160,500	$ 160,875	75%
Mode	$ 44,000	$ 44,000	10%

Figure 6-12. Hypothetical statistics resulting from the addition of a $20M player

Notice that the mean is far more sensitive to the addition of this new outlier. It jumped from $164K to almost $200K, while the median increased by less than $100. Relative insensitivity to outliers is another reason to consider using the median when communicating "typical" values of skewed distributions.

Visualizing Typical Values of Non-Normal Distributions

If we create box plots of player salary for each of the teams similar to the way we created box plots in the RBI example, we would end up with the view shown in Figure 6-13.

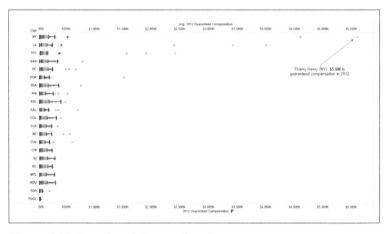

Figure 6-13. Box plot of player salary by team

Notice how the mean (the dots colored red) don't even fall within the interquartile range for the three teams at the top of the chart. It's no coincidence that these are the teams with the three highest paid players in the league. The presence of these outliers "pulled" the mean to the right. I'm sure the players on the New York team wouldn't agree if you told them the "typical" player salary was $518K.

Summary

In this chapter, we covered measures of central tendency—mean, median, and mode—and how to visualize these values for different types of distributions. We also touched on how the notion of "average" can be problematic in communicating data. To recap: blindly using the mean can be dangerous. It conveys a notion of "typical" when it may not be typical at all, depending on the distribution of the data. This is important to remember when communicating measures of central tendency.

Does knowing this make the task a little more difficult? Yes, but we wouldn't want to make it simpler than it is, would we?

In the next chapter, we'll consider two very important topics that are often overlooked in communicating data: variation and uncertainty.

CHAPTER 7

Variation and Uncertainty

"There is nothing so uncertain as a sure thing."

—Scotty Bowman

It's easy to get cocky when armed with a little bit of data. We get a sense of knowing something about the world, and it increases our confidence in what we have to say. That can be a good thing. But the world is a noisy, chaotic, ever-changing place. If the data set we're working with is noisy, or if the inferences we're making are dubious at best, we'll need to proceed with caution.

The core principle to employ when communicating data is to be honest about what we know and what we don't know, and to represent reality to the best of our ability. If there is a high degree of variation in the data, or if we're only working with a limited sample, we should make that clear to our audience. Doing otherwise would be misleading.

In this chapter, we'll consider two humbling and unavoidable aspects of communicating data: variation and uncertainty. By *variation*, we mean the degree to which individual observations differ from others in a group. By *uncertainty*, we mean the lack of confidence in inferences about a population based on data collected from samples.

Respecting Variation

In Chapter 6, we considered measures of central tendency, like mean and median. In so doing, we touched on some basic measures of variation, such as standard deviation and the interquartile range, concepts visualized once again in Figure 7-1.

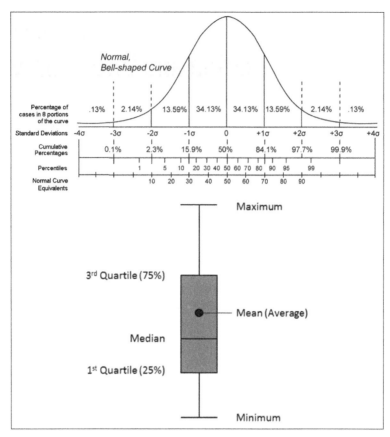

Figure 7-1. Visualizing variation

We also considered two very different types of variables from the world of sports in Chapter 6: baseball batting statistics (RBI) and soccer players' salaries, as shown in Figure 7-2.

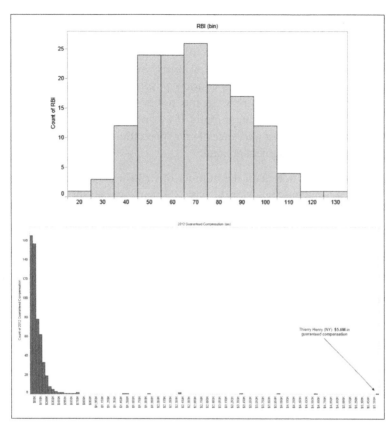

Figure 7-2. Two different distributions: normal/Gaussian/bell-shaped (top) and non-normal (bottom)

These variables are fundamentally different in the type of distribution their values form. The former demonstrates the Gaussian properties of the bell-shaped curve, while the latter is characterized by extreme outliers that make up the bulk of the total amount.

The importance of this distinction and what it means to the way we deal with data has been articulated by Benoit Mandelbrot, and more recently by Nicholas Nassim Taleb. In a nutshell, applying measures of variance like standard deviation to describe and predict phenomena that are decidedly non-normal—such as just about any parameter in the world of economics and finance—is fraught with error and should be avoided. It's the wrong tool for the job.

Visualizing Variation

One way to respect the variation inherent in our data is to show it. Merely showing averages yields an overly simplistic picture of the world. Not every person in a country possesses the most common physical traits in that country. So, too, not every value in a data set is equal to the mean, median, or mode. If we only show the most typical value, then we rob our audience of an appreciation of the rich texture to be found in the subject at hand.

If we consider once again the number of strikeouts per nine innings in professional baseball over the past 100 years, we can show a simple line plot of average strikeouts per nine innings, as shown in Figure 7-3.

Figure 7-3. Average number of strikeouts per nine innings

What we don't know from this chart, however, is how the different teams in the league each year differed in their strikeout rates. What's the difference between the team with the highest strikeout rate and the team with the lowest rate each year? We just don't know from this view. We can give a sense of the variation inherent in the data in a number of different ways, as shown in Figure 7-4.

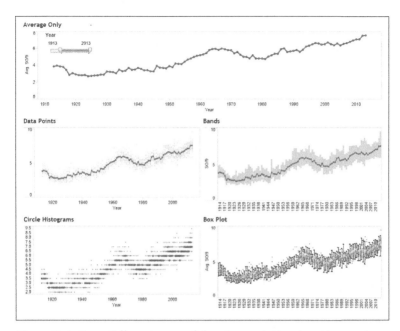

Figure 7-4. Four different ways of showing variation in a time series

The top-left view is the most straightforward—each team has its own circle in each year. The top-right view includes reference bands from the minimum to the maximum for each year. The bottom-left view is a series of circle histograms, wherein the area of each circle is proportional to the number of teams in each bin. The bottom-right view shows a series of box plots for each year. Each view gives a sense of how much the average number of strikeouts per nine innings varies from team to team each year.

It may not be important to our message, but if we only showed the average values for each year, then the assumption many would make is that each team was very close to the points plotted. Showing variation can be helpful, and there are ways to do so without "hitting the audience over the head" with all that variation.

Variation Over Time: Control Charts

Control charts illustrate whether data collected over time has any statistically significant signals, or whether the variation in the data is merely noise. They were invented at the Western Electric Company by Walter Shewhart in the 1920s, in the context of industrial quality control. The recent Six Sigma movement has brought this type of chart into prominent use, as legions of "black belts" use them to measure process behavior in an attempt to reduce variation and thereby improve quality.

The theory is that less variation results in fewer defects. The theory definitely holds water in manufacturing, and—more generally—any time a process should be producing the same thing over and over again. As drab as that sounds, it's what we expect when we order a burger from a fast food chain or go to start up a new car. Variation in those contexts would most likely be unwelcome.

In order to reduce variation, process specialists first need to figure out whether there are any sources of *special-cause variation*—or signals— in the historical data.

Let's first break down the elements of the control chart as shown in Figure 7-5, and then we'll consider how to make them step by step.

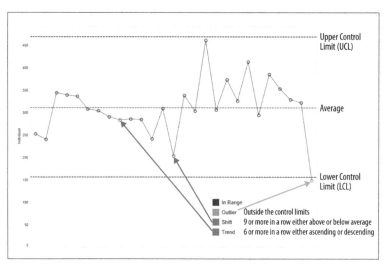

Figure 7-5. The elements of a Shewhart Control Chart

Anatomy of a Control Chart

A control chart contains the following basic elements:

- The time series data itself
- The average line
- The control limits, computed in various ways from the data itself:
  - UCL (the upper control limit)
  - LCL (the lower control limit)
- Signals:
  - Outliers (data points either above the UCL or below the LCL)
  - Trends (six or more points either all ascending or all descending)
  - Shifts (nine or more points either all above or all below the average line)

How to Create a Control Chart in Tableau

Now that we've got the basics covered, let's see how it's done using two different methods—the *quick method* and the *rigorous method*. The difference between the two is how the control limits are calculated. The quick method uses what's called a *global measure of dispersion*, or the standard deviation of all of the points. The rigorous method uses a *local measure of dispersion*, called Sigma(x), which is derived from the differences between successive data points.

For the next few pages, we'll take into consideration the total number of earthquakes recorded worldwide that registered magnitude 6.0 or higher on the Richter scale from 1983 through 2013. The source for the data is the USGS Earthquake Archive Search website (*http://bit.ly/ earthquake-search*). There were 4,136 such events recorded, and Figure 7-6 gives a view of the most recent records in the data set.

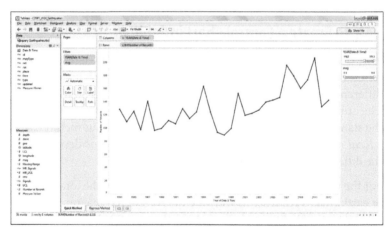

Figure 7-6. Sample of global earthquakes data set, registering magnitude 6.0 or greater

The quick method

Create a simple timeline with a YEAR(Date & Time) on the Columns shelf, and SUM(Number of Records) on the Rows shelf, fit to width as shown in Figure 7-7.

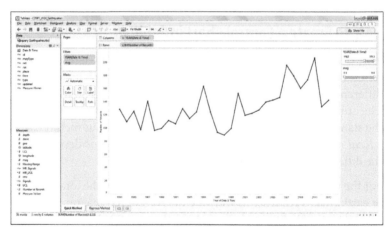

Figure 7-7. A simple timeline of the number of annual earthquakes

Right-click on the y-axis, select Add Reference Line, and add an average line by filling out the resulting dialog box. Then right-click on the y-axis, select Add Reference Line again, and this time add a distribution of +3 and −3 times the standard deviation, with dotted red lines and no fill. Both reference line dialog boxes are shown in Figure 7-8.

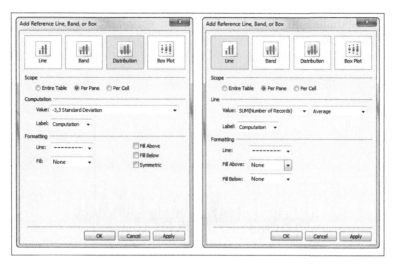

Figure 7-8. Adding reference lines to the line chart

We now have a simple control chart showing the annual number of earthquakes worldwide, as shown in Figure 7-9.

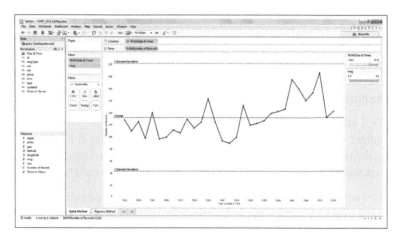

Figure 7-9. Simple control chart of annual earthquakes of magnitude 6.0 or greater

This version doesn't show any points "out of control," or beyond three standard deviations from the mean. If we change from YEAR to MONTH, then the control chart changes to show a number of points above the 3 sigma line, including a sharp outlier in March 2011 corresponding to the Great East Japan earthquake, as shown in Figure 7-10.

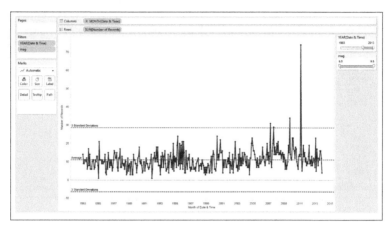

Figure 7-10. The simple control chart showing monthly counts of worldwide earthquakes

Also note that the lower limit is not real. It's below 0, and it's not possible to have a negative number of earthquakes recorded.

Let's see how a more rigorous approach can enlighten us further about whether any statistical outliers are included in the data.

The rigorous method

We'll add a few extra elements to this version, including a "Moving Range" timeline that shows the absolute value of the change from quake to quake, control limits calculated from this moving range, and data points colored by their type—in range, outliers, trends, and shifts.

Start with a new Sheet, and repeat Step 1 of the quick method described in the previous section to create a basic timeline, duplicating SUM(Number of Records) and creating a dual-axis plot with axes synchronized. The first set of Marks should be a line, and the second set of Marks should be circles, as shown in Figure 7-11.

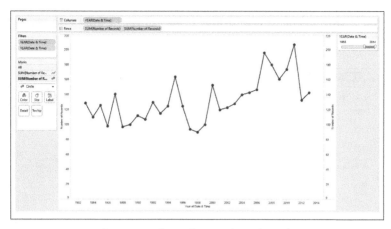

Figure 7-11. Dual-axis timeline of annual earthquake count

Create the "Moving Range" timeline underneath the main "Individuals" timeline by dragging another instance of SUM(Number of Re cords) to the Rows shelf to the right of the first two, and change this new pill to a Quick Table Calculation showing the difference, as shown in Figure 7-12.

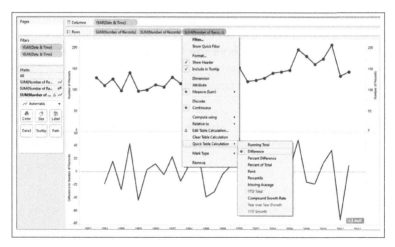

Figure 7-12. Adding a Moving Range chart

Edit the Table Calculation and click Customize to open the edit dialog, adding ABS() around the entire equation, as shown in Figure 7-13. Also, make the new Moving Range chart a dual-axis chart with a line and circle marks for the individual data points as we did with the top chart.

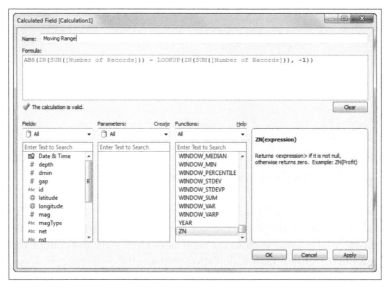

Figure 7-13. Modifying the Moving Range table calculation to make it an absolute value

Add the average lines for both the Individuals chart (top) and the Moving Range chart (bottom) by right-clicking on each of the y-axes and selecting *Add Reference Line*, similar to Step 2 in the quick method. Do this for both charts.

Create the following three calculated fields, MR_UCL, UCL, and LCL, which are Shewhart's original equations to determine the control limits:

```
MR_UCL = 3.267*WINDOW_AVG([Moving Range])
UCL = SUM([Number of Records]) + 3*WINDOW_AVG([Moving
Range]) / 1.128
LCL = SUM([Number of Records]) - 3*WINDOW_AVG([Moving
Range]) / 1.128
```

Figure 7-14 shows these equations in Calculated Field dialog boxes.

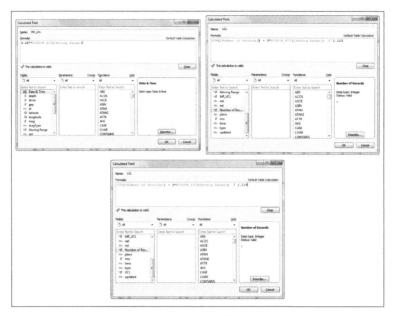

Figure 7-14. Creating Shewhart's control limits via calculated fields

Add these three new calculated fields to the level of Detail for All Marks, and use them to create three new reference lines: UCL and LCL in the top Individuals chart, and MR_UCL in the bottom Moving Range chart.

Create two new Calculated Fields for the signals, one called Signals (to be used in the top Individuals chart) and the other called MR_Sig nals (to be used in the bottom Moving Range chart) by copying and pasting the equations available in *Signals.doc (http://bit.ly/cdwt-ch7-signals)* and *MR_Signals.doc (http://bit.ly/cdwt-ch7-mr-signals).* You can also find these files to download at *http://dataremixed.com/books/cdwt.*

Drag these new calculated fields to their respective Colors shelves— Signals should be placed on the Individuals Circle Color shelf and MR_Signals should be placed on the Moving Range Circle Color shelf.

The final rigorous control chart is shown in Figure 7-15.

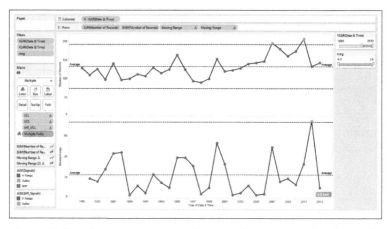

Figure 7-15. The rigorous control chart showing worldwide earthquake count by year

There are a few new insights we can glean from this more rigorous approach:

- Both 2009 and 2011 are statistical outliers: they are above the upper control limit for this time period.

- 2012 and 2013 represent a shift in the data: they are the ninth and tenth points all on one side of the average line (higher).

- The drop in earthquake count from 2011 to 2012 was a statistically significant *change* in the number of annual earthquakes, further highlighting the extraordinary amount in 2011, largely accounted for by the crisis in Japan that year.

If we change from YEAR to MONTH, then we see a number of other statistically significant outliers and shifts, but no trends, as shown in Figure 7-16.

Control charts have a broad application to anything that can be thought of as a process. Creating control charts in Tableau is a great way to track that process and be alerted to signals in the data, as well as save time and effort by filtering out the noise. When creating control charts, users can either opt to employ the quick method or the rigorous method, depending on their level of skill and the degree of statistical rigor warranted by the situation.

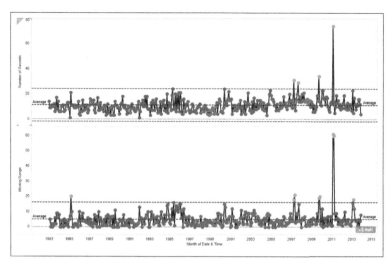

Figure 7-16. A monthly view of global earthquakes using the rigorous method

Understanding Uncertainty

When we present data to an audience, it's important to make clear whether we are presenting data from the entire population, or from just a sample of the population.

Often, the data set we're working with is the whole enchilada—all sales for the past quarter, total inventory levels, a team's win percentage for the entire season. But sometimes we're only presenting data from a sample of the population—quality inspection results for a sample of the day's production, or the results of a customer satisfaction survey sent to 1% of the customer base.

In these cases, we should do our best to follow good statistical practices and randomize the sample, and we should also present the results with confidence intervals included so our audience isn't misled into thinking that they can conclude more than the data allows.

To illustrate the point, let's consider a fictional case of chess club participation rates of students in ten different cities in the peaceful country of Chesslandia. The President of Chesslandia, Garry Fischer, wanted to know whether students in his country were involved in chess club or not, and which cities were more successful in getting students to participate. He sent out his amateurs to ask a handful of students in

each city whether they were in chess club or not, and the spreadsheet
they brought back to him is shown in Figure 7-17.

	A	B	C	D
1	Grade	Town	In Chess Club	Not in Chess Club
2	5th-6th grade	Kingston	29	40
3	5th-6th grade	Queensville	39	30
4	5th-6th grade	Rooktown	39	31
5	5th-6th grade	Bishop Village	18	32
6	5th-6th grade	Knightfield	35	33
7	5th-6th grade	Pawnford	36	18
8	5th-6th grade	Castleborough	38	22
9	5th-6th grade	Checkshire	33	31
10	5th-6th grade	Fianchettoberg	32	33
11	5th-6th grade	Gambitopolis	31	30
12	3rd-4th grade	Kingston	14	28
13	3rd-4th grade	Queensville	16	22
14	3rd-4th grade	Rooktown	13	21
15	3rd-4th grade	Bishop Village	7	26
16	3rd-4th grade	Knightfield	15	26
17	3rd-4th grade	Pawnford	14	21
18	3rd-4th grade	Castleborough	22	14
19	3rd-4th grade	Checkshire	15	27
20	3rd-4th grade	Fianchettoberg	14	27
21	3rd-4th grade	Gambitopolis	11	27
22	1st-2nd grade	Kingston	7	20
23	1st-2nd grade	Queensville	6	12
24	1st-2nd grade	Rooktown	8	20
25	1st-2nd grade	Bishop Village	4	17
26	1st-2nd grade	Knightfield	6	20
27	1st-2nd grade	Pawnford	6	12
28	1st-2nd grade	Castleborough	10	14
29	1st-2nd grade	Checkshire	7	20
30	1st-2nd grade	Fianchettoberg	8	15
31	1st-2nd grade	Gambitopolis	6	16

Figure 7-17. Spreadsheet of results of chess club student survey

Being a big believer in data visualization, the president uploaded the
numbers into his computer, Deep Purple. The enlightening bar charts
that he saw are shown in Figure 7-18.

He was about to call up the mayors of Castleborough and Pawnford
to congratulate them on their results when he noticed that the sample
sizes were very small relative to the thousands of students in each city.
For some of the grades, as few as 18 students had been surveyed.

He demanded to know what level of confidence he could place on the results, and so he summoned his chief statistician, who was busy calculating how many chess moves were possible.

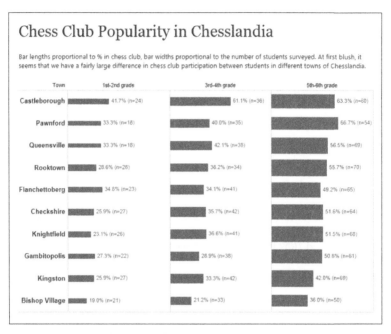

Figure 7-18. Visualization of the survey results

The chief statistician explained to him the concept of sample statistics and population parameters, the central limit theorem, and binomial proportion confidence intervals. The survey was not unlike flipping coins—the possibilities were two-fold: either a student was in chess club, or not. Given a certain number of students surveyed, it was possible to compute an interval for each city and grade at a certain degree of confidence.

The statistician used the normal approximation interval formula to put error bars around each proportion.

To do so, he first needed to create a parameter that allowed the president to select his desired degree of confidence, as shown in Figure 7-19.

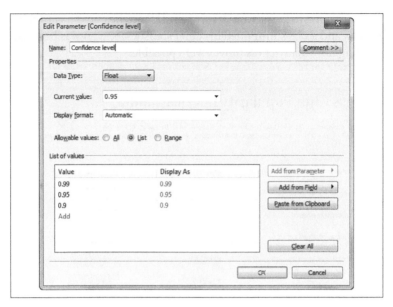

Figure 7-19. A new parameter to select desired confidence level

Next, he needed to create a number of calculated fields to generate the error bars:

- **% in Chess Club**, p = [In Chess Club]/([In Chess Club]+[Not in Chess Club])
- Sample Size, **n** = [In Chess Club]+[Not in Chess Club]
- **Standard Error** = SQRT((([% in Chess Club]*(1-[% in Chess Club]))/[n])
- **z upper** = CASE [Confidence level]
  - — WHEN 0.99 THEN 2.575829
  - — WHEN 0.95 THEN 1.959964
  - — WHEN 0.90 THEN 1.644854
- **Margin of Error** = [Standard Error]*[z upper]
- **Lower limit** = [% in Chess Club]-[Margin of Error]
- **Upper limit** = [% in Chess Club]+[Margin of Error]
- **Error Bar Line** = [Upper limit]-[Lower limit]
- **np** = [n]*[% in Chess Club]

Finally, he created a dual-axis dot plot with error bars as follows:

- He created a Circle plot with Town on Rows and SUM(% in Chess Club) on Columns, sorted descending, and added np to the Filter shelf, including only values of np greater than or equal to 5 (to satisfy the criteria for using the Normal approximation interval).

- Next, he created a Quick Filter for Grade and selected only one of the grades to show (fifth and sixth grade).

- He dragged Lower limit and Upper limit to the Details card and created reference lines for each cell, one for each of the two calculated fields.

- He then dragged SUM(Lower Limit) to Columns, made it a Gantt Bar chart, and added SUM(Error Bar Line) to the Size shelf of the Gantt Bar chart, reducing the Size of the bar so that they were thin lines rather than thick bars.

- Finally, he changed the new Gantt Bar chart to a dual-axis with synchronized axes.

The resulting dot plot with error bars is shown in Figure 7-20.

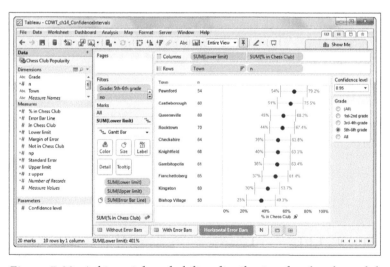

Figure 7-20. A binomial probability distribution for the chess club survey results

The confidence intervals are shown for each city and each grade in Figures 7-21, 7-22, and 7-23.

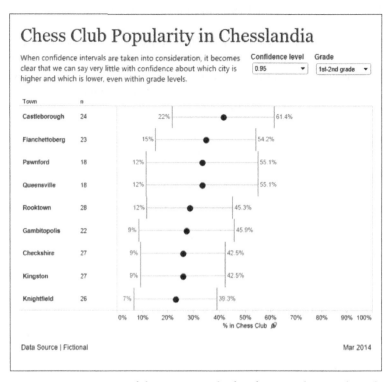

Figure 7-21. 95% confidence intervals for first- and second-grade chess club participation

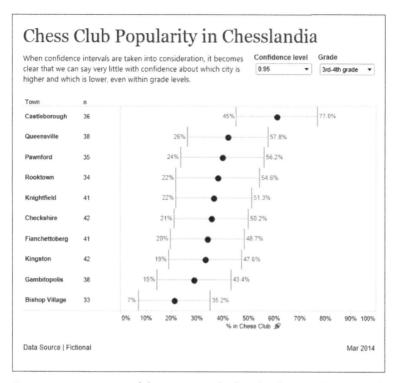

Figure 7-22. 95% confidence intervals for third- and fourth-grade chess club participation

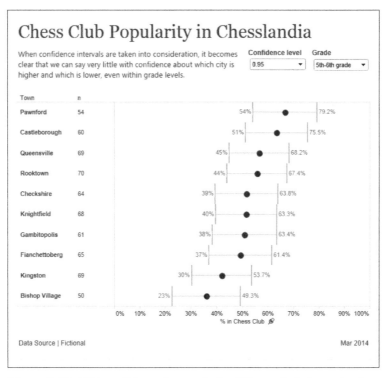

Figure 7-23. 95% confidence intervals for fifth- and sixth-grade chess club participation

From these charts, it's apparent that based on these survey results, the president can be confident about far less than he originally thought. In fact, nothing can be said about the relative difference of chess club participation between the first and second graders of each city. The intervals completely overlap one another.

Additionally:

- Bishop Village has been filtered out of the first and second grade results because the sample size times the proportion (np) was less than 5, meaning that the normal approximation isn't legitimate.

- While Castleborough seems to have much higher participation rates for third and fourth graders, we can only be confident at the 95% level that rates are higher at Castleborough than Gambitopolis and Bishop Village.

- We can be 95% sure that Pawnford fifth and sixth graders participate at higher rates than at Kingston and Bishop Village, and we can be 95% sure that Castleborough fifth and sixth graders participate at higher rates than at Bishop Village.

Lastly, we can't really combine these results to compare *all* students in each city, because the sampling plan was somewhat haphazard. If President Fischer wanted to compare the overall picture, he would need his statistician to create a stratified sampling plan that took into account the relative differences of students in each of the grade groupings.

Summary

Variation and uncertainty really matter when communicating data. It's easy to take the simple route and just show averages or percentages, glossing over the complexity of the situation at hand. But how much the data points vary, and how confident we can be in the proportions can have a huge impact on the conclusions and decisions that follow.

The methods we've used in this chapter—the control chart and the binomial confidence interval plot—don't come close to covering every situation, and the wise communicator of data will research principles and techniques that may apply to the specific circumstances.

In the next chapter, we'll consider ways to communicate multiple quantities in the same views.

CHAPTER 8

Multiple Quantities

"Correlation does not imply causation."

—Unknown

So far, we've been creating views that focus on one variable at a time. While focus can be great, there is a whole world of relationships between multiple variables to explore, understand, and communicate. Finding these relationships can change the world (think carbon dioxide and global temperature).

One thing to keep in mind when exploring two or more variables at a time is that "correlation does not imply causation." What does this oft-quoted phrase mean? Just because two variables seem to change together doesn't necessarily mean that one causes the other to change, or vice versa. A third factor could be causing them both to change, or it may be coincidence and there may not be any causal relationship at all.

You've probably heard the example of rising ice cream sales and shark attacks. They both may rise together, but as the college textbook example goes, they're both caused by increasing numbers of people at the beach, which is in turn caused by increasing temperature. It's a silly example intended to illustrate the point, but there's some truth to it. We're very quick to assume causal relationships exist when all we really have is evidence of correlation. It's something to watch out for, but we shouldn't let it derail our exploration altogether, either.

In this chapter, we'll consider a number of ways to explore and communicate multiple quantities in the same individual chart. Later, in

Chapter 12, we'll tackle dashboards, where many different charts can be added to the same view.

Scatterplots

I'll come right out and say it: I love scatterplots. I love them because they create a two-dimensional plane in which a whole host of comparisons can be made in an instant. It's almost effortless to spot groups of points and individual points that stand apart from the rest, or outliers. The first visualization I created with Tableau Public was a scatterplot of the top 100 career points leaders in professional hockey history, shown in Figure 8-1.

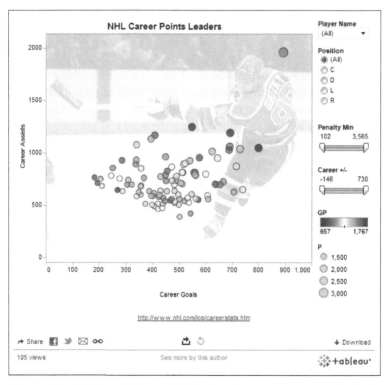

Figure 8-1. My first Tableau Public visualization: a scatterplot dashboard of career stats (photo by B. Bennett/Getty Images) (http://bit.ly/great-one)

In professional hockey, players earn a point toward their career statistics in one of two ways: they either score a goal themselves or they earn an assist by enabling a teammate to score a goal. A player's point total is simply the sum of their goals and assists. Goals and assists are also recorded individually, and you can find an updated table of career stats online (*http://bit.ly/nhl-career-stats*) that can be searched and filtered.

As we discussed in Chapter 3, tables are helpful for gleaning a small number of precise values, but they're not so helpful when it comes to recognizing patterns or comparing many values at the same time. That's where visualization comes in handy. The scatterplot shown in Figure 8-1 makes use of two axes to locate the circles on the plane according to the players' career goals (the x-axis) and their career assists (the y-axis).

Let's explore how to create this scatterplot. First, we'll connect to the spreadsheet that contains the top 100 players, which you can find online here (*http://bit.ly/nhl-career-stats*). Once we've connected to the spreadsheet, it's a simple matter of Ctrl-selecting Player, G (for goals), and A (for assists), and then clicking on *scatterplots* in the Show Me panel, as shown in Figure 8-2.

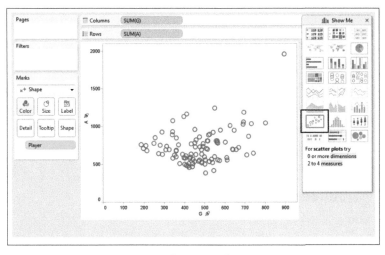

Figure 8-2. Creating a scatterplot using Show Me

Notice that Tableau has placed SUM(G) on the Columns shelf, SUM(A) on the Rows shelf, and Player in the Marks card (in the level of Detail). We could also have dragged these fields out to their corresponding places instead of using Show Me to create the scatterplot.

We'll consider how to add trend lines later in this chapter, but for now we can see that there is a large cloud of dots in the middle and a single dot in the upper-right corner that stands apart from the rest of the pack. The outlier is Wayne Gretzky, the player who wore jersey number 99 for Edmonton, Los Angeles, St. Louis, and New York. This view makes it clear that Gretzky's career statistics were something remarkable, even when compared to the rest of the players that together with Gretzky make up the top 100 of all-time. There are the 99, and then there is number 99. To me, this chart shows why Gretzky is regarded by many as the greatest athlete to play any team sport, ever.

So far we've compared two variables: goals and assists. With the scatterplot, we can add two more variables to the view rather easily. If we drag P (for points) to the Size shelf and GP (for games played) to the Color shelf, we now have a scatterplot that allows us to compare these 100 players along four different dimensions, as shown in Figure 8-3.

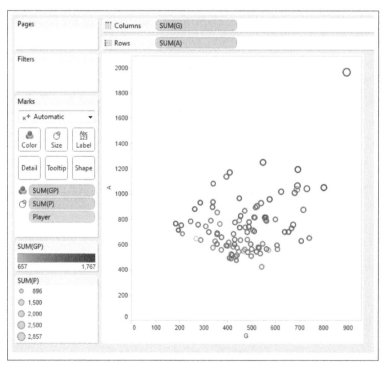

Figure 8-3. Scatterplot with added encodings for size and color

The larger the ring, the more career points a player has. The darker the ring, the more games a player played. These new comparisons are based on area and color ramp encodings, respectively. Refer back to Figure 1-6 and notice that area and color ramp are below position in the Quantitative list. The scatterplot still primarily facilites a comparison of the goals and assists, which are encoded based on position.

When deciding which variables to use where, consider which are the most important comparisons to make, and then encode them with the most effective encodings.

I made some changes purely based on aesthetics: first, I changed the Marks type from *Automatic* to *Circles*, then I changed the color palette from *Green Sequential* to a reversed *Orange-White-Blue Diverging*. Finally, I gave the circles some transparency and added light gray borders using the Color shelf, as shown in Figure 8-4.

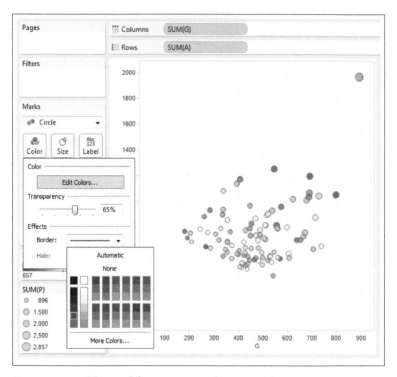

Figure 8-4. Additional formatting to the scatterplot

Who Is Who?

One challenge with the view so far is that it's a guessing game as to which players the dots correspond to. Where is Mark Messier, Gretzky's teammate on the Edmonton Oilers and the New York Rangers? Where is Gordie Howe, the player that Gretzky surpassed when he claimed the career points leadership? We can't tell. If that's part of our message, then we have a problem.

There are three ways to communicate who is who: labels, tooltips, and annotations. Let's consider them one at a time.

Labels

If we take Player from the Dimensions panel and drag it onto the Label shelf, Tableau attempts to add as many labels as it can without creating a messy view. The result is shown in Figure 8-5.

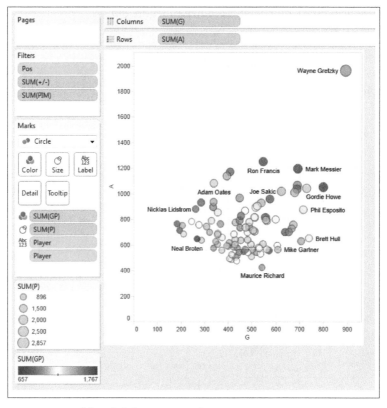

Figure 8-5. Adding labels to scatterplots

From this view, you can see a handful of other players around the cloud of points, including Messier and Howe. Conveniently, the algorithm tends to label the outliers, or at least the players on the fringes.

Adding these labels is helpful and allows the audience to pick out a few other stories from the view. For example, I can recall my father telling me about Maurice "the Rocket" Richard when I was a boy. He was known as a legendary goal scorer, and now I can see why: he is one of the few players in the top 100 with more career goals than assists, so he did little else than put the puck in the back of the net, relatively speaking.

It's possible to force Tableau to show all the labels, but I don't recommend it. Go ahead and try it out if you feel the need to, by clicking *Label* and checking the box at the bottom where it says *Allow labels to overlap other marks*. Don't say I didn't warn you, though. Sometimes more is less.

Tooltips

What about the other points without labels? How can we see who they are? Tableau has a great feature called Tooltips, which appear when a person interacting with the chart hovers the mouse cursor over an individual mark (or circle, in this case).

What would be an interesting data point to investigate further? How about the blue point just below Messier? We know blue means the player played relatively few games. Who is this player, and how did he rack up so many goals and assists in such a small number of games? Let's hover the mouse over the point or click on it to discover who it is. The mystery is revealed in Figure 8-6.

Hovering over the blue circle in the upper right reveals that the player is none other than former Pittsburgh center Mario Lemieux, another remarkable player whose career was interrupted by a number of injuries and health problems, including Hodgkin's lymphoma. We can only imagine how many points he would have tallied had he played as many games as Gretzky.

It's possible to modify the tooltip, and we'll cover formatting of tooltips later in Chapter 13. But if you want to play with them yourself now, just click *Worksheet → Tooltip* and the dialog box shown in Figure 8-7 appears.

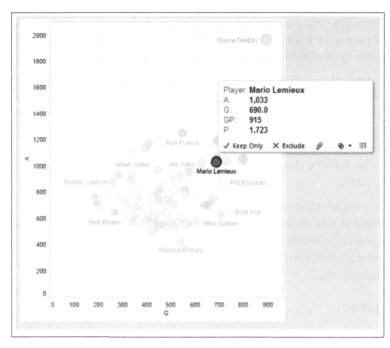

Figure 8-6. Hovering and clicking reveals tooltips

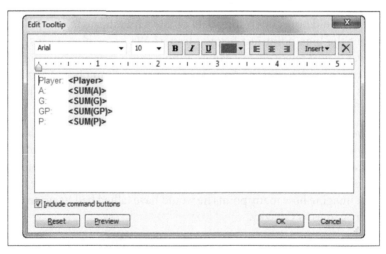

Figure 8-7. Editing tooltips

What does the checkbox in the bottom left mean? It says "Include command buttons," and if the checkbox is checked, then the footer of the tooltip shown in Figure 8-6 will appear, allowing the user to perform a variety of filtering and grouping actions with the selected points. Only check this box if you want the user to be able to filter or group points directly. I almost always uncheck this box, as I prefer to use Quick Filters to allow the user to control what data is shown and what is not shown in the view.

Annotations

Let's say we don't want to show a whole bunch of player names as labels, we just want to show Gretzky and Lemieux. How can we do that? First, let's get rid of the labels by dragging the blue Player pill next to the Abc symbol out of the Marks area. Next, right-click on the circle for Gretzky and select *Annotate → Mark*. In the resulting dialog box, let's delete everything except <Player> and click *OK*. After we do the same for the blue circle for Mario Lemieux, we get the scatterplot shown in Figure 8-8, with the annotations moved to a convenient place on the view.

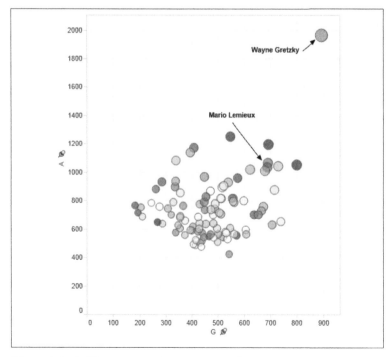

Figure 8-8. Adding annotations to scatterplots

Labels, tooltips, and annotations are three different ways to call attention to specific marks, or data points, in our views. Which we decide to use depends on whether we want to label many points, no points, or specific points. We can also use a combined approach as we did in the previous examples, showing some labels and allowing a user to discover other names through interaction.

Making it Exploratory

The last element we'll add with this scatterplot are the Quick Filters you see in Figure 8-1 on the righthand side. Why would we bother adding these filters? If our goal is to *explain* how remarkable Wayne Gretzky was, our job is done. However, if we'd like to give our audience the ability to *explore* the data to find other insights about the top 100 players, we still have some work to do.

We've mentioned it already, but it's worth repeating: adding Quick Filters is an easy and powerful way to explore data in Tableau. In the case of the hockey player career points data set, we'd like to add the ability to filter by position, career penalty minutes, and career +/− (pronounced "plus-minus"). To determine a player's plus-minus, stats keepers add up every goal the player's team scored while the player was on the ice, and subtract every goal the opposing team scored while the player was on the ice.

To add the three Quick Filters to the view, right-click on the three fields (Pos, +/−, and PIM) one at a time, and select *Show Quick Filter* for each one. Tableau adds a Multiple Values (combo box) list for Pos and Range of Values sliders for +/− and PIM, as shown in Figure 8-9.

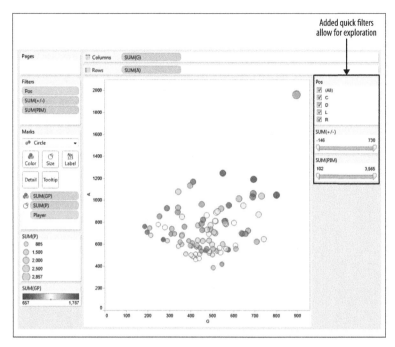

Figure 8-9. Quick Filters turn a scatterplot into an exploratory interactive

Now we can explore this data set in a number of different ways to ask and answer a variety of questions. We can also configure the filters to be different types. To change the position filter from a multiple select to a single select "radio button" style, we can hover over the filter box, click the small down arrow that appears in the upper-right corner, and then select *Single Value (list)*. We can also change the sliders to be one-sided: "At Least" or "At Most."

Our choice of filter type depends on what we want users to do with the filters. In this case, allowing the users to select only one position at a time makes it more likely that they will create the views shown in Figure 8-10, wherein certain patterns emerge about the different positions.

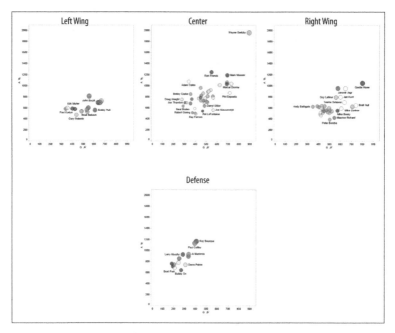

Figure 8-10. Viewing the scatterplot one position at a time

Among offensive players, there are relatively few left wingers in the group, and players who played the center position have some of the highest point totals, including Gretzky. Defensemen cluster to the lefthand side of the cloud, meaning they have a higher ratio of assists to goals than the offensive players, and they are mostly dark orange, meaning they played a relatively high number of games in their careers. What other patterns do you notice?

Adding Background Images

The next step is motivated purely by aesthetics, and it involves adding a background image that gives the effect of Wayne Gretzky sweeping through the other 99 players with a slap shot. To do this, I selected *Map → Background Images → [File Name]* and then *Add Image*, which resulted in a dialog box, which I filled out as shown in Figure 8-11, browsing to select the image file and specifying how to center the image.

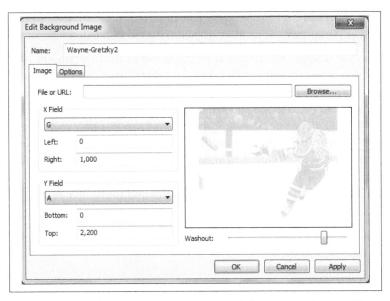

Figure 8-11. Adding a background image (photo by B. Bennett/Getty Images)

In the *Options* tab, I made sure to select both *Lock Aspect Ratio* and *Always Show Entire Image*, because I didn't want to either distort the image or chop off any of the sides.

 I try to use background images sparingly, as they are kind of like playing with fire: you either have a nice campfire going, or you burn down the forest. If you're going to use one, proceed with caution.

What's your opinion? Does the background image add to the overall impact of the visualization or does it take away from it? The dialog that emerges from these preferences and opinions is the part about data visualization that I enjoy the most.

Stacked Bars

Scatterplots aren't the only way to show multiple quantities in the same view. Another visualization type we can use is the stacked bar chart. Let's create a stacked bar chart as we explore a different angle of the data: *per game rates*. Recall from Chapter 4 that a rate is a ratio in which the numerator and the denominator have different units. Rates that are *per game* have the number of games played as the denominator.

Let's see whether Gretzky also stands alone in his career point production rate, or whether he has any company when it comes to scoring efficiency. The data table doesn't include the per game rates, so we'll have to create them using calculated fields, just like we did in Chapter 4. We'll create `Goals per Game`, `Assists per Game`, and `Points per Game` by right-clicking in the Dimensions or Measures area, selecting *Create Calculated Field*, and then filling out the dialog boxes similar to the one shown in Figure 8-12 for all three fields—the only difference being the calculated field names and the numerators.

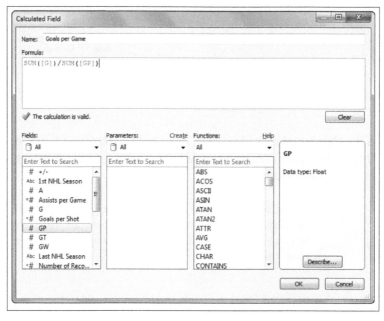

Figure 8-12. Creating per game rates with Calculated Fields

Now that we have these three new calculated fields in our Measures area, we can use them to visualize the rate of point production as a stacked bar plot. The way we'll need to create the stacked bar plot isn't straightforward in this case, because the values we want to stack are different Measures. Here are the steps:

1. Drag `Player` to the Rows shelf, creating an alphabetical list of player names.

2. Drag `Measure Values` from the Measures area to the Columns shelf, creating bars that are the sum of all Measures for each player.

3. Drag `Measure Names` from the Dimensions area to the Colors shelf, breaking up the bars by color.

4. Drag everything except `AGG(Assists per Game)` and `AGG(Goals per Game)` out of the Measure Values area below the Marks card, which leaves only two corresponding bars for each player.

5. Change the colors by clicking on the down arrow to the right of the `Measure Names` area header and clicking *Edit Colors*.

6. Click the down arrow in the blue `Player` pill on the Rows shelf and select *Sort*, choosing a descending sort order by the `Points per Game` field.

Figure 8-13 shows what the Sheet should look like after following these steps.

We can see right away that Gretzky has company at the top of this list. He and Mario Lemieux both stand apart from the rest, don't they? Their overall points per game are substantially higher than the rest of the top 100. We can also see that Lemieux scored goals at a higher rate than Gretzky, as indicated by the dark gray bars, and that Mike Bossy scored more goals per game than either of them.

It's a little more difficult to compare their Assists per Game rates, though, wouldn't you say? This is one drawback of the stacked bar chart: it's easy to compare the lengths of the first bars (dark gray in this case) and the overall lengths of the stacked bars, while the bars without a common baseline are much more difficult to compare. What if it was more important to enable a comparison of assists?

 If it's more important to be able to communicate the comparison of the two variables themselves, and less important to compare the overall sum, then a dual dot chart is preferred to the stacked bar.

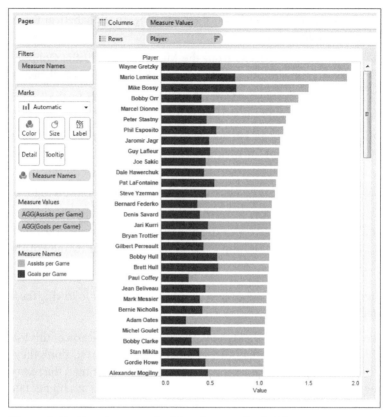

Figure 8-13. Creating a stacked bar from multiple Measures

To make the change from the stacked bar to the dual dot chart plot, simply change the Marks type from *Automatic*, or bars, to *Circles* or *Shapes*, whichever you prefer. Figure 8-14 shows the view with Shapes selected and Row grid lines added from the Format panel, which can be opened by right-clicking anywhere in the view and selecting *Format*.

The sort is a little difficult to make sense of. Try sorting by either Goals per Game or Assists per Game by editing the Sort dialog box (accessed by clicking the down arrow of the blue Player pill in the Rows shelf) and see which you prefer.

You can see how these different sort options allow you to communicate slightly different messages to your audience. Knowing your precise message helps you make the right choice.

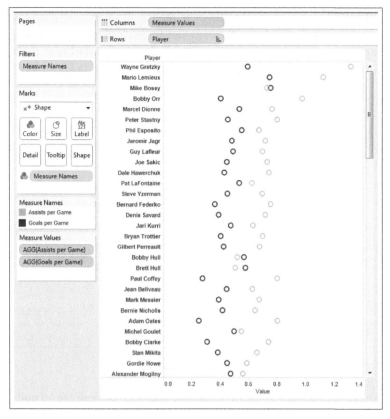

Figure 8-14. Per game rates shown in a dual dot chart view

Regression and Trend Lines

When comparing two variables, it's common to apply statistical regression analysis to estimate the strength of the correlation between the two variables. Regression analysis can be visualized by adding a trend line to a scatterplot, and the indication of how well the points fit the trend line is known as the coefficient of determination, R^2 (pronounced "R Squared").

While making use of Tableau's regression functionality, let's consider a new combination of rates: shots and goals. Shots can result in goals (and not the other way around), so we want to place the `Shots` field on the x-axis (the Columns shelf), because this is typically where the *independent* variable is placed. `Goals` would then be placed on the y-axis (the Rows shelf), the typical orientation of the *dependent* variable. We'll also need to add `Player` to the Detail shelf so we don't just have one single dot, but rather one dot for each player. After taking these steps, and also adding `Pos` to the Color shelf and `Player` to the Label shelf, we have the standard scatterplot as shown in Figure 8-15.

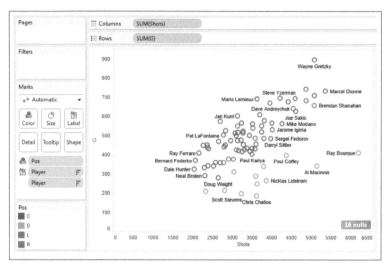

Figure 8-15. Scatterplot of shots versus goals

Notice the message at the bottom right that tells us there are 16 nulls. What does this mean? It turns out that the league didn't start collecting the number of shots in their statistical monitoring of games until after some of the players in the top 100 had already started playing, so this information isn't available for all players. In the spreadsheet, there is a blank (as opposed to a value of 0) for these 16 old-timers. We'll filter them out by clicking on the message and selecting *Filter Data*.

Further notice that the axes do not have the same ranges. While both start at 0, the y-axis extends upward to just under 1,000 goals, while the x-axis extends to the right past 6,500 shots. This is typical of scatterplots, as the primary goal is to understand the nature of the grouping of the points. Having the axes be of equal length would result in the data points lying very close together above the x-axis, making it difficult to see any trend.

How do we add trend lines? Just right-click anywhere in the grid defined by the axes and select *Trend Lines → Show Trend Lines*. The resulting view shows four trend lines, one for each position, as shown in Figure 8-16.

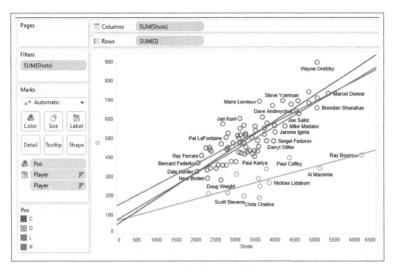

Figure 8-16. Scatterplot with multiple trend lines

As we can clearly see, defensemen (the orange line) have a very different shots-to-goals relationship than the offensive players, whose trend lines are all very similar.

If we want to show only one trend line for all of the points together, we can right-click anywhere in the grid area and select *Trend Lines* → *Show Trend Lines*. Then, we can uncheck the box that says "Allow a trend line per color"—and I'd also recommend checking "Force y-intercept to zero," because no shots means no goals. The resulting view is shown in Figure 8-17.

As we would imagine, the line slopes upward, indicating a positive correlation between shots and goals. The points are somewhat scattered about the line, but how can we describe the relationship in mathematical terms? If we hover over any point along the trend line, a pop up appears with a linear equation and a p-value, as shown in Figure 8-18.

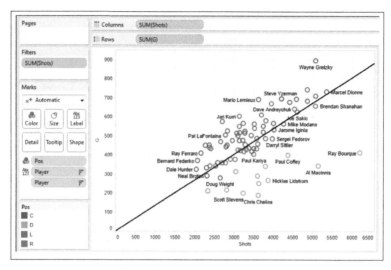

Figure 8-17. Scatterplot with a single trend line

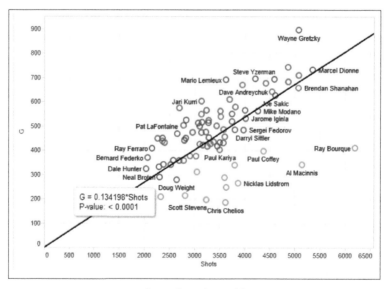

Figure 8-18. Equation and p-value of trend line

The equation tells us that the line has a slope of 0.134198, meaning that for every increase of one shot (along the x-axis), the line rises 0.134198 units (along the y-axis). The p-value indicates that there is a very small chance (< 0.0001, or < 0.01%) that two variables without any correlation at all would produce such a relationship. They are definitely correlated, and this comes as no surprise.

But how good is the fit? We can find that and much more by right-clicking on the trend line and selecting *Describe Trend Model*. The window shown in Figure 8-19 appears.

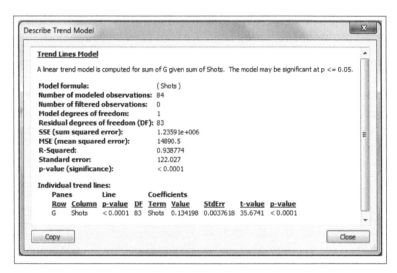

Figure 8-19. Describe Trend Model window

From this window, we can see a number of different aspects of the model, including its coefficient of determination (R-Squared) and its Standard error. Since we forced the trend line to cross the y-axis at y=0, we can't use the R-Squared value in the typical way, namely, to understand how well the model fits the data. Try editing the trend line by unchecking the "Force y-intercept to zero" box and then choose "Describe Trend Model" once again. You'll notice that the R-Squared value drops from 0.938774 to 0.302579.

The line divides the grid area into two sections. The data points that lie above and to the left of the upward sloping line can be thought of as having higher accuracy: it took these players fewer shots to achieve a certain number of goals, as compared to the model. The data points that lie below and to the right of the line can be though of in the opposite way: it took a relatively high number of shots to achieve a certain number of goals. The farther away from the line, the more the player deviated from the typical ratio of shots to goals.

The Quadrant Chart

Another way to compare these same points is to divide the grid area into four sections instead of two. I have a predilection for dividing everything into quadrants, so let's explore how to do that now.

First, let's turn off the trend line by right-clicking in the grid area, selecting *Trend Lines*, and deselecting *Show Trend Lines*. Next, let's create the four panels using reference lines as we've done before.

How should we divide the plane into quadrants? Let's create horizontal and vertical lines at the mean, or average values. This would allow us to determine right away if a player was above or below the group averages for both shots and goals. To do that, we'll just right-click in each of the axes and select *Add Reference Line*, completing the dialog boxes as shown in Figure 8-20.

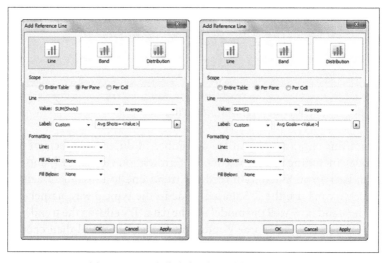

Figure 8-20. Adding vertical (left box) and horizontal (right box) reference lines

The resulting cartesian plain is now divided into quadrants, as shown in Figure 8-21, with the Row and Column grid lines removed.

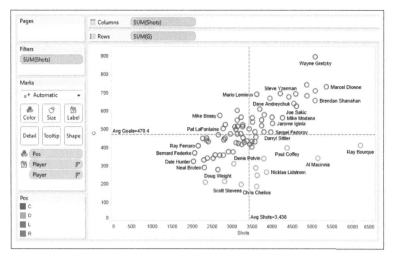

Figure 8-21. The four quadrant scatterplot

Don't you think this is an interesting way to compare the players? They're divided based on whether they scored an above or below average number of goals, and whether they took an above or below average number of shots in their careers. (Remember that when we say "average," we're referring to the mean value of the top 100 players (minus the 16 without shot statistics), so there's nothing "average" about this group from an overall point of view. Our comparison is relative to players within this group.)

I would consider the relative few number of players in the top-left quadrant to be the most accurate shooters of the group. Why? They scored an above average number of goals while shooting a below average number of times. In contrast, the group in the bottom-right quadrant (populated mostly with defensemen) are the least accurate shooters of the group. They scored a below average number of goals while shooting an above average number of times. If you've watched hockey, you know that the defensemen typically stay the farthest from the goal, unleashing powerful slapshots from greater distances, so let's not be too harsh in our assessment of their accuracy. Nevertheless, in the bottom-right quadrant they remain.

The top right and bottom left are the high and low relative producers, respectively, We can label these areas by right-clicking in the grid area and selecting *Annotate → Area*, and then typing in the quadrant names. The finished quadrant scatterplot is shown in Figure 8-22.

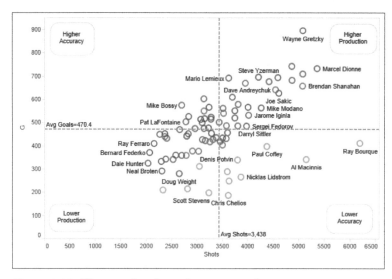

Figure 8-22. The completed quadrant scatterplot

This is an interesting way of grouping the players. If you want, you can add the trend line back to the quadrant view and use both comparison aids together. I'd recommend going with soft, light lines if you do so, as you don't want to obstruct the data points themselves with thick, dark lines.

Summary

In this chapter, we explored but a few of the ways to compare multiple variables at the same time, and my admiration of the scatterplot has been evident. We also touched on annotations and background images, topics we'll pick up again later. In addition, we exlored how to create stacked bar charts using Measure Names and Measure Values, a tricky technique that is a little mind-bending at first, I'll admit. Lastly, we covered how to add trend lines and reference lines to aid in comparison.

In the next chapter, we'll explore the all-important factor of time.

CHAPTER 9

Changes Over Time

"Perfection is attained by slow degrees;
it requires the hand of time."

—Voltaire

When it comes to communicating data, it's all about time. Time is the one factor that simply can't be removed from the equation. Look at any presentation of data on the Web, in print, or at the office. You won't have to look very hard to see the element of time. It's usually right on the surface: monthly unemployment rate, quarterly earnings per share, top-grossing movies of the weekend. If the element of time isn't explicitly stated somewhere, it probably should be.

So far, we've compared quantities summed up over a period of time, like total points in a player's career or tons of trash collected in New York City during the month of September. While time was a factor, we didn't consider how these quantities varied *over the course of time*, other than control charts in Chapter 7. We simply defined the start and stop points, and lumped everything between into one bucket.

But we can unlock a whole new dimension of insight if we consider how the measurable universe has changed, is changing, or likely will change with time:

- Is the situation getting better or worse, or continuing the same?
- Has time treated one variable differently than another?

- Are there trends, outliers, or shifts in the data over a specific period of time?
- Is the degree of variation over time significant or just mere noise?

These are all questions that are central to communicating data with respect to time. There are many ways to communicate change over time, and we'll consider a number of them in this chapter, starting with the simple and effective line plot.

The Origin of Time Charts

Scottish engineer and political economist William Playfair (*http://bit.ly/wiki-William-Playfair*) is credited with inventing the line chart in 1786, when he visualized the balance of trade between countries in his book, *The Commercial and Political Atlas* (see Figure 9-1).

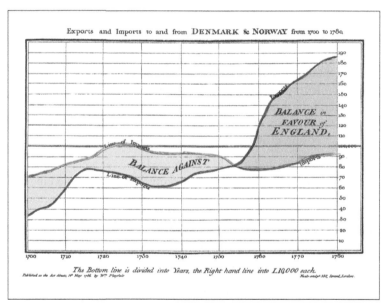

Figure 9-1. The first line chart, by William Playfair in 1786

Two lines are depicted, showing imports and exports over time, and the caption at the bottom describes the two axes. We're so accustomed to seeing line charts today that it's almost amusing to see the axes explained in this way, and yet line charts aren't even as old as the United

States. William Playfair had the pioneer's task of introducing his readers to this new form of communication.

As we seek to communicate how quantities change over time, we'd do well in most cases to follow Playfair's lead and place time on the x-axis, proceeding from left to right. This orientation will be well understood by those we are communicating with, and they'll need to invest relatively little time and effort to begin gleaning insights from what we show them.

Let's look at some examples.

The Line Chart

Let's start with a pre-aggregated data set (*http://bit.ly/mlb-pitching-data*): average strikeouts per game (SO), number of teams (Tms), and the total number of pitchers (#Pitch) of each professional baseball season (Year) since 1871. In this data set, Year is a simple quantitative measure. An image of the data set is shown in Figure 9-2.

	A	B	C	D
1	Year	Tms	SO	#Pitch
2	2012	30	7.5	662
3	2011	30	7.1	662
4	2010	30	7.06	635
5	2009	30	6.91	664
6	2008	30	6.77	651
7	2007	30	6.62	666
8	2006	30	6.52	635
9	2005	30	6.3	606
10	2004	30	6.55	632
11	2003	30	6.34	612
12	2002	30	6.47	609
13	2001	30	6.67	591
14	2000	30	6.45	606

Figure 9-2. Average game stats data set

In order to visualize how these variables have changed over time, we can first connect Tableau to the spreadsheet, and then take the following steps to create a line chart:

1. Left-click the Measure SO, and drag and drop it onto the Rows shelf.

2. Right-click on the Measure Year, and drag it to the Columns shelf. When you release the right mouse button, select the top option, *Year*.

The resulting line chart is shown in Figure 9-3.

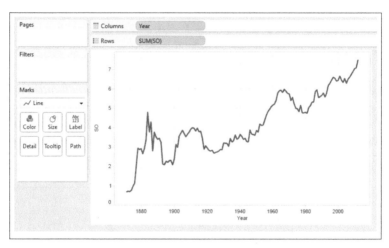

Figure 9-3. A simple line chart showing the increase

How would we describe this pattern? There is no doubt that there is an increasing trend in the number of strikeouts per game over the past century and a half. The climb looks dramatic, but if we add a trend line by right-clicking in the chart area and selecting *Trend Lines*, then *Show Trend Lines*, we can see that the average number of strikeouts per game has increased at a glacial rate of 0.033 strikeouts per game each year, on average. So every decade, pitchers struck out one extra batter every three games, on average. The time chart with added trend line is shown in Figure 9-4.

There are a number of departures from the trend, though, aren't there? Before the turn of the twentieth century, the rules of baseball were in a state of flux. For example, the definition of the strike zone underwent a number of changes, and until 1887, batters could actually request a high pitch or a low pitch. Correlated with these changes to the rules, we see a relatively high degree of flux in the number of strikeouts per game until about 1920, when the rules of the game stabilized.

Strikeouts per game began steadily climbing, and then something changed in the late 1960s.

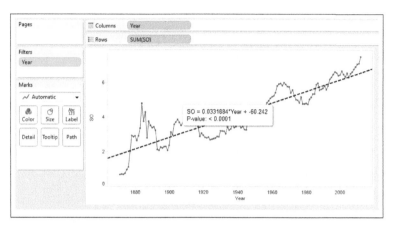

Figure 9-4. Strikeout line chart with trend line added

Researching the rules of the game, we discover that the mound was lowered and the strike zone was reduced in 1969. The league implemented these changes in response to the increasing dominance of pitchers in the league. They wanted teams to score more runs during games, in hopes of boosting attendance. We can see that this change to the rules coincides with a decrease in the average number of strikeouts per game that lasted until 1981, when the trend once again began climbing.

We can add a vertical reference line at 1969 by right-clicking in the chart area and selecting *Add Reference Line*, and then filling out the resulting dialog box as shown in Figure 9-5, resulting in the updated line chart shown.

So far, we've only been able to show how one quantitative variable has changed over time. While we've added a trend line and a reference line, we haven't yet matched the degree of sophistication of Playfair's original line charts.

Let's see how we can gain further insight into the history of strikeouts by adding a second line to the chart: pitchers per team.

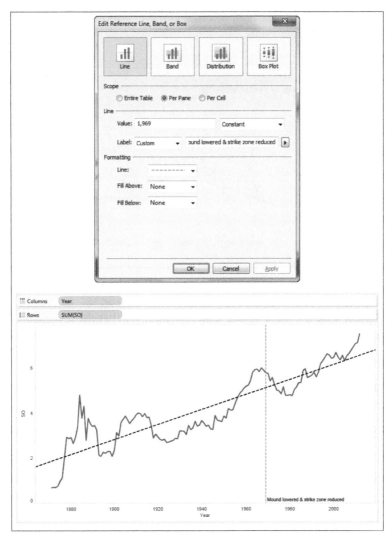

Figure 9-5. Updated line chart with added reference line

The Dual-Axis Line Chart

What else changed in 1981 that could give us a clue as to the reason for the reversal in the strikeout trend? The data set also includes a field called #Pitch, representing the total number of pitchers that played in each season. It also includes the number of teams in the league each year in a field called Tms. We can create a simple ratio by dividing the total number of pitchers by the total number of teams each year, re-suling in `Pitchers per Team`.

Let's see how the number of pitchers used by teams changed over the course of the same period of time. If we drag the `Pitchers per Team` Measure onto the Rows shelf next to strikeouts, we create a sec-ond line chart below the first, as shown in Figure 9-6, with the trend line for the new time chart added.

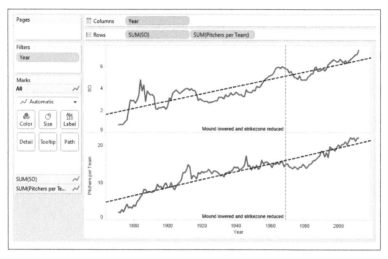

Figure 9-6. Two line charts, shown one above the other

Notice that these two charts share the same x-axis, but they have dif-ferent y-axes. The new chart showing the increase in the number of pitchers per team has been added to the view directly below our strike-out chart.

How can we superimpose them on top of each other? If we hover over `SUM(Pitchers per Team)` in the Rows shelf and click on the small down arrow that appears, we can select *Dual Axis* in the menu that pops up, as shown in Figure 9-7, resulting in a dual-axis line chart.

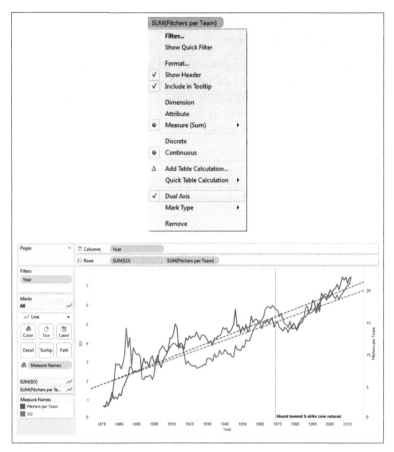

Figure 9-7. The dual-axis line chart

Notice that a number of elements have changed:

- First, and most obviously, the lines have been placed together and Tableau has automatically colored one chart (and its trend line) red to differentiate it from the other.

- Second, notice that the second y-axis (`Pitchers per Team`) has been placed on the righthand side of the chart, and that it has a different scale than the lefthand y-axis (`SO`).

- Third, notice that the green pills in the Rows shelf have changed shape: their adjacent edges are flat instead of round.

- Finally, notice that the Marks card area to the left of the lines now has three different sections: All, SUM(SO), and SUM(Pitchers per Team). Click on these headers to see how the Marks card changes to allow us to control each line separately, or both together.

One challenge to reading the dual-axis chart is that it's difficult to know which y-axis applies to which line. To find out, we need to look from the lines to the color legend to the y-axes. To reduce the time and effort required to match each line with its corresponding y-axis, we can change the color of both y-axes by right-clicking the axis and selecting *Format*, changing the properties as shown in Figure 9-8. We can also double-click on the leftmost y-axis and change the title from "SO" to something more meaningful, like "Average Strikeouts per Game."

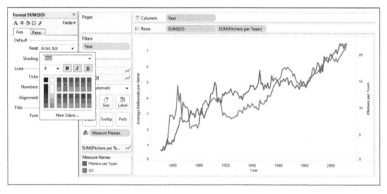

Figure 9-8. Dual-axis line chart with y-axes formatted

What can we glean from this dual-axis line chart? We can see right away that teams added pitchers starting in 1871 until about 1940, and then held their rosters steady at about 15 pitchers per team until the early 1980s, when they began adding pitchers once again. Thus, the turnaround in average strikeouts per game correlates with the point in time when teams began adding more pitchers to their rosters. Correlation does not imply causation, but we could come up with a causal theory to test: more pitchers per team means each batter is likely to encounter a pitcher who has thrown fewer pitches, and therefore has a "fresher arm" (*http://nyti.ms/U0weNo*).

Let's consider another way of showing how these two variables are correlated: the connected scatterplot.

The Connected Scatterplot

We haven't yet strayed from the rule of thumb that time should be encoded on the x-axis increasing from left to right. An innovative way to encode time is to make a scatterplot of the two variables in question and connect dots that represent successive years. Let's create one to see what it would look like.

To start with, we can create a standard scatterplot as we did in Chapter 8 with pitchers per team on the x-axis (or Column shelf) and SO, or average strikeouts per game, on the y-axis (or Rows shelf). If we do so and then add a trend line as before, we will find that the variation in pitchers per team explains 71% of the variation in strikeouts (from the R-Squared value). The basic scatterplot with trend line is shown in Figure 9-9.

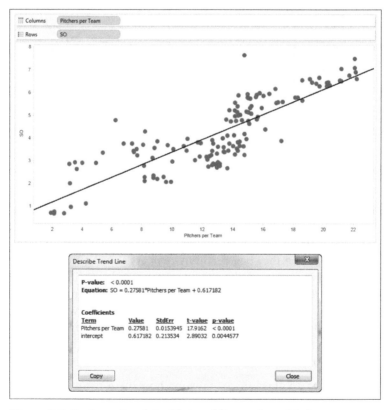

Figure 9-9. Basic scatterplot with trend line and model shown

It's difficult to tell from this view in what *order* the points occurred. Which circle corresponds to which year? The basic scatterplot doesn't tell us anything about time. We could add Year to the Color shelf and the Label shelf, resulting in the view shown in Figure 9-10.

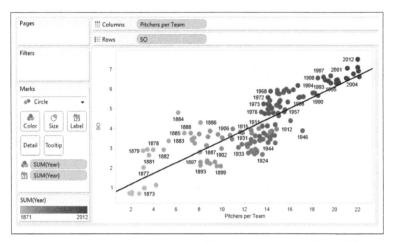

Figure 9-10. Basic scatterplot colored by year and year labels added

This helps somewhat: we can tell that the circles in the lower-left region correspond to the earliest seasons and the circles in the upper right are more recent. Yet another way to show the pattern is to connect the dots of successive years with a straight line. To do so, we'll need to change the Marks type from *Circle* to *Line*, and move SUM(Year) from the Color shelf to Path, resulting in the somewhat scrambled view shown in Figure 9-11.

From this view, we can see that the points start in the lower left and ricochet their way upward and to the right, indicating an increase in both variables over the years. Depending on the data, connected scatterplots are generally easier to read when we plot fewer points. Let's filter the view to just the years in question: 1981 to the present. To do so, we can right-click on Years in the Measures panel and select *Show Quick Filter*, entering 1981 into the left parameter of the quick filter, as shown in Figure 9-12.

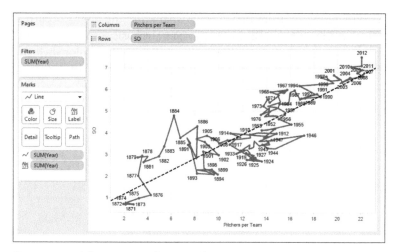

Figure 9-11. The connected scatterplot

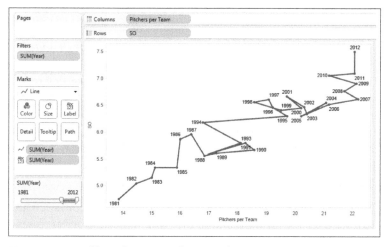

Figure 9-12. A filtered connected scatterplot

This view is much easier to read, and the pattern is now obvious. In addition, another pattern has become clearer: between 2007 and 2012, strikeouts per game increased, while pitchers per team did not.

I prefer to format connected scatterplots to look like the view shown in Figure 9-13. To do this, the following steps are required:

1. Drag a second `Pitchers per Team` pill onto the Columns shelf to the right of the first and make it a dual-axis plot.

2. Right-click in the top x-axis and select *Synchronize Axis*, then uncheck "Show Header." The top x-axis should disappear.

3. Take `Measure Names` off of the Color shelf of "All" by dragging and dropping it back into the Measures area.

4. Change Mark type for `Pitchers per Team (2)` from *Line* to *Circle*, and take `SUM(Year)` off of the Labels shelf.

5. In the Marks panel for `Pitchers per Team (2)`, change the Circle color from blue to white and give each circle a gray border.

6. In the Marks panel for `Pitchers per Team`, change the color of the line to gray and reduce the size.

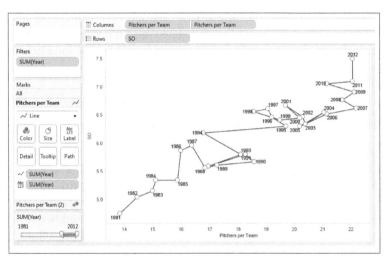

Figure 9-13. The formatted connected scatterplot

Take a look back at the different ways of showing the change in average strikeouts per game and pitchers per team over time. Which would be most effective in communicating this data to an audience? The answer depends on which insights we want to highlight, and how "captive" the audience is:

- Can we be present to explain the chart to the audience or not?
- Are they highly motivated to understand the content or not?

If the answer to either of these questions is "yes," then a connected scatterplot may work just fine. If the answer to both is "no," then the connected scatterplot is a risky choice.

 In my experience, the connected scatterplot takes more effort up front to decipher what is being shown, simply because we're less accustomed to seeing time shown in this way. If we can't be present when the audience sees it, and if they're not that motivated regarding the subject matter, then they'll be less likely to put in the effort and we should probably stick with a chart type that will be easier to understand: one with time on the x-axis.

The baseball strikeout data was an easy "learner" data set for us because it was pre-aggregated and the only date type we needed to consider was year. In the real world, we often get data in logs or long lists of records with a time-date stamp field. Let's consider how we can explore changes over time with this type of data next.

The Date Field Type and Seasonality

Let's return to the New York City rat sightings data we considered in Chapter 3. Recall that this data is formatted as a list of reported occurrences, and each row in the spreadsheet is a single occurrence. The location, time, and date are reported, as well as a number of categorical fields such as type of location. We considered the total number of rat sightings for each borough, but we didn't consider how those sightings were spread out over time.

A number of questions could be asked of the list of records, such as:

- What time of the year do the most rat sightings occur?
- Is the number of rat sightings increasing, decreasing, or staying steady?
- How many rat sightings can we expect to see in the coming year?

Let's explore this data to find some answers. If you recall from Figure 3-12, the rat sightings data set included a field called Created Date, in the form of *mm/dd/yyyy*. Let's see how Tableau treats a date field like this.

If we drag Created Date onto the Column shelf and then drag Number of Records from the Measures area to the Rows shelf, Tableau creates a yearly line plot by default, as shown in Figure 9-14.

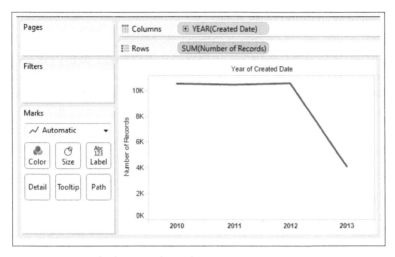

Figure 9-14. Default annual timeline

Notice that the color of the Year(Created Date) is blue, indicating that Tableau is treating the field as a discrete, or categorical, data type, and that there is a + sign to the left of the field. Clicking on the + sign disaggregates (or breaks down) the line plot by quarter, as shown in Figure 9-15.

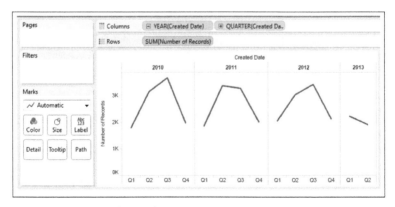

Figure 9-15. Rat sightings by quarter

Notice that Year(Created Date) now has a - sign next to it. Clicking on the - sign returns the view to the one shown in Figure 9-14, and clicking the + sign next to Quarter breaks down the data by month. By using the + and - symbols, we can either increase or decrease the level of aggregation of the data.

We can also change the Created Date field from discrete to continuous by clicking the down arrow in the Year(Created Date) pill and selecting either *Year, Month, Week Number,* or *Day* from the options below the line, resulting in the line charts shown in Figure 9-16 (shown with the partial month of June 2013 excluded).

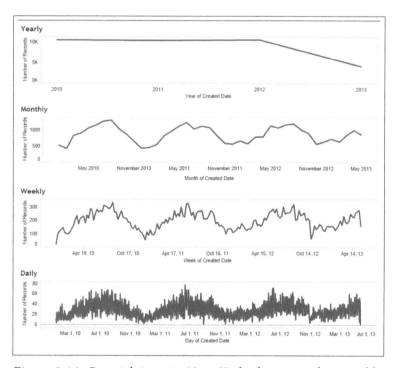

Figure 9-16. Rat sightings in New York shown yearly, monthly, weekly, and daily

Notice the seasonality of the reported rat sightings. Summer months have seen the highest number of rat sightings, and winter months the lowest. Is this seasonality the same for all boroughs? All we need to do is drag the Borough data field from Measures to the Color shelf to find out, resulting in the view shown in Figure 9-17.

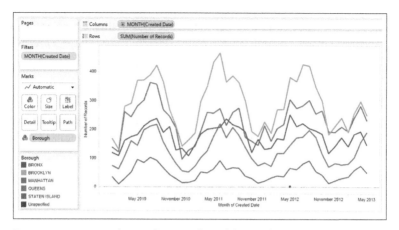

Figure 9-17. Rat sightings by month and borough

Now we can see the line plot for each borough, and it's clear that this seasonality holds true for all boroughs.

Do you notice the one lone brown dot in May of 2012 associated with the borough "Unspecified"? It seems that a single reported sighting did not include an address or borough. I clicked on this point and chose to exclude it from the analysis.

Another feature that is new to Tableau is the ability to add a forecast to a line plot such as this one. If we right-click in the graph area, and then select *Forecast* and *Show Forecast*, the line plots update to show lighter colors for months stretching into the future, as shown in Figure 9-18.

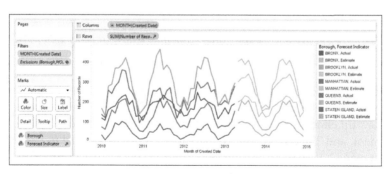

Figure 9-18. Rat sightings by month and borough, forecast added

There are a number of options associated with the forecast, such as the forecast length and whether to include seasonality. These options can be accessed by right-clicking and selecting *Forecast → Forecast Options*. To see the full details associated with the forecast, choose *Describe Forecast*.

The line plot is the simplest and clearest way to show how quantities vary over time. But what if we're interested in showing event durations in order over time, like the various presidential administrations? That's where a timeline comes in handy.

The Timeline

Two decades prior to William Playfair's line plots, English theologian and chemist Joseph Priestley created the first known timelines, in which each bar represents the life span of an influential person of history (see Figure 9-19).

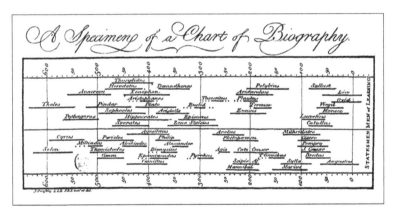

Figure 9-19. Joseph Priestley's first timeline: Chart of Biography, 1765 (http://bit.ly/priestley-chart)

This may seem like a rather obvious way to depict this type of information to us now, but it was innovative to Priestley's readers. In our day, timelines such as these are used extensively in project management, and Tableau includes a chart type known as a *Gantt Bar chart* to make it easy to create one. Let's consider the history of presidents of the United States of America as we examine how to create this type of timeline.

Wikipedia records the day of birth (*http://bit.ly/wiki-president-birth*) and death (*http://bit.ly/wiki-president-death*) of each of the 44 U.S. presidents, as well as their first and last days in office (*http://bit.ly/wiki-president-terms*). These dates can be combined into a single spreadsheet, as shown in Figure 9-20.

	A	B	C	D	E	F	G	H
1	Number	President	Took office	Left office	Party	Born	Died	Birth State
2	1	George Washington	4/30/1789	3/4/1797	Independent	February 22, 1732	December 14, 1799	VA
3	2	John Adams	3/4/1797	March 4, 1801	Federalist	October 30, 1735	July 4, 1826	MA
4	3	Thomas Jefferson	3/4/1801	3/4/1809	Republican	April 13, 1743	July 4, 1826	VA
5	4	James Madison	3/4/1809	3/4/1817	Republican	March 16, 1751	June 28, 1836	VA
6	5	James Monroe	3/4/1817	3/4/1825	Republican	April 28, 1758	July 4, 1831	VA
7	6	John Quincy Adams	3/4/1825	March 4, 1829	Republican	July 11, 1767	February 23, 1848	MA
8	7	Andrew Jackson	3/4/1829	3/4/1837	Democratic	March 15, 1767	June 8, 1845	SC/NC
9	8	Martin Van Buren	3/4/1837	March 4, 1841	Democratic	December 5, 1782	July 24, 1862	NY
10	9	William Henry Harrison	3/4/1841	April 4, 1841	Whig	February 9, 1773	April 4, 1841	VA
11	10	John Tyler	4/4/1841	3/4/1845	Whig	March 29, 1790	January 18, 1862	VA
12	11	James K. Polk	3/4/1845	3/4/1849	Democratic	November 2, 1795	June 15, 1849	NC
13	12	Zachary Taylor	3/4/1849	July 9, 1850	Whig	November 24, 1784	July 9, 1850	VA
14	13	Millard Fillmore	7/9/1850	March 4, 1853	Whig	January 7, 1800	March 8, 1874	NY
15	14	Franklin Pierce	3/4/1853	3/4/1857	Democratic	November 23, 1804	October 8, 1869	NH
16	15	James Buchanan	3/4/1857	3/4/1861	Democratic	April 23, 1791	June 1, 1868	PA
17	16	Abraham Lincoln	3/4/1861	April 15, 1865	Republican	February 12, 1809	April 15, 1865	KY
18	17	Andrew Johnson	4/15/1865	3/4/1869	Democratic	December 29, 1808	July 31, 1875	NC
19	18	Ulysses S. Grant	3/4/1869	3/4/1877	Republican	April 27, 1822	July 23, 1885	OH
20	19	Rutherford B. Hayes	3/4/1877	3/4/1881	Republican	October 4, 1822	January 17, 1893	OH
21	20	James A. Garfield	3/4/1881	September 19, 1881	Republican	November 19, 1831	September 19, 1881	OH

Figure 9-20. Spreadsheet of U.S. president milestones

If we connect a new Tableau workbook to this spreadsheet, we will first need to create two calculated fields: Life Span and Time in Office. These two calculated fields are simple enough, but need to take into account that not all presidents have died yet, and that the current president hasn't yet left office. If these fields are null (blank), then the formula uses today's date to calculate these two spans of time, as shown in Figure 9-21.

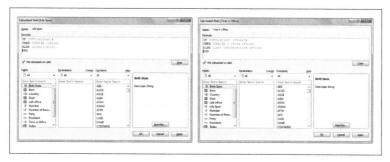

Figure 9-21. Calculating life span and time in office

Now that we've created these two fields, we can begin creating time-lines using the Gantt Bar option by following these steps:

1. Drag `Took Office` to the Columns shelf and change the pill to *Day, continuous*.

2. Change the Marks type from *Automatic* to *Gantt Bar* using the drop-down selector.

3. Drag `Time in Office` from the Measures pane to the Size shelf.

4. Drag `Party` from Dimensions to the Color shelf.

The resulting simple timeline is shown in Figure 9-22.

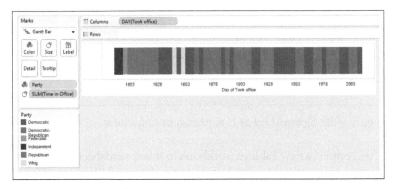

Figure 9-22. A simple timeline of U.S. presidential administrations, colored by political party

If we want to break this timeline out by president, we can simply drag `President` from the Dimensions pane to the Rows shelf. Doing so lists each president in alphabetical order, so we can change the sort to be in chronological order by clicking in the `President` pill on the Rows shelf, selecting *Sort*, and applying the sort rule shown in Figure 9-23.

After doing so, the timeline changes to appear as shown in Figure 9-24.

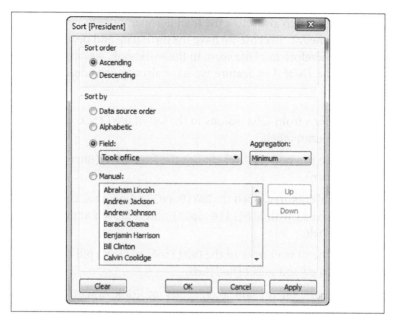

Figure 9-23. Sorting presidents by "Took office" date

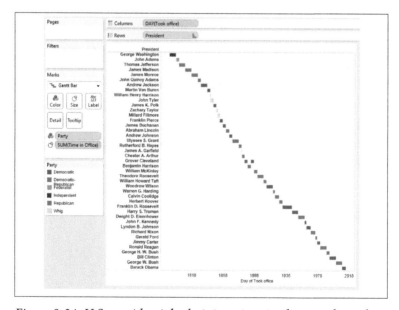

Figure 9-24. U.S. presidential administration timeline, in chronological order

It would be nice to also show the total life span of each president on the same timeline. Because we have the birth date and death date figures, and therefore total life span, in the workbook, we can add them by using the *Dual Axis* feature we have already considered. Follow these steps:

1. Drag Born from Dimensions to the left of DAY(Took office) in the Columns shelf.

2. Click in the new pill and change the from YEAR(Born) to green DAY(Born).

3. In the Marks area, open the DAY(Born) section, replace SUM(Time in Office) with SUM(Life Span) and remove Party from the color shelf.

4. Click the down arrow in the DAY(Took office) pill in the Columns shelf and select *Dual Axis*.

5. Right-click on the top x-axis (Day of Took office) and select *Synchronize Axis*.

6. Right-click on the top x-axis again and uncheck "Show Header."

The resulting view is shown in Figure 9-25 with a few reference lines added for context.

This turns out to be a very interesting and useful way to show events over time, as it's easy to identify presidents who died while in office, as well as to see the number of previous and future U.S. presidents who were alive during the Civil War, for example.

The timeline is a visual history, and because it's visual, patterns and relationships emerge in ways that are difficult to explain using only words.

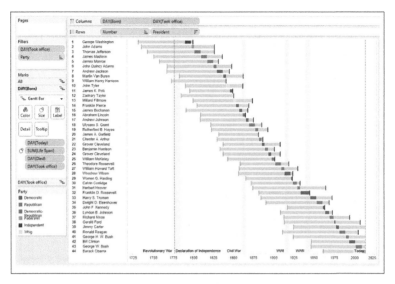

Figure 9-25. The completed U.S. presidential timeline

The Slopegraph

The following project was inspired by a blog post by Andy Kirk, who compares the change in points earned by professional English soccer teams in the first 15 games of successive seasons.[1]

If we only want to show changes in time of a number of different items from one point in time to another, the slopegraph can be useful. Let's walk through how we can make this type of chart in Tableau.

Step 1: Get the Data

League tables for each season up to a chosen game number are available online (*http://bit.ly/league-standings*). The teams' results up to game 15 for both the 2012/2013 and 2013/2014 seasons were copied and pasted into an Excel spreadsheet, with an added column for Year, as shown in Figure 9-26.

---

1. Andy Kirk, "In praise of slopegraphs," Visualising Data, December 2012 (*http://bit.ly/kirk-slopegraphs*)

	A	B	C	D	E	F	G	H	I	J	K	L
1	POS	Year	LP	CLUB	P	W	D	L	GF	GA	GD	PTS
2	1	2013	-1	Arsenal	15	11	2	2	30	11	19	35
3	2	2013	-2	Liverpool	15	9	3	3	34	18	16	30
4	3	2013	-3	Chelsea	15	9	3	3	30	17	13	30
5	4	2013	-4	Manchester City	15	9	2	4	41	15	26	29
6	5	2013	-5	Everton	15	7	7	1	23	14	9	28
7	6	2013	-6	Tottenham	15	8	3	4	15	16	-1	27
8	7	2013	-7	Newcastle	15	8	2	5	20	21	-1	26
9	8	2013	-8	Southampton	15	6	5	4	19	14	5	23
10	9	2013	-9	Manchester	15	6	4	5	22	19	3	22
11	10	2013	-11	Swansea City	15	5	4	6	21	20	1	19
12	11	2013	-10	Aston Villa	15	5	4	6	16	18	-2	19
13	12	2013	-13	Hull City	15	5	3	7	13	19	-6	18
14	13	2013	-12	Stoke City	15	4	5	6	15	20	-5	17
15	14	2013	-14	Norwich City	15	5	2	8	14	28	-14	17
16	15	2013	-15	West Bromwich	15	3	6	6	17	21	-4	15
17	16	2013	-16	Cardiff City	15	3	5	7	11	22	-11	14
18	17	2013	-17	West Ham	15	3	4	8	13	19	-6	13
19	18	2013	-18	Fulham	15	4	1	10	14	26	-12	13
20	19	2013	-19	Crystal Palace	15	4	1	10	10	22	-12	13
21	20	2013	-20	Sunderland	15	2	2	11	12	30	-18	8
22	1	2012	-1	Manchester	15	12	0	3	37	21	16	36
23	2	2012	-2	Manchester City	15	9	6	0	28	11	17	33
24	3	2012	-3	Chelsea	15	7	5	3	25	16	9	26
25	4	2012	-4	Tottenham	15	8	2	5	28	23	5	26
26	5	2012	-5	West Bromwich	15	8	2	5	24	19	5	26
27	6	2012	-6	Everton	15	5	8	2	25	19	6	23
28	7	2012	-7	Swansea City	15	6	5	4	23	17	6	23

Figure 9-26. The first 15 game results in Excel

If you read Andy's blog post, you'll notice that this spreadsheet is structured differently than Andy's. He had one column for 2012/2013 results and another column for 2013/2014 results. I've structured the spreadsheet in this way so that I can use `Year` as a Measure in Tableau.

Step 2: Connect Tableau

This is a very straightforward step: Open Tableau, click *Connect to Data*, and find your results spreadsheet.

Step 3: Create a Parameter and Matching Calculated Field

Before creating the slopegraph, let's make a Parameter that will allow users to choose which stat to chart. This is a technique we'll explore more in later chapters as well.

Right-click anywhere in the Dimensions or Measures panel to the left, and select *Create New Parameter*. Fill out the dialog box as shown in Figure 9-27.

Figure 9-27. Creating a Parameter in Tableau

Click *OK*, and then right-click the newly created Parameter in the area to the bottom left and select *Show Parameter Control*. You'll see a drop-down select appear in the upper right. You can use this to change the value of the parameter.

We now need to create a calculated field to link to the different team stats based on the user's choice. Right-click on the parameter, select *Create Calculated Field*, and fill out the dialog box as shown in Figure 9-28.

Figure 9-28. Mapping a Calculated Field to a Parameter

Step 4: Create the Basic Slopegraph

Now that we have this Selected data field mapped to the Parameter, we can use it to create our basic slopegraph as follows:

1. Drag Year to the Columns shelf, and change it to discrete (blue pill) by clicking the down arrow and selecting *Discrete*.

2. Drag the Selected calculated field to the Rows shelf.

3. Change the Marks type from *Automatic* to *Line*.

4. Drag the CLUB Dimension to the Detail card and resize the view (making it wider).

5. Drag another instance of the CLUB Dimension to the Label card, and then click on *Label* and select *Line Ends* in the "Marks to Label" area.

Step 4, numbers 1–5 are shown in Figure 9-29.

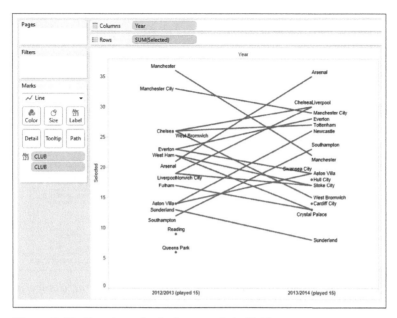

Figure 9-29. Creating a basic slopegraph in Tableau

Step 5: Add Line Coloring and Thickness

In order to make the lines one color for increasing values and another color for decreasing values, and to change their thickness based on the magnitude of the change, we'll need to create three more calculated fields:

Delta
>	The first calculated field computes the change in value of the selected statistic from one year to the next, as shown in Figure 9-30.

Direction
>	The second calculated field gives one string for values that got better and another for values that got worse. This will be useful for coloring the lines. See Figure 9-31.

Magnitude
>	This final calculated field yields the absolute value of the change, or the magnitude. This will be helpful for making lines thicker or thinner based on the magnitude of the change. See Figure 9-32.

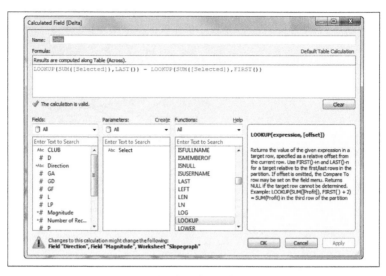

Figure 9-30. Creating a Calculated Field to compute the change in values

Figure 9-31. Creating a Calculated Field to categorize the direction of change

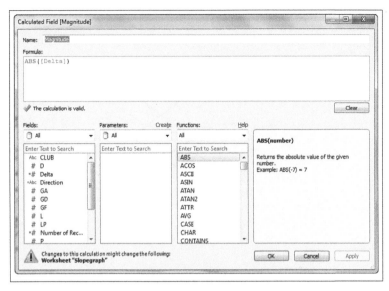

Figure 9-32. A Calculated Field that determines the absolute value, or magnitude, of the change

Now that these fields are created, let's do the following to complete the slopegraph itself:

1. Drag Direction to Color.

2. Drag Magnitude to Size.

3. Drag Selected to Label and change the label so that the Club name and the value are in line, with a comma separating them.

4. Filter out the Clubs that were either promoted or relegated after the 2012/2013 season.

5. Clean up the fonts (change them all to Gill Sans MT).

Step 5, numbers 1–5 are shown in Figure 9-33.

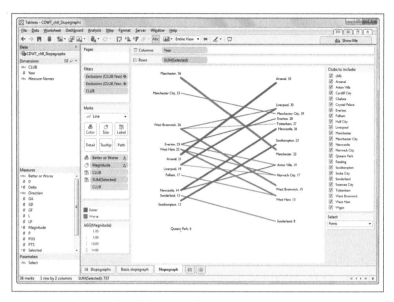

Figure 9-33. An updated slopegraph

I've also formatted the tooltips to yield a nice result when mousing over any of the line ends, and I've hidden Marks that were placed in awkward positions on the slopegraph that I couldn't adjust.

Step 6: Design the Dashboard

We'll cover dashboards much more starting in Chapter 12, but let's see how a finished dashboard could look using this slopegraph example. After creating the slopegraph, we can add it to a new dashboard, add the parameter control and a drop-down filter for Clubs as floating dashboard objects, and then add a title and data source/reference information at the bottom.

With this view, we can do a whole lot more than find out what's behind Manchester's performance; we can also notice other big changes, such as Liverpool's suddenly prolific offense (select "Goals For"), or Southampton's dramatic improvement in defense ("Goals Against" drops from 32 in 2012/2013 to only 14 in 2013/2014). See Figure 9-34.

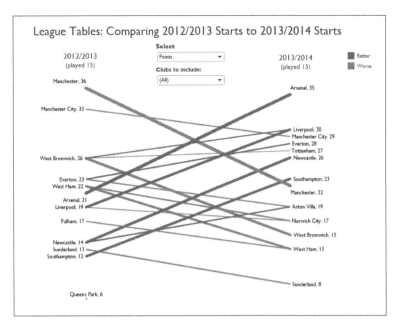

Figure 9-34. A slopegraph comparing the points earned by clubs through 15 games

This is the value of the slopegraph. It allows us to make a whole host of point-to-point comparisons, and the largest magnitude changes literally jump to the surface.

Summary

In this chapter, we took a close look at a number of different ways to show quantities and events over time. We considered simple line plots, dual-axis line plots, connected scatterplots, different levels of aggregation, forecasts, timelines, and finally slopegraphs.

In the next chapter, we'll move from time to the other ubiquitous element of our universe: space.

CHAPTER 10

Maps and Location

"There's just something hypnotic about maps."
—Ken Jennings,
74-time Jeopardy winner

Not only are maps hypnotic, but they are also very practical. Simply, maps are our way of communicating where things are in relation to one another. When I say the word "map," you probably think of a world map, but the earliest known maps are of the heavens. Dots on the walls of the Lascaux caves in southwest France date back to 16,500 B.C, and are interpreted to depict constellations: the position of stars in relation to one another (*http://bit.ly/star-map*).

There are many, many different types of maps. Architectural floor plans are also maps, as are dental charts and heat maps that show the location of pitches in a baseball game. What they all have in common is that at least one of their encodings is location in physical space.

In this chapter, we'll focus on maps with two positional encodings: latitude and longitude, or more generally, x and y. Of course the earth is not actually a flat plane, so we will need to make use of what's called a *standard projection* to avoid requiring a three-dimensional medium. There are many different types of projections, and Tableau uses the Web Mercator (sometimes referred to as EPSG 3857) projection common in online mapping applications such as Google Maps and Bing Maps.

One Special Map

One year before he died at the age of 89, French civil engineer Charles Joseph Minard left the world with a truly remarkable map depicting the ill-fated march of Napoleon's army to Moscow and back in the winter of 1812, shown in Figure 10-1.

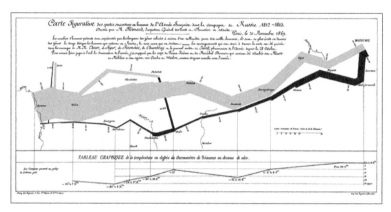

Figure 10-1. Minard's "carte figurative" of Napoleon's March of 1812

The thickness of the band represents the size of Napoleon's army, with the pale colored band showing the French soldiers' advance on Moscow and the black band their return. The gradual narrowing of the band conveys the staggering loss of life that occurred during the campaign. The line plot at the bottom charts the temperature during the return.

What's most remarkable about this now-famous map is that it was created by a man who wasn't a professional cartographer at all. Minard spent his career working on dams, canals, bridges, and railroads, and his map was largely ignored by professional cartographers of his day. Minard was an expert in the flow of masses across a terrain, and he applied his professional expertise to his hobby: history.

With a little effort using today's tools, anyone can become a hobbyist cartographer like Minard. In this chapter, we're going to consider how to communicate positional data using circle maps, filled maps (or choropleths), and maps that combine both of these approaches. In later chapters, we'll consider different types of maps, including maps with shapes and maps using custom imported background images.

Circle Maps

So far, we've created a number of charts and graphs of various places (chiefly New York City), but we have yet to create a map. At its simplest, a map shows a graphical depiction of some place, with markings for objects in that place. The markings on the map, like roads, borders, or bridges, are spaced in proportion to their spacing in the real world.

A map, then, becomes an ideal chart on which to visualize data. One way to visualize data on a map is to place a circle at a particular location, the size or color of which is proportional to some quantity associated with that location. This type of map is sometimes called a "bubble map."

 Why use a circle? Because we quickly identify a circle with its center point; there are no corners that would suggest another intended location.

There are plenty of ways to make these types of maps, including using the D3.js library or the Processing environment. Tableau provides an incredibly easy way to create a circle map using the same drag-and-drop interface we've been exploring. Let's try it out.

If we go back to the New York City boroughs population data we considered in Chapter 2, we can see that creating a map with circles is easy. There are three ways to do it:

1. Double-click on any geographic data field (one that has a globe icon next to it).

2. Select the geographic field by clicking on it, open the Show Me panel, and select *symbol maps*.

3. Drag `Latitude (generated)` to the Rows shelf, drag `Longitude (generated)` to the Columns shelf, and then drag `County` to Detail.

All three of these methods result in the view shown in Figure 10-2, in which Tableau places a blue circle at the center point of the coordinates of the geographic field.

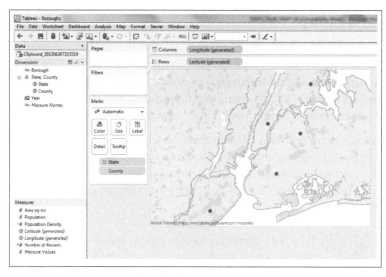

Figure 10-2. Creating a "symbol map" with circles

Recall from Chapter 2 that Tableau automatically generated these co-ordinates for us. We didn't need to find, download, and import the coordinates of New York City counties ourself: Tableau contains these values natively. Tableau also comes with coordinates for every country and state or province in the world; cities with population greater than 15,000; and other geographic fields such as zip code, area code, and metropolitan district for certain parts of the world. A complete list of the types of geographic fields is shown in Figure 10-3.

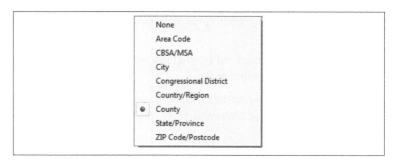

Figure 10-3. Different types of geographic fields in Tableau

Now, all the map in Figure 10-2 really tells us is that our data set contains at least one record for five different counties. That's not very interesting, is it? What we really want to show is how many people live in each of these places. To do that, all we need to do is drag `Popula tion` from the Measures shelf to the Size shelf, as shown in Figure 10-4.

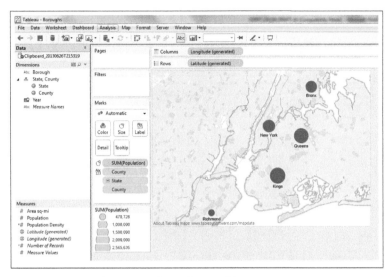

Figure 10-4. Circle map with circles sized by a Measure

We can do this with any numeric data field type, but it's best to use Continuous (green) fields, as they will result in maps with circles that are sized proportionately to the quantity. You can change the sizing by clicking on *Size* and moving the slider up or down. To create the map in Figure 10-4, I dragged the Size slider to the second notch, which increased the size of each of the circles proportionately. I also added `County` to the Label shelf so that those less familiar with New York will be able to know the place names.

Now we can see the circles and their size and position relative to each other, but comparisons aren't as precise as they are with bar lengths. Is the circle for New York county larger or smaller than the circle for Bronx county? How much larger is the population in Kings than in Richmond? Why not just make a bar chart, then? The map adds something to the equation: relative position.

Adding a Second Encoding

We've encoded population with circle size, but we haven't used color yet. We could use the Population Density calculated field to make circles darker proportionate with the number of people per square mile.

This would be a very intuitive thing to do, as we naturally identify darker colors with more and lighter colors with less. By now you get it: it's as easy as dragging the `Population Density` field to the Color shelf. The resulting view is shown in Figure 10-5.

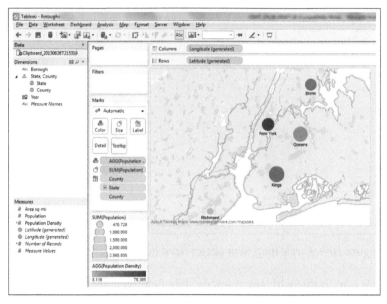

Figure 10-5. Circle maps with two encodings: size and color

Now we can make a number of different comparisons. It's more complex, but also more useful if we invest the time to learn the map. While there are fewer people in New York County as compared to Queens, the inhabitants of New York County are much more tightly packed. Richmond has both the fewest inhabitants as well as the lowest population density.

This isn't any different than the comparisons we were able to make with the bar chart shown in Figure 2-12 (the borough names have been replaced with county names), but the map provides the added benefit of being able to know *where on the planet* these place names are located. That's valuable.

When Marks Multiply

We've made a very simple map: there are only five circles on it. What does it look like if we create a map with a lot of marks? Let's try it out.

Because the world is a bigger place than just New York City, let's take a look at some global numbers: the growth of the Internet, by country, from 2000 to 2010. The data is available as part of the World Bank Indicators sample set that comes along with Tableau Desktop. Open a new workbook, click *Connect to Data* and find *Sample – World Bank Indicators (Excel)* in the *Saved data sources* section.

Let's build our circle map by taking the following steps:

1. Double-click on `Country / Region` in the Dimensions area.

2. Drag the Measure called `B: Internet users (per 100)` to the Size card.

3. Drag the Dimension `Region` to the Color card.

4. Click on the down arrow in the Region color legend area and change `The Americas` to blue and `Other` to pink. (This is a matter of preference, but I prefer using primary colors as much as possible.)

Let's pause and take a look at what we have, shown in Figure 10-6.

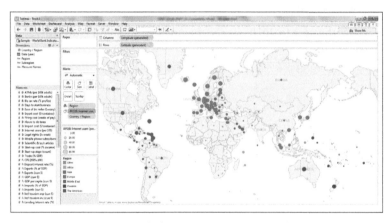

Figure 10-6. Average global Internet usage rates, by country, 2000– 2010

First, notice that when we dragged `B: Internet users (per 100)` to the Size card, Tableau created a green pill called `AVG(B: Internet users (per 100)`. There is more than one value for each country/ region for the field `B: Internet users (per 100)` in the data set, so Tableau had to do something with the set of rates for each country to give us a single circle on the map for each country. It could have summed up each value, given us a count, shown only the maximum or the minimum, and a handful of other options you can see by clicking the down arrow in the green pill and looking at the *Measure* menu.

But why is there more than one value for each country? If we look in the Dimensions panel, we see that there is also a field called Date (year). Every country has a rate for each year. We know the Internet grew rapidly over the first decade of the twenty-first century, so we likely don't want to show the *average rate*. Instead, let's add a Quick Filter for year so we can see Internet usage rates for one specific year.

To do that, right-click on Date (year) in the Dimensions pane, select *Show Quick Filter*, then click the down arrow in the upper-right corner of the resulting multiple values list and change the filter type to a single value list or single value slider.

Why do this last part and change the filter type? Well, it's not likely that users will want to know the average of the rates for a handful of years, like 2000, 2002, and 2009. So instead of giving them this ability and risk confusing them, let's keep it simple and let them see the world map for a single year.

If we set the year to 2010, we see the updated map in Figure 10-7.

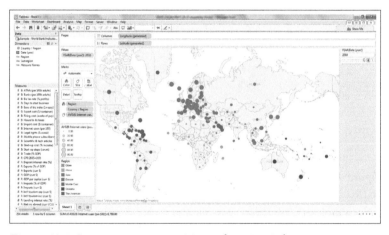

Figure 10-7. Internet usage per 100 people in 2010, by country

Notice how Europe has become a giant red blob. The same is true for the the Caribbean, only the blob is blue. What do we do about that? Two things: we can change the formatting to allow for transparency and circle borders, and we can add a filter for country/region to allow users to zoom in on one particular part of the world.

1. Click on the Color card and change the Transparency to 60%.

2. Still in the Color card options, add a gray border in the Effects area. Steps 1 and 2 are shown in Figure 10-8.

3. Right-click on the Country / Region field in the Dimensions area and select *Show Quick Filter*.

4. Change the Country / Region quick filter to the type of filter you'd like to use. I'll select the *Single Value (Dropdown)* style.

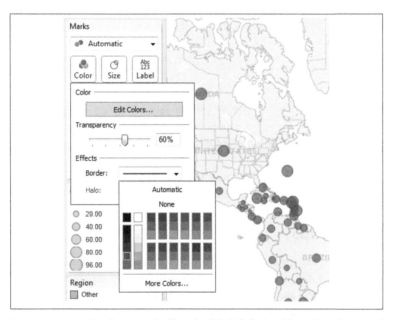

Figure 10-8. Dealing with "circle blobs" by adding borders and transparency

Our final circle map of global Internet adoption by country is shown in Figure 10-9.

Was coloring by Region the best choice in this case? It makes for a prettier picture, but is it helpful?

Well, we had a number of options, including double encoding color based on the same field dictating size. The only function coloring based on Region performs, because we can already tell which countries belong together based on their proximity, is to resolve a few groupings of countries close to the boundaries between the regions, like Greenland and Iceland. What it will do, though, is set us up to create a dashboard with multiple sheets, where regional colors are cues to link the map with other charts. We'll set that aside for later.

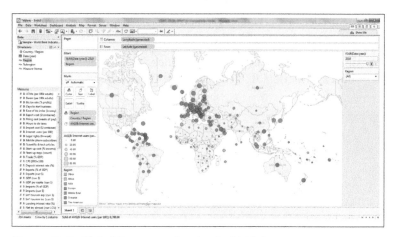

Figure 10-9. Global Internet adoption in 2010, by country

Next, let's consider another way to show data on a map of the world using a choropleth, or a filled map.

Filled Maps

Filled maps are great ways to show concentration by location, where location is a distinct area on the map with borders separating it from other areas. We see these very often with election results data, where certain regions are shaded a certain color according to how they voted.

The Internet usage statistics are a great example of a data set that is perfect for a filled map, because the data is in the form of a *rate*: users per 100 in the population. This metric is a type of density, not mass. If I see a map with circles, and place A has a bigger circle than place B, my first assumption is that place A has more of something. But a place with a higher rate than another place may have a greater concentration, while having a far fewer number overall.

To consider an example, compare Iceland with India in 2010, as shown in Figure 10-10.

Country / Region	B: Internet users (per 100)	P: Population (count)	B: Internet users (calculated)
Iceland	96	0.3M	305,319
India	8	1,224.6M	97,969,146

Figure 10-10. Comparing Internet usage in Iceland and India, 2010

The World Bank data set includes the first three columns, and the fourth was made with a simple calculated field, as shown in Figure 10-11.

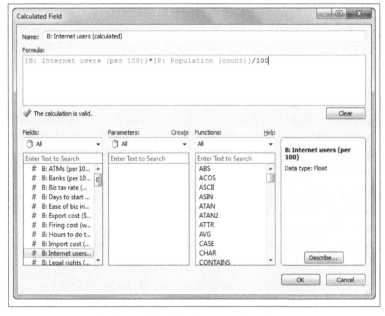

Figure 10-11. Calculating the absolute number of Internet users

As we can see, while Iceland has a far higher rate of Internet adoption than India, the sheer number of Internet users in India overwhelms the number in Iceland by more than 300:1. Mass versus density. Quantity versus rate.

Before we create the filled map, let's rename the Sheet for the circle map we just created and duplicate it. That way we can retain both maps in our workbook and we can use either one. Once we've done that, changing the map in the duplicated sheet from a circle map to a filled map is a simple as selecting the *filled map* tile in Show Me. The result is shown in Figure 10-12.

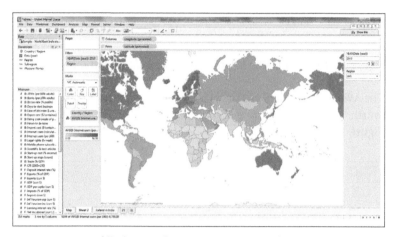

Figure 10-12. A filled map of Internet usage rates by country, 2010

Tableau automatically gets rid of the circles and replaces them with country shapes colored an increasingly darker green in proportion to the Internet adoption rate in each country. In this type of coloring, termed "Sequential" in Tableau, only one color (or *hue*) is used.

This allows us to communicate rate very effectively, and there is less risk that we'll mislead viewers about the absolute number of Internet users. We can clearly see that the rate is higher in North America, Europe, and Australia, somewhat lower in South America and most of Asia, and dramatically lower in Africa.

But can we easily tell which countries are at the halfway point, with around 50 Internet users out of 100? That would be a difficult list to come up with using the map as we have designed it. Let's try a different style of coloring: a diverging scale, in which more than one color is used.

We'll start with a color palette that evokes the notion of hot versus cold: *Orange-White-Blue Diverging*. To aid cognition, let's change the defaults so that the deepest blue (cold) corresponds to 0 Internet users out of 100, and the deepest orange (hot) corresponds to exactly 100 Internet users out of 100. Tableau defaulted to 0 and 96, which are the min and max values in the data set, but this places the white midpoint at an awkward 48 users out of 100, a meaningless value. The dialog box used to edit colors is shown in Figure 10-13.

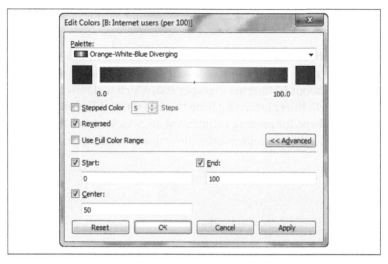

Figure 10-13. Editing the color palette for the global Internet user filled map

Once we make this change, the all-green filled map changes to the filled map shown in Figure 10-14.

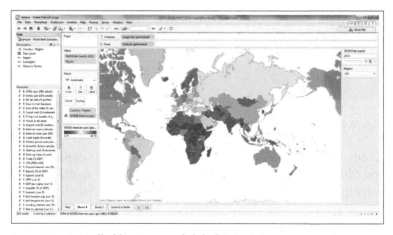

Figure 10-14. Filled heat map of global Internet usage

Which gives a clearer picture of the state of Internet usage in 2010, the all green version in Figure 10-12, or the hot/cold version in Figure 10-14? Now is it easier to tell which countries are at about 50% Internet usage—the halfway point? We can tell pretty easily that Italy, Portugal, Morocco, and Uruguay are at around 50 Internet users out of 100.

But what about North Korea? As Figure 10-15 shows, this version of the map is not without its problems. It seems at a glance that North Korea is at about 50 Internet users per 100, which we know to be false. In fact, North Korea is missing from the data set, and Tableau does not include a shape for missing countries at all, which makes them seem close to the halfway usage point of the color scheme we've chosen.

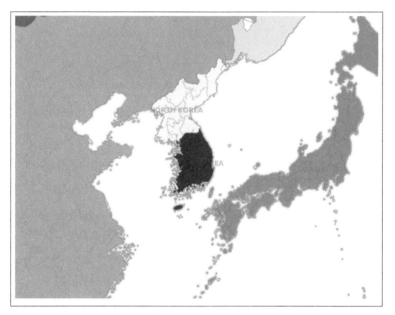

Figure 10-15. North Korea is missing data, not at 50 users per 100

Another example is shown in Figure 10-16. Portugal (51 users per 100) and Morocco (49 users per 100) are both very close to the halfway point in 2010, but data for the territory of Western Sahara is missing.

We can see that we've solved one problem and created another, which is often the case with color choices. We could go with an orange-blue diverging color palette rather than an orange-white-blue to make the situation a little better, but if you try it for yourself you'll see that it isn't a perfect solution either, as the gray of the base map is close to the blue of Morocco.

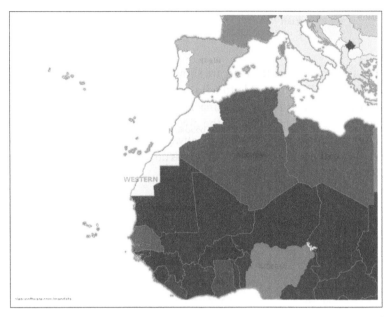

Figure 10-16. Western Sahara is missing data; Morocco and Portugal are not

Another possible solution is to change the style of base map from "Gray" to "Dark." To do this, just click *Map* from the menu, select *Map Options*, and change the *Background Style* from *Gray* to *Dark*. The result for this and the orange-blue color choice are shown in Figure 10-17.

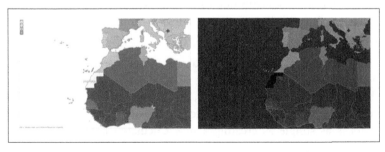

Figure 10-17. Two solutions to the missing values problem: orange-blue (left) and a dark map (right)

One further consideration when choosing a color scheme is whether the viewer of the visualization will be able to view it in color, or will see it only in grayscale. If there's any chance the viewer will see a grayscale version, steer clear of diverging color palettes and stick with sequential.

The two versions of the map are shown in grayscale in Figure 10-18. Notice how it's impossible to tell the difference between the dark of very high values (like in Scandinavia) and the dark of very low values (like in Africa) when viewing the diverging color palette in grayscale. With sequential, higher values are always darker than lower values, so it's perfectly clear in grayscale. If there's any chance your viewer won't have a color display, use sequential.

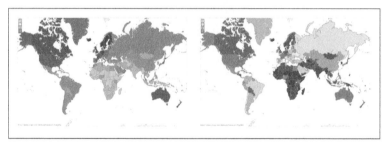

Figure 10-18. Sequential (left) and diverging (right) color palettes shown in grayscale

Dual-Encoded Maps

Now we've created a version of the Internet usage map with circles, and a couple others with filled country shapes using different color schemes. Both types communicated one variable: Internet usage per 100 users. But what if we also wanted to communicate which countries have the most *overall* Internet usage?

The first thing we'll have to do is to create a new variable for the number of Internet users, because that isn't included. What is included is the rate of Internet users per 100, and the overall population of the country, so creating the measure for the absolute number of Internet users is as simple as creating a new calculated field, as shown in Figure 10-19.

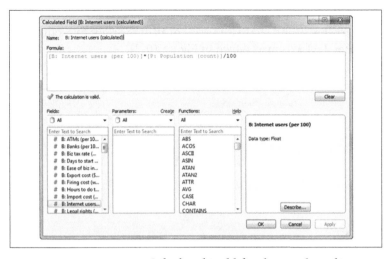

Figure 10-19. Creating a Calculated Field for the number of Internet users

We could create two different maps, one for each variable, or we could create a single map that encodes both variables. Let's take a look at two ways to show both variables on a single map: the first makes use of the dual-axis feature, and the second makes use of the two attributes of circles: size and color.

A Dual-Axis Map

Let's start with the filled map we created (shown in Figure 10-14). We'll take the following steps to create a dual-axis map:

1. Drag another Latitude (generated) pill to the Rows shelf to the right of the first one.

2. Click the small down arrow in the second Latitude (gener ated) pill and select *Dual Axis* (as shown in Figure 10-20).

3. In the Marks card, open the panel for Latitude (generated) (2) and change the Mark type from *Automatic* (or Filled Map) to *Shape*.

4. Still in the Marks card area for Latitude (generated) (2), re-move AVG(B: Internet users (per 100) from the color shelf and add B: Internet users (calculated) to the Size shelf.

5. Use the Color and Size cards to change the color of the rings to a darker gray and increase the size of all of the rings to produce the final dual-axis map shown in Figure 10-21.

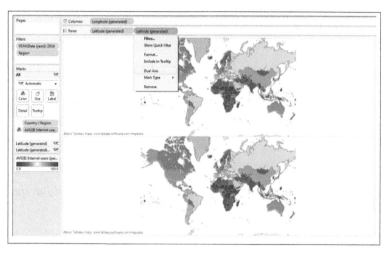

Figure 10-20. Create a dual-axis map

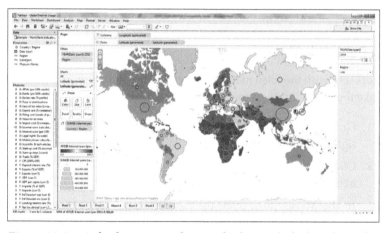

Figure 10-21. A dual-axis map showing both rate (color) and number (circle sizes) of Internet users

If we pause a moment to take a look at what we've created, we'll notice that this version of the map would probably be slightly more intimidating to the first-time viewer. We're communicating two different measures via totally separate encodings, so viewers will need to invest a little more time to "learn the map," especially if we don't have the luxury of explaining it to them in person. Once they understand the cipher though, they'll get more in-depth insights in return.

Viewers can easily see, for example, that while the rate of Internet users in China is relatively low (light blue color), it represents the highest absolute number of Internet users in any country in the world in 2010. That might not be very surprising, but other interesting comparisons can be made. Compare Japan with India, for example. Both had around 100 million Internet users in 2010, but Japan had a much higher rate of adoption. The Scandinavian countries, while still the darkest on the map, contribute a fairly low total number of users to the global pool. These types of comparisons can be made relatively quickly with this type of map.

A Dual-Encoded Circle Map

The second way to show both variables on a single map is to use the fact that we can encode measures to two different shape properties in Tableau: color and size.

Let's return to the circle map we created earlier in the chapter (see Figure 10-9). If we review this first version of the circle map, we'll notice that we encoded circle size by the rate of Internet users per 100, and we encoded circle color with region. Instead, let's duplicate this sheet (right-click on the *Sheet* tab and select *Duplicate Sheet*), and rearrange the pills to encode number of Internet users to size and rate of usage to color, as follows:

1. Remove Region from the Marks card area so that it no longer encodes circle color (click the blue Region pill and drag and drop it back into the Dimensions area).

2. Change the Marks type from *Automatic* to *Circle*.

3. In the Marks card area, click the *Size* icon next to the green AVG(B: Internet users (per 100)) pill (shown as two rings), and change this encoding to *Color*, as indicated in Figure 10-22.

4. Change the color palette to *Orange-White-Blue Diverging*, starting a 0 and ending at 100.

5. Drag the calculated field B: Internet Users (calculated) to the Size shelf.

6. Increase the size of the circles.

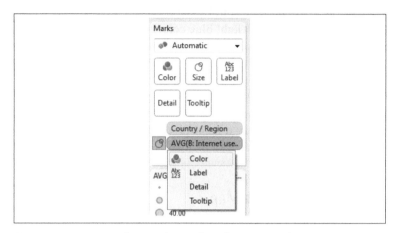

Figure 10-22. Using the Marks card to change encodings

The resulting dual-encoded circle map is shown in Figure 10-23.

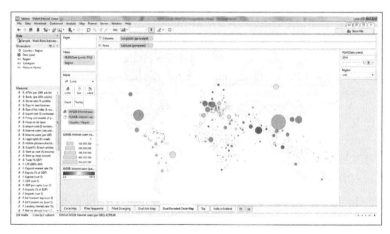

Figure 10-23. A dual-encoded circle map of Internet usage

It's hard to say which does a better job of communicating the two variables, the dual-axis map or the dual-encoded circle map. They both are probably adequate, and a choice of which to use likely comes down to a matter of preference. To me, the dual-encoded circle map shown in Figure 10-23 is easier to read, because (by definition) the dual-axis map in Figure 10-21 involves occlusion of marks, as the circles are overlaid on the country shapes. For this reason, it feels more "jumbled" to me, which increases the intimidation factor upon viewing it for the first time.

Summary

In this chapter, we created a number of different map types in Tableau without ever dealing directly with GIS shapefiles or having to find latitude and longitude coordinates. We compared symbol maps and filled maps, and found ways to show more than one quantitative measure at a time.

In the next chapter, we'll dive into some more advanced mapping topics.

CHAPTER 11

Advanced Maps

"The map is not the territory."

—Alfred Korzybski, philosopher and
scientist, 1931

I remember my first job interview after engineering school. The year was 2000, and online maps and driving directions were relatively new. Feeling confident and wearing my best suit, I headed out the door with a printout of my driving directions in hand for what should have been a ten-minute drive north on the Ventura Freeway. Forty-five minutes later and in the middle of a strawberry field in Camarillo, I felt the sting of this quote like never before.

Korzybski's statement is helpful because it points out that often we confuse an abstraction (like a map) derived from something with the thing itself. Indeed, this idea is applicable to each of the data visualizations we've created so far in this book, and is a healthy reminder any time we are communicating data. We're showing abstract representations of reality, not reality itself. Just because some map says a particular road goes over a creek doesn't mean the road has to obey, no matter how much a tardy job seeker may want it to. Maps contain approximations, uncertainties, and errors.

So far, we've looked at circle maps and choropleth (or filled) maps. In this chapter, we'll consider a number of other types of maps, including maps with shapes, maps showing paths, and views that plot map shapes on axes. While these additional types of maps may contain their fair share of inaccuracies, they can also serve a purpose as we communicate data to others.

Maps with Shapes

We love to look at maps with shapes on them. Online maps have symbols for freeways, national parks, and hotels. Shopping mall maps have store logos and the universally recognized bathroom icons to guide us to the right places in the least amount of time (hopefully!). As children, we learn to read maps with icons like the ones at zoos that show the different animal exhibits.

Why are these so effective? If we refer back to our data encoding effectiveness diagram (Figure 1-6), we'll get a clue as to why shapes on maps can be such a powerful communication tool: notice that the two most effective encodings for nominal values are position and shape. Think of the proverbial tiger in the savannah: we are very quick to spot images and to associate them with the place in which we saw them. It's just how our brain works.

We can also see from Figure 1-6 that we wouldn't want to use shapes to encode quantitative or ordinal values. Think of the way shapes are used in the world around us: we use traffic signs with different shapes to indicate the *type of action* to be performed (like stop or yield), but we don't use the shapes themselves to tell us the speed limit, for example. This is an issue of nominal versus quantitative information.

Let's consider a few examples of how we can make good use of shapes on maps to communicate data.

If I wanted to communicate where the 32 different professional football teams are located in the United States, I could simply provide a list of team names and locations in table form, as shown in Figure 11-1, obtained from Wikipedia (*http://bit.ly/wiki-nfl-stadiums*).

As accurate as this list may be, it's not very useful or interesting. Our brains just can't process it very efficiently for a whole host of tasks, such as determining whether there are any clusters of teams, or figuring out which areas of the country have relatively few teams.

Alternatively, I could show a map of the team names using Tableau, as shown in Figure 11-2, by connecting to the table, double-clicking on *City*, dragging Team(s) to the Text shelf, and changing the Marks type from *Automatic* to *Text*.

	A	B	D	E	F	G	H	I
1	Tm	Team(s)	City	State	Capacity	Playing surface	Roof type	Opened
2	WAS	Washington D.C.	Landover	Maryland	85000	Bermuda Grass (Latitude 36)	Open	1997
3	NYG	New York	East Rutherford	New Jersey	82566	UBU-Intensity Series- S5-M Synthetic Turf	Open	2010
4	NYJ	New York	East Rutherford	New Jersey	82566	UBU-Intensity Series- S5-M Synthetic Turf	Open	2010
5	GBP	Green Bay	Green Bay	Wisconsin	80750	Desso GrassMaster	Open	1957
6	DAL	Dallas	Arlington	Texas	80000	Matrix RealGrass artificial turf[7]	Retractable	2009
7	KC	Kansas City	Kansas City	Missouri	76416	Grass	Open	1972
8	DEN	Denver	Denver	Colorado	76125	Desso GrassMaster	Open	2001
9	MIA	Miami	Miami Gardens	Florida	75540	Prescription Athletic Turf (Natural Grass)	Open	1987
10	CAR	Carolina	Charlotte	North Carolina	73778	Grass	Open	1996
11	NO	New Orleans	New Orleans	Louisiana	73208	UBU-Intensity Series- S5-M Synthetic Turf	Domed	1975
12	CLE	Cleveland	Cleveland	Ohio	73200	Kentucky Bluegrass	Open	1999
13	BUF	Buffalo	Orchard Park	New York	73079	A-Turf Titan	Open	1973
14	ATL	Atlanta	Atlanta	Georgia	71228	FieldTurf	Domed	1992
15	HOU	Houston	Houston	Texas	71054	419 Tifway Bermuda Grass	Retractable	2002
16	BAL	Baltimore	Baltimore	Maryland	71008	Sportexe Momentum Turf	Open	1998
17	SD	San Diego	San Diego	California	70561	Grass	Open	1967
18	SF	San Francisco	San Francisco	California	69732	Kentucky Bluegrass	Open	1960
19	TEN	Tennessee	Nashville	Tennessee	69143	419 Tifway Bermuda Grass	Open	1999
20	NE	New England	Foxborough	Massachusetts	68756	FieldTurf	Open	2002
21	PHI	Philadelphia	Philadelphia	Pennsylvania	68532	Desso GrassMaster	Open	2003
22	JAC	Jacksonville	Jacksonville	Florida	67246	419 Tifway Bermuda Grass	Open	1995
23	SEA	Seattle	Seattle	Washington	67000	FieldTurf	Open	2002
24	STL	St. Louis	St. Louis	Missouri	66000	AstroTurf GameDay Grass 3D	Domed	1995
25	TB	Tampa Bay	Tampa	Florida	65890	419 Tifway Bermuda Grass	Open	1998
26	CIN	Cincinnati	Cincinnati	Ohio	65535	UBU-Intensity Series- S5-M Synthetic Turf	Open	2000
27	PIT	Pittsburgh	Pittsburgh	Pennsylvania	65050	Grass	Open	2001
28	DET	Detroit	Detroit	Michigan	65000	FieldTurf	Domed	2002
29	MIN	Minnesota	Minneapolis	Minnesota	64121	UBU-Intensity Series- S5-M Synthetic Turf	Domed	1982
30	ARI	Arizona	Glendale	Arizona	63400	419 Tifway Bermuda Grass	Retractable	2006
31	IND	Indianapolis	Indianapolis	Indiana	62421	FieldTurf	Retractable	2008
32	CHI	Chicago	Chicago	Illinois	61500	Grass	Open	1924
33	OAK	Oakland	Oakland	California	53200	Grass	Open	1966

Figure 11-1. List of NFL teams and stadiums sourced from Wikipedia

Figure 11-2. Mapping football team cities

Note that three places aren't automatically given latitude and longitude coordinates and therefore don't appear on the map at first: Miami Gardens, FL; Landover, MD; and East Rutherford, NJ. This is because these are not cities: they're unincorporated communities or they have fewer than 15,000 residents, so Tableau doesn't autogenerate their coordinates.

To make them appear, click on the 3 unknown pill in the bottom right of the map, select *Edit Locations*, and then enter the coordinates shown in Figure 11-3 for each of the three respective locations.

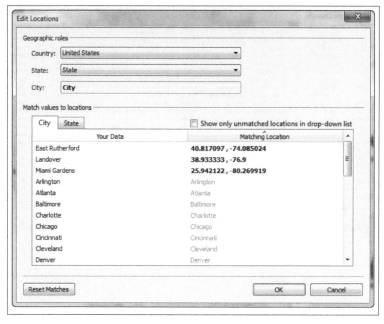

Figure 11-3. Entering coordinates for cities that are unknown to Tableau

The map with team name labels is much easier to digest than the list, even if a few of the team names are difficult to read due to proximity to another team. We can immediately see the clustering of teams in the Northeast, and I can see right away that the Seattle players probably fly the farthest over the course of a season to play their games.

But there's still some ambiguity in this map, as I don't know the exact location of each team's city relative to the text displayed. Are the cities located near the first letters, the last letters, in the middle, or somewhere else?

To resolve this ambiguity, we can change the Marks type from *Text* back to *Circles*, and we see very quickly that each city is located in the center of the text and slightly above it, as shown in Figure 11-4.

Figure 11-4. Mapping football teams with name and circle

This seems like a missed opportunity, though, because all of the blue circles are the same shape and color. These symbols have the potential to communicate more information than just latitude and longitude. Is there a way to make use of this opportunity to either enhance interest, cognition, or memory?

I could place Team on the color shelf, or I could change the Marks type to *Shape* and add Team to the Shape shelf, as shown in Figure 11-5.

I'm not a big fan of either one of these. In the first case, Tableau automatically mapped 20 different colors to the 32 different teams, meaning that some teams got the same colors, like the Carolina and Pittsburgh teams (both are green). There is no reason for these two teams to be linked in this way; they simply got assigned the same color due to their position in the alphabetically sorted list of names.

It's even worse with the shapes: the 32 teams got assigned one of 10 default shapes, meaning there are groups of three teams that arbitrarily share the same shape. While I could edit the colors or shapes to give each team a unique assignment, I don't see how this would communicate anything more effectively than the circle map in Figure 11-4.

If we wanted to convey something about each team, such as what type of stadium they play in, we could use different shapes to communicate this information. There are stadiums with three different roof types: open, domed, and retractable (as indicated in Column H of the table shown in Figure 11-1).

Figure 11-5. Mapping football teams with different colors and standard shapes

We can create shapes for each of the roof types (as shown in Figure 11-6) and save them as individual image files (ideally in *.png* with transparent backgrounds) in a folder called, say, *stadiums*. Then we can make them accessible inside Tableau by placing that folder into *My Documents/My Tableau Repository/Shapes*.

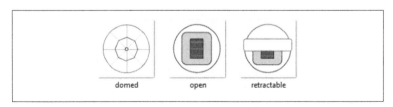

Figure 11-6. Images (.png files) corresponding to different stadium roof types

Once the files are in this location, we can then add them to the map by taking the following steps:

1. Change the Mark type from *Circle* to *Shape* (the Shape card should appear to the right of Tooltip)—Tableau changes the marks to rings.

2. Drag `Roof Type` from *Dimensions* to the *Shape* shelf—Tableau automatically assigns default shapes.

3. Click the *Shape* card (or click the small down arrow in the upper-right corner of the shape legend).

4. In the dialog box that appears (see Figure 11-7), select your folder in the *Select Shape Palette* and assign the appropriate icon to the roof type in the list to the left. If the folder does not appear, click the *Reload Shapes* button.

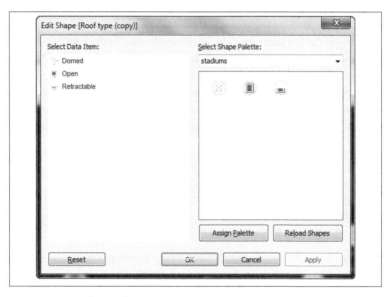

Figure 11-7. Editing shapes

The map changes to look like the map shown in Figure 11-8. (This map was also changed to a dark map by selecting *Map → Map Options → Style → Dark*.)

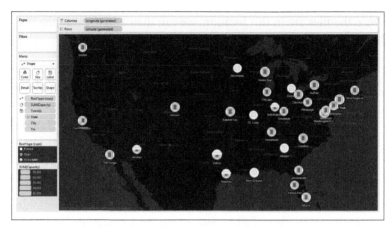

Figure 11-8. Mapping football team stadium types using custom shapes

If you were asked to quickly tell the locations of the domed roof stadiums (indicated by the white round shape a circle in the center), you could spot them rather quickly — all are located in the central section of the country. You could also quickly see that all but one of the retractable roofs are in the southern states. These patterns are very difficult to spot when the information is given in a table, but they reveal themselves with a minimum amount of interrogation when shown on a map: the audience gets an immediate return on very little effort.

But there are some issues with this map. Some shapes are hidden or partially covered, such as the stadium shape for San Francisco, which is almost entirely underneath the stadium shape for Oakland. I can't imagine fans of either team approving of this configuration. Similar occlusion of logos is happening in the Northeast, where the stadium shapes for the two New York teams overlap heavily.

This can be partially remedied by adding Annotations to the shapes that are clustered. If we right-click on each shape, select *Annotate* and then *Mark*, we can edit the resulting dialog box to make sure the data field <Tm> is displayed. The team acronym appears on the map with an arrow pointing to the shape.

We can move the resulting annotations to the desired locations on the map and then right-click each one and change its format. I prefer to remove the arrows from the line ends and change the line colors to a lighter gray. The updated stadium map is shown in Figure 11-9 (with the map changed to the Normal style and shapes changed to standard ones from the *Proportions* palette).

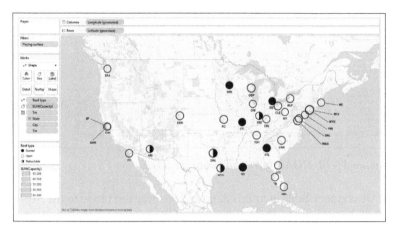

Figure 11-9. Updated football team city map with annotations

By now, we've established the usefulness of using shapes on maps to communicate data. So far, all of the maps we've created show shapes stuck to one place on a map. Sometimes, though, the point of showing a map is to show people the path taken along a particular route. Next, let's consider how to handle data when the location on a map isn't static, but dynamic, like a hurricane in motion.

Maps Showing Paths

Weather patterns are excellent examples of objects that move over time. When a hurricane makes its way across the surface of the ocean and toward land, the whole world watches. There are rich sources of historical hurricane data on the Web, such as the IBTrACS dataset (*http://bit.ly/IBTrACS*) maintained by the National Oceanic and Atmospheric Administration, NOAA.

The table shown in Figure 11-10 shows an Excel spreadsheet created from a *.csv* of 2012 hurricane data. Notice that each row contains a set of coordinates and information about a particular storm at a particular hour. There are multiple rows for each storm, and the series of coordinates contained in these rows provides a route that the storm followed over time.

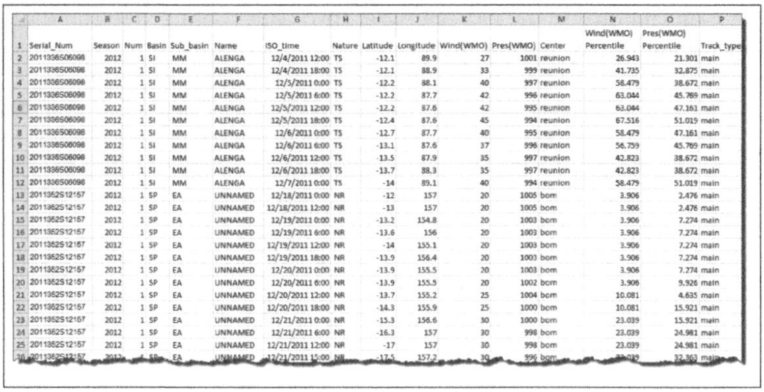

Figure 11-10. NOAA hurricane data for 2012

If we connect Tableau to this data, and we drag `Latitude` to the Rows shelf, `Longitude` to the Columns shelf, `Name` to the Label shelf, and `Basin` to the Color shelf, then we get the circle map shown in Figure 11-11.

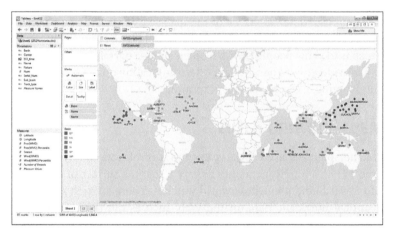

Figure 11-11. The average location of each hurricane recorded in 2012

There isn't really too much significance to the "average" latitude and longitude of a storm. In fact, the average position could be in a place that the storm never visited. What we'd really like to see is the route of each storm as it made its way across the face of the planet.

To create such a map, we can do the following:

1. Change the Marks type from *Automatic* to *Line*. Notice that a new landing pad called *Path* appears to the right of Tooltip in the Marks card.

2. Drag ISO_time to this Path landing pad/shelf. Notice that a new blue pill called YEAR(ISO_time) appears in the Marks card with a path icon to the left of it.

3. Click in the down arrow of the blue YEAR(ISO_time) pill in the Marks area and choose *More → Hour*, as shown in Figure 11-12.

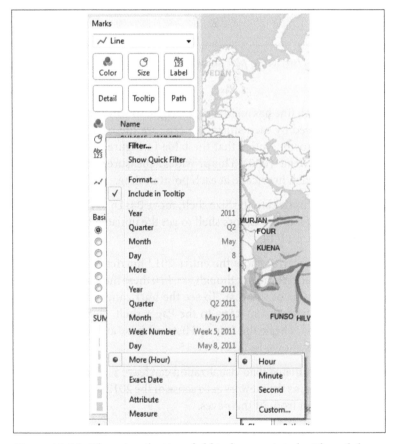

Figure 11-12. Changing the time field to be associated with each hour

The resulting hurricane plot is shown in Figure 11-13.

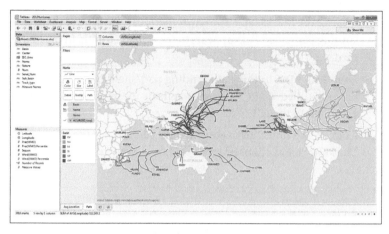

Figure 11-13. Hurricane plot showing the route of each hurricane of 2012

Notice that each line has an identical weight, so while we can visualize the path traveled by each storm, we can't see the relative strength or size of each storm. Notice that the table in Figure 11-10 contains a column called Wind (WMO). This provides a measure of the wind speed (in knots) of each hurricane at each point in time.

We can drag this field to the Size shelf, move Basin to the Filters shelf and Place Name to the Colors shelf to get the updated hurricane map shown in Figure 11-14.

This is a great way to show the entire 2012 hurricane season in one snapshot. What isn't shown, though, is *when* these hurricanes occurred during the course of the year. To see the hurricanes move their way across the map, drag ISO_time to the Pages shelf, change the pill to DAY(ISO_time), check the "Show History" box, and then press the *Play* button, as shown in Figure 11-15.

This type of animated data visualization can leave a lasting impression on an audience, as the viewers get a sense of the 2012 hurricane season "playing out" in front of their eyes.

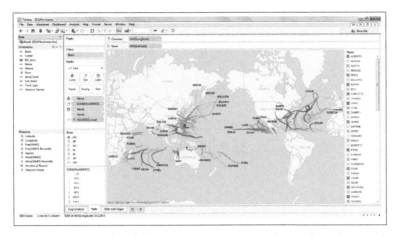

Figure 11-14. Updated hurricane map showing the path and strength of each hurricane

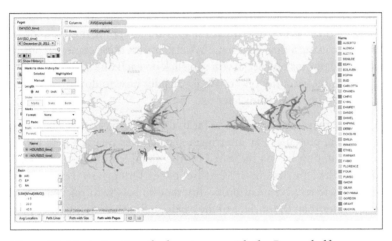

Figure 11-15. Animating the hurricanes with the Pages shelf

Here's another example of using the Path shelf to show routes on a map. My two sons and I like to track our hikes using a GPS app for my smart phone. Afterward, we download the data from the app site and connect Tableau to see our trek. A recent hike in the hills near Mount Si in Washington is shown in Figure 11-16.

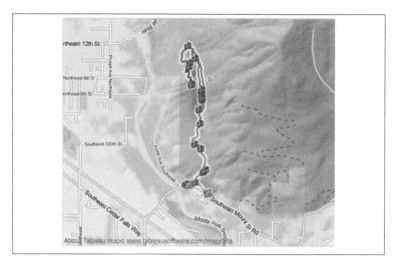

Figure 11-16. The Little Si hike, May 26, 2013

You can also see that we captured the spots where we took photos, showing them as custom camera shapes and mapping them on top of our route using a dual-axis map. We also linked these camera icons to the actual photos online, so you can click on each one and be taken to a website showing the photo. We'll consider how to do this when we cover Dashboard Actions later on.

All of the maps we've created so far in this book have made use of the Urban Mapping tiles that are triggered whenever we use a field with a "Geographic Role" (as indicated by the globe icon next to the field name in the Dimensions or Measures pane). Often, however, we want to show the relative position of different objects with reference to a space other than the surface of the earth, such as a building floor plan or some other object projected onto a plane.

Lastly, we're going to make use of Tableau's built-in geographical filled maps to make a different kind of filled map: one in which the shapes of the regions are placed on types of views we considered earlier in the book: scatterplots and bar plots.

Plotting Map Shapes Using Axes

The 2012 U.S. presidential election pitted the Democratic candidate and incumbent, Barack Obama, against the Republican candidate and former governor of the state of Massachusetts, Mitt Romney. After the votes were tallied, a whole host of comparisons could be made, such as how the voting record compared with other demographic variables, including unemployment levels, degree of urbanization, and education levels, among many others. We'll consider a few of these variables in tandem, and see if there is any correlation between them.

The trick with these types of comparisons is to remember that correlation does not imply causation.

First, we'll start with the data. At a state level, we can obtain the voting percentages and demographic statistics from governmental sites (*http://bit.ly/fed-elec-2012*, *http://bit.ly/reg-state-employment*, *http:// bit.ly/2010-UR-census*, and *http://bit.ly/educ-attainment*), and combine them into the table shown in Figure 11-17.

	A	B	C	D	E	F	G	H	I
				Advanced degree	Bachelor's degree	Unemployment	High school graduate	Urban	Voted for
1	State	State ID	Region	or more	or more	Rate	or more	Population	Obama
2	Alabama	AL	South	7.7%	22.0%	8.3%	82.1%	59.0%	38.4%
3	Alaska	AK	West	9.0%	27.0%	7.5%	91.4%	66.0%	40.8%
4	Arizona	AZ	West	9.3%	26.0%	8.2%	84.2%	89.8%	44.6%
5	Arkansas	AR	South	6.1%	19.0%	7.1%	82.4%	56.2%	36.9%
6	California	CA	West	10.7%	30.0%	10.2%	80.6%	95.0%	60.2%
7	Colorado	CO	West	12.7%	36.0%	8.0%	89.3%	86.2%	51.5%
8	Connecticut	CT	Northeast	15.5%	36.0%	8.9%	88.6%	88.0%	58.1%
9	Delaware	DE	South	11.4%	29.0%	6.8%	87.4%	83.3%	58.6%
10	Florida	FL	South	9.0%	25.0%	8.7%	85.3%	91.2%	50.0%
11	Georgia	GA	South	9.9%	28.0%	9.0%	83.9%	75.1%	45.5%
12	Hawaii	HI	West	9.9%	30.0%	5.7%	90.4%	91.9%	70.6%
13	Idaho	ID	West	7.5%	24.0%	7.1%	88.4%	70.6%	32.6%
14	Illinois	IL	Midwest	11.7%	31.0%	8.8%	86.4%	88.5%	57.6%
15	Indiana	IN	Midwest	8.1%	23.0%	8.2%	86.6%	72.4%	43.9%
16	Iowa	IA	Midwest	7.4%	25.0%	5.2%	90.5%	64.0%	52.0%
17	Kansas	KS	Midwest	10.2%	30.0%	5.9%	89.7%	74.2%	38.0%
18	Kentucky	KY	South	8.5%	21.0%	8.4%	81.7%	58.4%	37.8%
19	Louisiana	LA	South	6.9%	21.0%	7.0%	82.2%	73.2%	40.6%
20	Maine	ME	Northeast	9.6%	27.0%	7.6%	90.2%	38.7%	56.3%
21	Maryland	MD	South	16.0%	36.0%	6.9%	88.2%	87.2%	62.0%
22	Massachusetts	MA	Northeast	16.4%	38.0%	6.5%	89.0%	92.0%	60.7%
23	Michigan	MI	Midwest	9.4%	25.0%	9.3%	87.9%	74.6%	54.2%
24	Minnesota	MN	Midwest	10.3%	32.0%	5.8%	91.5%	73.3%	52.7%
25	Mississippi	MS	South	7.1%	20.0%	9.2%	80.4%	49.4%	43.8%
26	Missouri	MO	Midwest	9.5%	25.0%	6.9%	86.8%	70.4%	44.4%

Figure 11-17. Spreadsheet of voting rates and demographics

By now you're familiar with how to connect Tableau to this data source and you're probably already thinking of a number of ways to visualize these variables from the earlier chapters. It's helpful to remember that as soon as we connect Tableau to the data, we have at our disposal three other geographic elements for each U.S. state: its latitude, longitude, and shape. In this section, we'll see how to make use of the built-in shape library to enhance our common chart types so as to aid cognition and memory.

Before we begin visualizing the data, let's do some extra setup to create a Parameter that we can use to quickly toggle between views with different variables. Right-click in the Dimensions area and click *Create Parameter*, then fill out the resulting dialog box with the information shown in Figure 11-18.

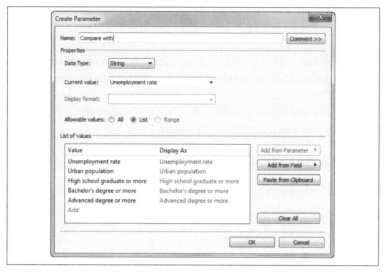

Figure 11-18. Create a Parameter to change the "compare with" variable

Once you click *OK*, a Parameters area appears in the lower-left corner of the sheet, and "Compare with" appears in that area. Now that we have this Parameter created, we can right-click it and select *Show Parameter Control*. The drop-down selector should now appear in the upper-right corner of the sheet. While you can now change the value of the Parameter by using the drop-down menu, it isn't linked to anything.

We need to link a new calculated field to it first. To do so, right-click on *Compare with* in the Parameters area in the bottom left, select *Create Calculated Field*, and fill out the resulting dialog box as shown in Figure 11-19, making sure the text you enter is exactly as it appears in the Parameter dialog box (it's case-sensitive).

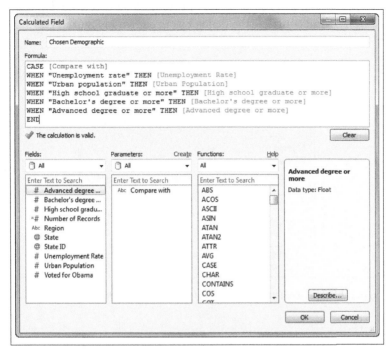

Figure 11-19. Creating a Calculated Field for the Parameter to control

Now that we have this calculated field called "Chosen Demographic" in the Measures area, let's use it to create a scatterplot comparing the various state demographics with the voting record using the following nine steps:

1. Drag `Chosen Demographic` to the Columns shelf.

2. Drag `Voted for Obama` to the Rows shelf.

3. Drag `State` to the Level of Detail.

4. Change the Marks type from *Automatic* to *Filled Map*.

5. Click the Size card and increase the size to the second notch.

6. Drag `State ID` to Label.

7. Drag `Voted for Obama` to the Color shelf and edit the colors as shown in Figure 11-20.

8. Right click in the scatterplot and select *Trend Lines* → *Show Trend Lines*.

9. Right click on the y-axis and select *Add Reference Line, Band, or Box...* and complete the dialog box as shown in Figure 11-21.

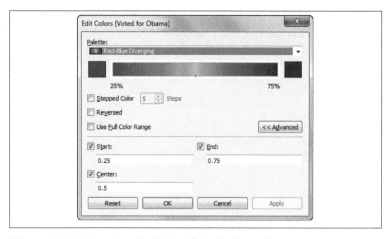

Figure 11-20. Creating the U.S. political color scheme

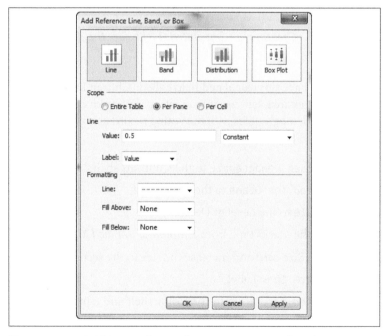

Figure 11-21. Adding a reference line at 50% voting for Obama

The resulting scatterplot (with grid lines removed) is shown in Figure 11-22. Notice that we can use the Parameter control in the upper right to quickly change the x-axis variable to any of the five fields we included in the Parameter.

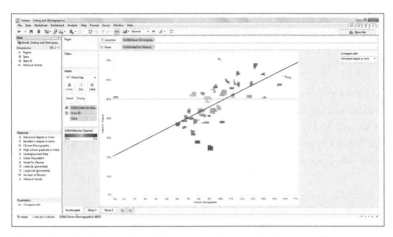

Figure 11-22. Scatterplot of demographics and voting results

We can figure out which of the five variables is most closely correlated with the voting record by clicking on the trend line, right-clicking, and selecting *Describe Trend Model*. The trend model when "Advanced degree or more" is selected is shown in Figure 11-23.

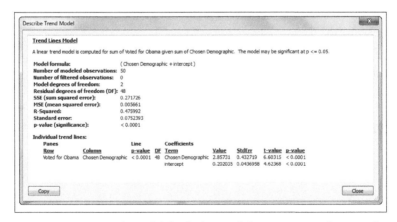

Figure 11-23. Trend Model for "advanced degree or more" versus "% voted for Obama"

Variable	p-value	R-Squared	Slope
Unemployment rate	0.024	10.0%	1.828
Urban population	0.007	14.0%	0.286
High school graduate or more	0.388	1.6%	0.376
Bachelor's degree or more	<0.0001	39.0%	1.344
Advanced degree or more	<0.0001	47.5%	2.857

Figure 11-24. Significance and strength of correlation for five variables

Another way to show two variables at a time using these shapes is to create a dual-axis bar chart with the state shapes at the end of the bars, as shown in Figure 11-25. The key to building this chart is to change the Marks type of the second axis to *Filled Map*, as we did in step 4 when we created the scatterplot.

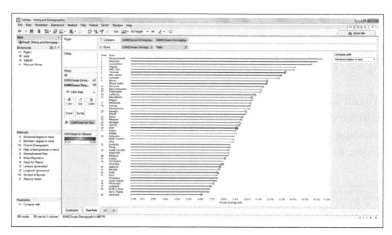

Figure 11-25. Using state shapes on a dual-axis map

The same can be done with country shapes, as shown in Figure 11-26, comparing trade and GDP for the G-20 nations.

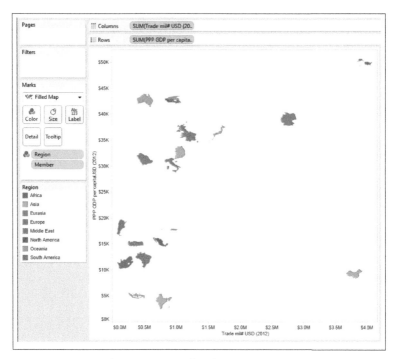

Figure 11-26. Trade versus GDP for the G20 nations

Summary

In this chapter, we've considered a number of advanced mapping functions in Tableau. We've added shapes to maps, mapped moving objects via the Path and Pages shelves, and used geographic region shapes on common chart types.

We've now considered how to communicate data using many different types of individual charts, graphs, and maps. The focus has been on communicating effectively using the abilities of Tableau to use data fields as encoding types, and to quickly filter the view using the power of Tableau's visual analytics engine.

In the subsequent chapters, we'll consider how to bring multiple views, filters, parameters, and various objects into richly interactive data dashboards.

CHAPTER 12

The Joy of Dashboards

"You don't have to cook fancy or complicated masterpieces—just good food from fresh ingredients."

—Julia Child

If we compare communicating data with cooking, then what we've covered so far in this book amounts to a course on individual ingredients. Just as a master chef knows how to combine ingredients to serve up a meal, so an expert communicator of data can mix different charts, graphs, and tables to deliver a multifaceted message.

The analogy to a meal in this context is known as a *dashboard*. In this chapter, we'll consider different types and styles of dashboards, and we'll outline key factors to consider before creating them for consumption.

But first, it's important that we distinguish between two different, but related meanings of the word:

A data dashboard

A single display that combines multiple data visualizations, tables, text, and figures to give a multifaceted view of a subject.

Dashboards in Tableau

One of two tab types (the other type is a Sheet) that allows users to combine one or more Sheets with other objects—such as text, images, and web pages—into a single display.

The first definition is a general term describing how data is shared, and the second relates specifically to Tableau. The main difference between the two is that a data dashboard *always* involves multiple views in the same display, while a Dashboard in Tableau doesn't *necessarily* include multiple views (though it often does).

In other words, it's possible to create a Tableau Dashboard that only contains a single Sheet. Why would anyone do this? As we'll show, Dashboards in Tableau can be used to add text and images and format even a single visualization in helpful ways, as the Periodic Table dashboard in Figure 12-1 illustrates.

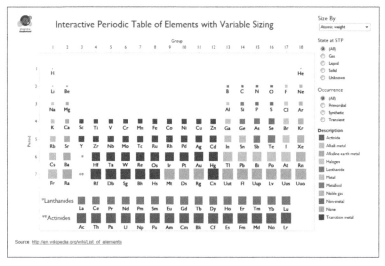

Figure 12-1. An example of a Tableau Dashboard with a single Sheet

Dashboards in Tableau

There are a number of advantages of using Dashboards in Tableau to create a final version of your message to share with your audience. In order to illustrate the advantages, we'll consider an example of a tiled dashboard, shown in Figure 12-2.

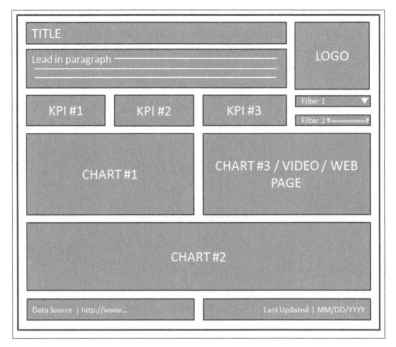

Figure 12-2. An illustrative example of a tiled dashboard

The following are six distinct advantages to using Dashboards over Sheets in Tableau, illustrated in Figure 12-3:

Descriptive text
> Titles, lead-in paragraphs, references, and attributions that describe the topic and give important background information can be added and positioned.

KPIs and metrics
> Important metrics, KPIs, or summary values can be added, often toward the top of the dashboard, that communicate the "big picture."

Multiple annotations
> In explanatory dashboards, multiple annotations can be added that explain outliers and patterns.

Filters
> In exploratory dashboards, filters can be added that change one, some, or all of the visualizations on the dashboard, allowing users to ask and answer a number of different questions about the data.

Sheet actions

> Each visualization on a dashboard can be configured to filter or highlight the other sheets, giving users the ability to interrogate the data to find hidden insights.

Multimedia

> Images, video, and even web pages can be added to the dashboard to provide additional context, aid cognition, and increase memory.

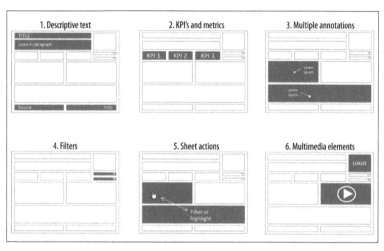

Figure 12-3. Six dashboard advantages illustrated

As these six advantages demonstrate, there is often a case to be made for creating a Dashboard rather than showing individual Sheets in sequence over the course of a presentation. Whether you're making one simple point with a single chart or illustrating a complex set of relationships with multiple visualizations, Tableau Dashboards afford you the design freedom and interactive capabilities to accomplish your objective.

A Word of Caution

Before we dive into data dashboards, let's pause for a moment and consider whether they're even necessary. When communicating data, is it really useful to combine a number of different visualizations into the same display? Won't that just overwhelm the audience? Overloading the audience is a very real concern, and often the dashboard designer is tempted to add more and more data to the display in a show of force.

As the epigraph to this chapter tells us, the best meals are often the least complicated, with the fewest ingredients. So, too, the least complicated data displays often convey the message in the strongest possible way. More is not always better, and care should be taken when adding anything to a dashboard that the additional pixels serve a real and useful purpose.

Showing multiple charts simultaneously on a dashboard is useful when:

- Juxtaposing different views provides a perspective that each one alone fails to provide; or
- Interactivity among different views, such as filtering or highlighting, allows viewers to answer a myriad of questions about the data ad hoc; or
- There is some inherent constraint such as limited time or space in which to present the data to the audience, and no single view will communicate all that is required.

"Begin with the End in Mind"

Before designing a data dashboard in Tableau or any other tool, you should be able to clearly state why a dashboard is needed. If it's because you want to impress your audience with data, or with your dashboard design skills, or because a particular software package makes it easy to do so, then you'd do well to revisit the Goal Triangle shown in Figure 1-4:

- Who is the target audience?
- What is your intended meaning?
- Why? What is the desired effect?

Once you've defined these three core elements, it's important to define the key objectives of the display in greater detail. What's the primary objective? Are there any secondary objectives?

Here are four additional questions to consider:

- Are you trying to make a specific point, are you trying to give the target audience the ability to ask and answer their own questions, or both?

- Is your target audience interested in the subject matter, and if so, why? What interests them most about the data?

- What questions will your audience have about the data?

- Does the data relate to specific tasks or decisions that your audience is responsible for? What are the tasks or decisions and how can the data help?

Once you have answers to these questions, you should be able to determine what type of dashboard will be most effective. In the next section, we'll consider five different types of dashboards.

Types of Dashboards

There are five different types of dashboards that you can create: explanatory, exploratory, explanatory/exploratory, storytelling, and infographics-style dashboards. Let's take a look at each:

Explanatory dashboards
> The primary objective is to point out a specific fact (or facts) about a certain subject to educate readers. Key features include annotations and informative text. Explanatory dashboards are often *static*, with very few, if any, interactive elements, such as the one in Figure 12-4.

Exploratory dashboards
> The primary objective is to allow users to delve into a subject ad hoc and find answers about a whole host of potential questions. Exploratory dashboards are often interactive, featuring various types of controls that allow the user to drill-down to specific subsets of the data, like the example in Figure 12-5.

Explanatory/exploratory dashboards
> Dashboards that explain central facts while also allowing for ancillary analyses can be very powerful. As such, they often include both annotations and interactive controls, such as the one about avalanches in the United States, shown in Figure 12-6.

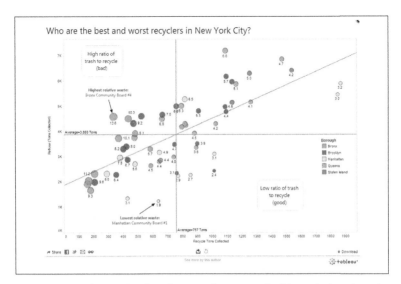

Figure 12-4. An example of an explanatory dashboard showing the best and worst NYC recyclers

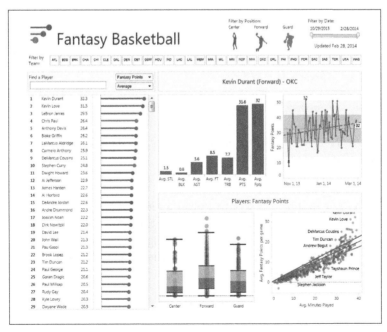

Figure 12-5. An example of an exploratory dashboard of basketball player stats

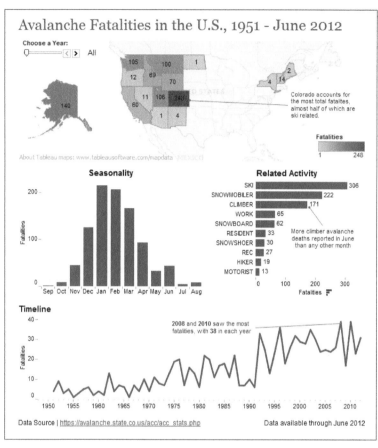

Figure 12-6. This explanatory/exploratory dashboard gives key facts and allows for interrogation

Storytelling dashboards

Often, dashboards seek to convey a series of events or show how a particular situation unfolded over time. Such dashboards are thus used to facilitate storytelling, like the example in Figure 12-7. The top three boxes, when clicked, step the viewer through various stages in a contest.

Figure 12-7. An example of a storytelling dashboard that conveys a development over time

Infographics

This style of data display includes a series of facts about a specific subject, often oriented in one tall column. Unfortunately, many infographics are merely tall posters full of cheesy images and individual percentages or figures. Often, the figures are accompanied by an ill-advised attempt at a visualization that skews the proportions horribly. But just because many abuse this format doesn't mean it's useless. Figure 12-8 shows one attempt to convey a series of facts about a particularly amazing feat of bravery.

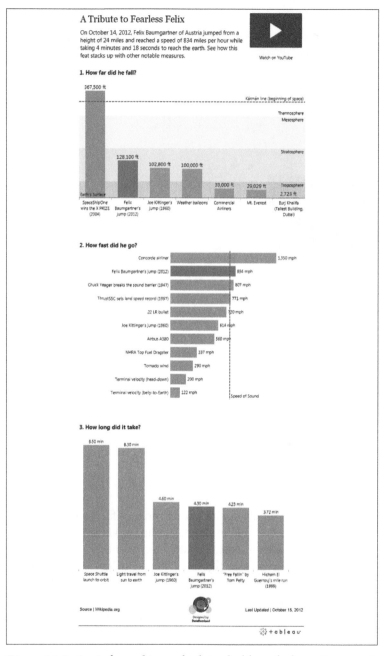

Figure 12-8. An infographics-style data dashboard about Baumgartner's 24-mile jump

Once you have a good handle on the type of data dashboard most appropriate to your objectives, it's also helpful to identify the context.

Context Is King

Data dashboards are used to communicate data in a variety of different contexts, including analytics/decision support, reference/open data, and data journalism. Let's take a closer look at each of these:

Analytics/decision support
>Organizations create data dashboards to show performance over time and to inform managerial decisions necessary to achieve growth objectives. Many Business Intelligence (BI) and web analytics dashboards, as well as Key Process Indicator (KPI) Scorecards, fall into this category. Figure 12-9 shows traffic to my blog, *http://dataremixed.com*, from the Google Analytics connector available in Tableau Desktop. This dashboard helps me answer the following questions:

>- What type of content should I focus on creating in order to drive traffic to my site?
>- What sites refer readers to my blog, and where are the opportunities to promote?
>- Where are my readers located in the world and how should that inform my strategy?

Data journalism
>Online newspapers often publish data dashboards in order to inform readers about topics in the news, and to allow them to "drill down" to uncover stories relevant to them. More focus is placed on visual appeal and aesthetics, as it's possible that readers' attention must first be captured. Figure 12-10 shows the history of mass shootings in the United States from 1982 through 2012.

Reference/open data
>Data bloggers around the world typically convert repositories of data into data dashboards, not to relay the news or inform a specific decision, but rather to educate their readers about specific topics of interest, such as the Type I Diabetes prevalence dashboard created and published by Ramon Martinez of Health Intelligence (*http://bit.ly/HI-diabetes*) shown in Figure 12-11.

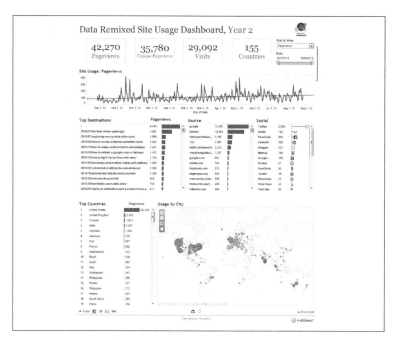

Figure 12-9. A web analytics dashboard: pageviews to http://datare mixed.com

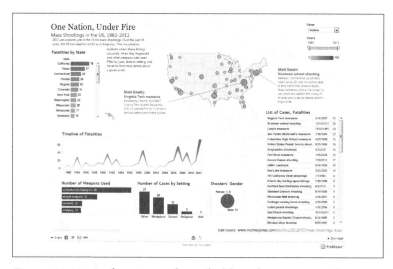

Figure 12-10. A data journalism dashboard: U.S. mass shootings, 1982–2012

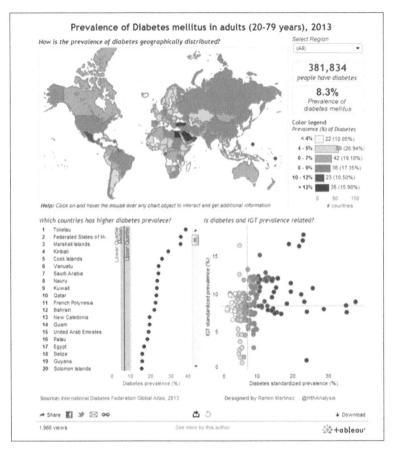

Figure 12-11. An open data dashboard: Prevalence of diabetes melli-tus in adults, 2013

While these different contexts may call for slightly different approaches, the fundamental way in which people interpret, or decode, data visualizations remains the same. Showing more than one data visualization in a particular view, such as in a data dashboard, means that the viewer must perform multiple decoding operations, which likely requires more effort on the viewer's part.

How much effort is your audience willing to put forward, and how much do they expect (or need) to get in return? The answer is different for different contexts.

Summary

In this chapter, we compared the act of creating dashboards to cooking. In both disciplines, it's easy to assume that more is better and thereby spoil the result. We also defined the various types of dashboards.

In the next chapter, we'll create some basic Dashboards in Tableau, and in the final chapter, we'll consider some more advanced usages.

CHAPTER 13

Building Dashboards

> *"'Data! Data! Data!' he cried impatiently.*
> *'I can't make bricks without clay.'"*
>
> —Sir Arthur Conan Doyle,
> "The Adventure of the Copper Beeches"

In this chapter, let's return to the analogy we used in the opening paragraphs of Chapter 1 and compare the act of communicating data with building a structure. As the famous fictional detective Sherlock Holmes relates emphatically in this chapter's epigraph, the raw material that we're using is data.

Now, neither we nor our audience have Holmes' superior powers of deduction, so we need to take the raw material and build a suitable structure in order to facilitate discovery. And if the data is the clay, then the bricks are the individual charts and graphs, and the overall structure is the dashboard.

Building a dashboard that communicates data well doesn't happen all at once. It requires some creative thought and diligent crafting. And like all creative processes, the process of building a data dashboard is rarely linear. There is typically a great deal of reworking and fine-tuning throughout.

That being said, it is useful to identify the different activities involved in creating dashboards in Tableau, and the general order in which they occur:

Design

Make a few rough sketches of dashboard layouts that use your data to help you accomplish your overall goal, taking into consideration the medium and channel that you will use to deliver the final version to your audience.

Sheets

Build each visualization as an individual Sheet and then add them to your dashboard, arranging them with their Quick Filters, Parameters, and Legends according to your chosen layout and dashboard size.

Annotations

Add titles, lead-in text, tooltips, labels, notes, instructions, sources, and other pertinent textual information to explain to your audience how to interact with the dashboard and/or how to interpret the data.

Objects

Add images, layout containers, blank spaces, and web page objects as needed to provide additional context to the visualizations, as long as they serve a real purpose.

Actions

Configure dashboard interactivity using actions to filter, highlight, and hyperlink the various Sheets and Objects in ways that help your audience explore and answer real questions.

Formatting

Configure the fit and finish of the dashboard by adjusting fonts, colors, borders, grid lines, and shading to remove distractions and enhance the visual appeal of the dashboard.

Delivery

Share the dashboard with your audience via your chosen medium and channel, whether guided or unguided.

Results

Find out whether your message was received, properly interpreted, and found effective in achieving your goals.

Let's use a few different examples to walk through these steps and build interactive dashboards in Tableau. We'll consider an updated version of the World Bank Internet usage data set we considered in Chapter 10. Let's start by first taking a look at a sample of the data set, as shown in Figure 13-1.

⬚	A	B	C	D	E
				Internet Users	
1	Country Name	Region	Year	(per 100)	Population
2	Afghanistan	Asia	2001	0.00	21,347,782
3	Afghanistan	Asia	2002	0.00	22,202,806
4	Afghanistan	Asia	2003	0.09	23,116,142
5	Afghanistan	Asia	2004	0.11	24,018,682
6	Afghanistan	Asia	2005	1.22	24,860,855
7	Afghanistan	Asia	2006	2.11	25,631,282
8	Afghanistan	Asia	2007	1.90	26,349,243
9	Afghanistan	Asia	2008	1.84	27,032,197
10	Afghanistan	Asia	2009	3.55	27,708,187
11	Afghanistan	Asia	2010	4.00	28,397,812
12	Afghanistan	Asia	2011	5.00	29,105,480
13	Afghanistan	Asia	2012	5.45	29,824,536
14	Albania	Europe	1995	0.01	3,357,858
15	Albania	Europe	1996	0.03	3,341,043
16	Albania	Europe	1997	0.05	3,331,317
17	Albania	Europe	1998	0.07	3,325,456
18	Albania	Europe	1999	0.08	3,317,941
19	Albania	Europe	2000	0.11	3,304,948
20	Albania	Europe	2001	0.33	3,286,084

Figure 13-1. World Bank Internet usage statistics by country, 1994–2012

At a glance, we can see that each country has an associated region, and both population and Internet usage statistics for a variety of years, including more recent data from 2011 and 2012. Of course, the format that the data set is in doesn't facilitate communication with an audience. That's where the skills we've learned in the first 12 chapters will be useful to craft something more informative.

There are two different angles to the Internet usage topic:

Proportion

What is the number of Internet users *per 100 people* in a given country and year? (For example, in China in 2012, there were 42.30 Internet users per 100 people.)

Quantity

How many total Internet users are there estimated to be in a given country and year? (For example, China had an estimated 571M Internet users in 2012.)

 To compute this value, we'll need to create a Calculated Field that multiplies Internet users per 100 with the population and divides by 100, as shown in Figure 13-2.

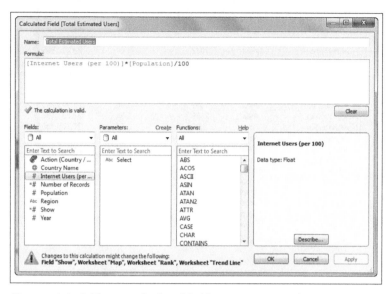

Figure 13-2. Adding a calculated field to estimate total Internet users

What we ultimately create for our audience strongly depends on what we hope to accomplish. Returning to our goal model in Chapter 1, we need to consider *who* we are presenting to, *what* meaning we hope to relate, and *why* we are doing so in the first place:

- If we want to allow them to ask and answer their own questions, we'll want to give them an exploratory dashboard that makes it easy to do so.

- If we want them to know the answer to a single specific or multiple specific questions, then we'll want to create an explanatory dashboard that makes those answers clear.

First, we'll build an *exploratory* dashboard that allows users to answer a whole host of questions, and then we'll build two different *explanatory* dashboards that clearly articulate specific (and completely different) insights from this data set.

Building an Exploratory Dashboard

As we discussed in the previous chapter, the primary objective of an exploratory dashboard is to allow the audience to delve into a subject ad hoc and find answers about a whole host of potential questions. Knowing that this is our objective, let's walk through the eight steps mentioned earlier.

Step 1: Design

To allow our audience to fully explore the subject, we'll want to include a few different types of views:

- A timeline that shows how usage has changed over time
- A world map to see where usage is the highest, geographically
- A chart to directly visualize usage by country from a common base

What could this look like? There are countless ways we could show these three views on the same dashboard. Take a minute to sketch some of your ideas.

We also want to allow the audience to explore both the proportion as well as the estimated total, and make it clear which aspect they are considering at any given moment.

Step 2: Sheets

It's critical that the audience be able to explore the subject of Internet usage by both proportion as well as quantity. In order to facilitate this dual function, we'll need to create a new Parameter (right-click in the *Dimensions and Measures* area and select *Create Parameter...*) and an associated Calculated Field (right-click on the Parameter once it's created and select *Create Calculated Field...*) as shown in Figure 13-3.

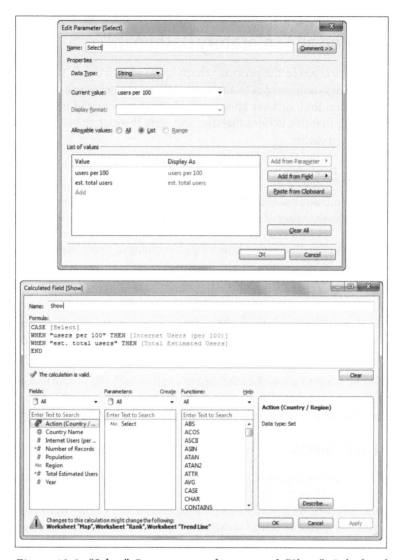

Figure 13-3. "Select" Parameter and associated "Show" Calculated Field

Now that we have these foundational types of "clay," we can start building the individual "bricks" for our dashboard, as shown in Figures 13-4, 13-5, and 13-6. If you need to review how to build these Sheets, go back to Chapter 3 (bar chart), Chapter 9 (timeline), and Chapter 10 (global map).

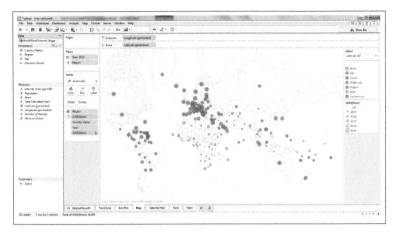

Figure 13-4. The global symbols map sized by Internet usage (propor-tion or quantity)

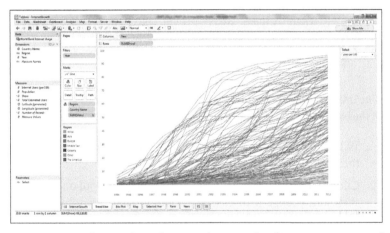

Figure 13-5. The timeline showing the growth of Internet usage and colored by region

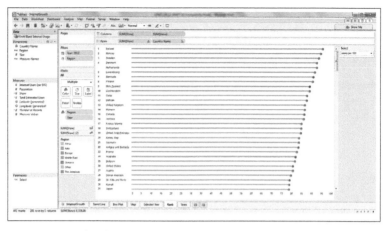

Figure 13-6. The dual-axis bar chart colored by region with rank added

Make sure to give each visualization an appropriate name; I renamed them "Map," "Trend Line," and "Rank." That will make it much easier when we go to add them to the Dashboard not to have to deal with "Sheet 1," "Sheet 2," and so on.

One important detail is the Rank column we have added at the far left of the bar chart. We used the Rank table calculation to add it as follows:

1. With the basic dual-axis bar chart already created, drag Show to the Rows shelf to add the green SUM(Show) pill.

2. Click on the down arrow in the green SUM(Show) pill on the Rows shelf and change it to *Discrete*. The pill changes from green to blue.

3. Click on the down arrow again and select *Quick Table Calculation → Rank*.

4. Click on the down arrow again and select *Edit Table Calculation*; then in *Running along*, select *Advanced*, updating the dialog box as shown in Figure 13-7.

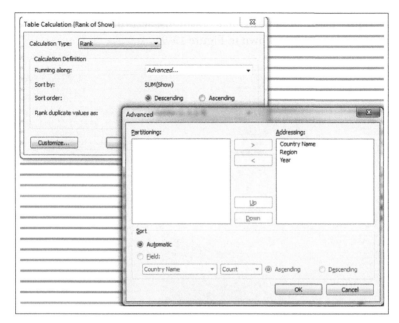

Figure 13-7. Updating the Rank field

We now have the three main Sheets built, and we can create a new Dashboard to bring them together onto the same canvas. From the top file menu, click *Dashboard → New Dashboard*, or click the ⊞ icon in the bottom.

I know that I want to embed this Dashboard on my website, which has a column width of 940 pixels, so in the bottom left corner of the newly created empty Dashboard, I'll set the *Size* to *Exactly* 940 by 700, as shown in Figure 13-8. I can always adjust the height later if I need to.

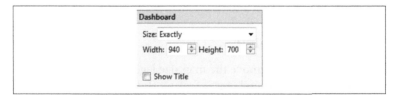

Figure 13-8. Setting the Dashboard size

Next, with the *Add new sheets and objects as:* set to *Tiled*, we'll simply drag the three Sheets from the *Dashboard* area on the left onto the

Dashboard in their approximate locations, according to our selected design. The result is shown in Figure 13-9.

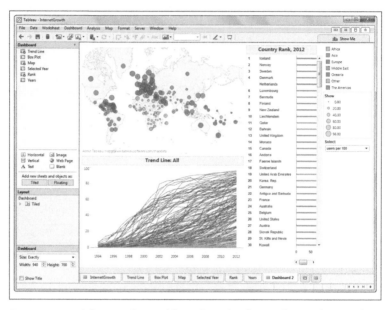

Figure 13-9. The rough Dashboard with Sheets dropped into place shown in their default locations

Notice that the Rank Sheet has both horizontal and vertical scroll bars. It's best to eliminate scroll bars as much as possible, as they hide information and require the user to interact to access that information. In this case, it would be difficult to fit all 204 countries in the vertical space allotted to our Dashboard, but we can certainly do something about the horizontal scroll bars. Click the arrow in the upper-right corner of the Rank Sheet and select *Fit → Fit Width*.

Moving Things Around

I'd argue that we can remove the map size legend altogether, because the map only gives a general sense of relative Internet usage by country. The main purpose is to show patterns by region (very high usage across Europe, very sparse usage in the middle of Africa, highly varied usage within Asia, etc.). More precise comparisons can be made using the Rank bar chart. To remove the size legend, just click the X in its upper-right corner.

Next, there's a large chunk of whitespace below the color legend and Parameter drop-down. Let's float these objects so they don't take up so much space. To do so, click the arrow in the upper-right corner of each, and set them to *Floating*, moving them to the most convenient and logical location as shown in Figure 13-10.

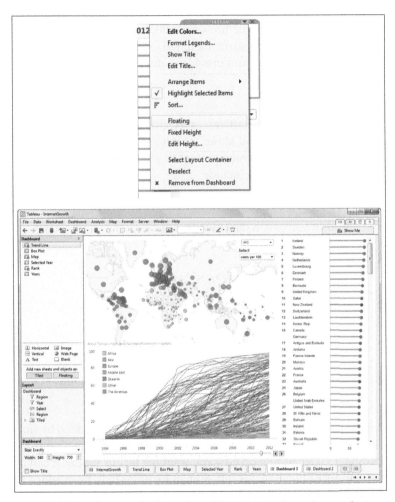

Figure 13-10. Floating the legend and Parameter drop-down selector

If you don't see the Quick Filters for Region and Year, or if you'd like to add more in the future, you can click on the Map and then from the top toolbar, select *Analysis → Quick Filters → Region*. Change it from a *Multiple Values (List)* type to a *Single Value (Dropdown)* type, and then float it somewhere near the Select Parameter dropdown. Click on the Timeline and select *Analysis → Quick Filters → Year*. Change it from a list to a Slider, customize it by removing the Read-out and Buttons, and place it below the x-axis of the timeline, sizing it so that the tick marks of the Slider align with the tick marks of the x-axis, as shown in Figure 13-10.

The basic frame of the structure we're building is now in place. Next, we'll add "signage" to the structure in the form of annotations: text to help orient our audience and provide useful information.

Step 3: Annotations

The annotation layer is critical, especially when we are creating a dashboard that will "stand alone," meaning that audience members will take it in without anyone present to guide them. Important elements to consider adding include:

- A title
- A lead-in paragraph or sentence
- A data source call-out
- A "created on" date
- A "created by" name
- Text that hyperlinks to reference websites
- Instructions on how to use the dashboard
- Call-outs or notes about the data
- Well formatted "tooltips" that pop up when the user hovers over or selects marks

With the exception of the last bullet, these items can be added by simply dragging Text objects from the middle of the left panel onto the Dashboard. Depending on how you want the text to appear, it can be either Tiled or Floating. Six different annotations have been added as shown in Figure 13-11, highlighted in yellow for illustrative purposes.

All of the annotations we just created can be seen without any interaction. They act as signage to give context and explain what the dashboard is all about and how to use it.

Sometimes we want to add context to the data themselves. By default, Tableau adds tooltips to each mark. Hovering over any mark results in a pop-up window that gives additional information about the mark. By default, the tooltips are functional but not very interesting (Figure 13-12).

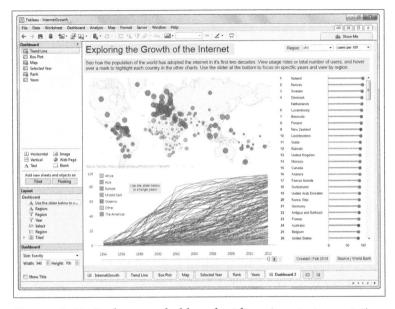

Figure 13-11. Exploratory dashboard with various text annotations added

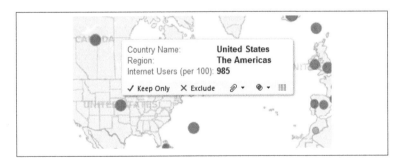

Figure 13-12. A default tooltip generated for the Map Sheet

Luckily, we can customize these tooltips using a rich text editor that also gives us the ability to add data fields and even Parameter values. For example, I edited the tooltips for each of the three Sheets, as shown in Figure 13-13. To add the data fields, which appear in <brackets>, I used the *Insert* button in the top toolbar of the Tooltip edit dialog box.

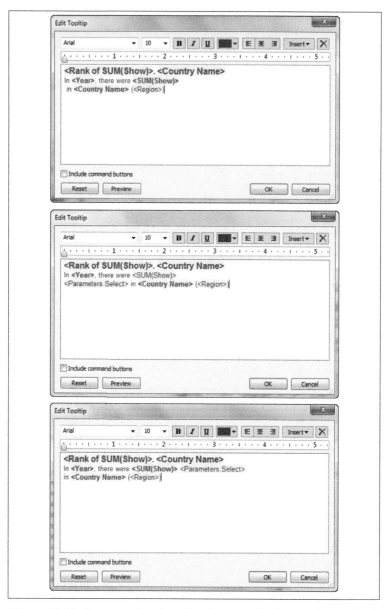

Figure 13-13. Formatted tooltips for the Map (top), Trend Line (middle) and Rank (bottom) Sheets

Note that in order for a data field to appear in the Insert menu, that data field needs to be used somewhere on the Sheet. If the data field you want to use doesn't appear in the menu, dragging it to the Tooltip card in the Marks area of a Sheet will do the trick.

Now, hovering over a mark yields a much nicer experience for the person interacting with your dashboard, as shown in Figure 13-14.

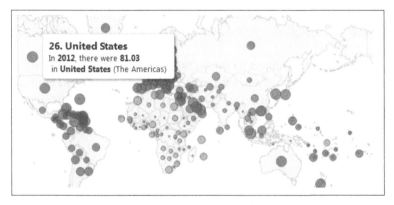

Figure 13-14. Hovering over a mark with a formatted tooltip

Next, we'll consider whether adding any other objects to the Dashboard would be useful.

Step 4: Objects

Tableau also gives us the ability to add images and web page objects to a dashboard to add additional context. For example, we might want to add our logo and make it link to our website.

To add my logo, I'll click on Image in the middle of the left panel, making sure *Floating* is highlighted, and then drag an Image object to the upper-right corner of the dashboard. When I drop it there, Tableau automatically opens a dialog box that lets me navigate to my image file. Once I find it, I'll click *Open*, and then resize the image to fit in the space I've made for it. I also dragged a "Blank" object to the right of the lead-in paragraph to make additional room for the logo, as shown in Figure 13-15.

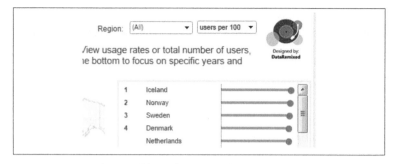

Figure 13-15. The Dashboard's top-right corner with Image object added

To link the Image object to my website, I'll click in the upper-right corner of the image itself, select *Set URL*, and fill out the resulting dialog box, as shown in Figure 13-16. Now, when a person interacting with my Dashboard clicks on my logo, a new browser window will open to take them to my site.

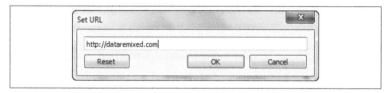

Figure 13-16. Adding a URL hyperlink to a Dashboard Image object

The logo is a good feature to add to a dashboard, provided that it serves a useful purpose. Adding frivolous images or "clipart" is not recommended, as it will only serve to detract from the data. As we discussed in Chapter 11, images and icons can be rich sources of emotional content, so they're a double-edged sword: they can do much good or much harm, depending on how they're used.

"Hover for More Info" icons

A small icon that provides detailed instructions and information when the user hovers over it can be a useful feature to add to an exploratory dashboard, especially when there's high complexity. Tableau doesn't allow us to add a tooltip to an Image object, so we'll need to jump through a few hoops to make a feature like this. It involves creating a new Sheet with a shape mark that has a tooltip. Here are the steps involved:

1. Create the icon image that you'd like to use and add it to a new folder in *Documents* → *My Tableau Repository* → *Shapes*. I named my folder *Hover*, and I'll be using this: ⓘ

2. Create a new Sheet in your Tableau Workbook and rename it Info or something like that.

3. Create a new Calculated Field, give it the name Info (or whatever you want to call it) and enter some simple text in quotes, like "Info."

4. In the new Sheet, change the Marks type from *Automatic* to *Shape* and drag the Info Calculated Field to the Shapes card.

5. Change the Shape from the default ring shape to your chosen shape by clicking the down arrow in the Shape legend, selecting *Edit Shape*, and navigating to your new *Hover* folder, as shown in Figure 13-17.

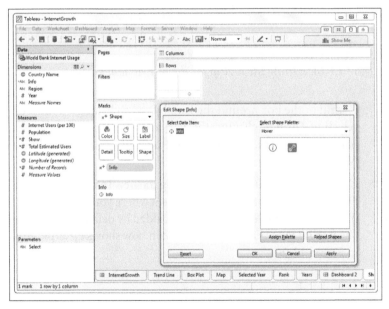

Figure 13-17. Changing the shape of your icon

6. Edit the tooltip for the icon by selecting *Worksheet* → *Tooltip* and entering the instructions and information that you'd like to include, as shown in Figure 13-18.

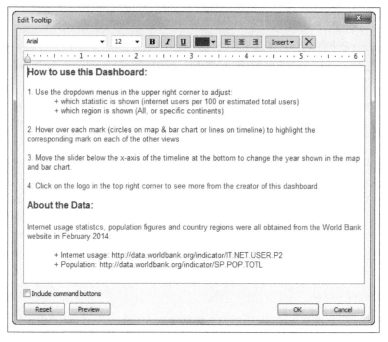

Figure 13-18. Editing the tooltip for the instructional icon

7. Get rid of the box around the icon by right-clicking on the icon, selecting *Format*, clicking the *Format Borders* icon on the left panel that appears, and setting the Row and Column Dividers to *None*, as shown in Figure 13-19.

8. Click on the *Dashboard* tab and drag the new Info Sheet onto the Dashboard as a floating object. Place it where you want, get rid of the sheet title and legend that are included by default, and size the Sheet to *Fit to the Entire View*. The icon now shows up as pictured in Figure 13-20.

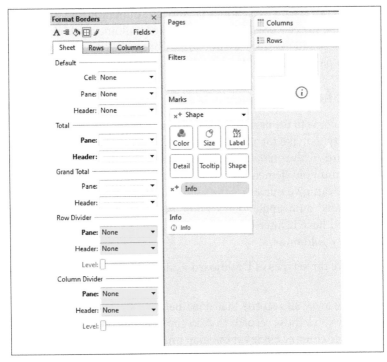

Figure 13-19. Formatting the borders of the icon

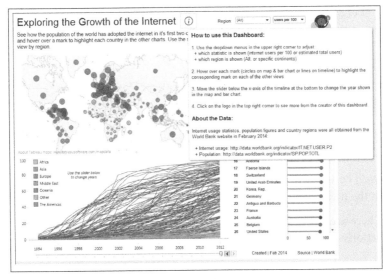

Figure 13-20. Dashboard shown with hover icon

This new hover icon we've added is more an annotation than an image, illustrating my earlier claim that dashboard building is a highly iterative process and the steps are not strictly linear. We'll consider how to add web page objects in the next chapter.

Step 5: Actions

Now we come to the part of Tableau that is perhaps the most powerful: the ability to make the visualizations we've created and added to our dashboard *richly interactive*. This can give users the ability to rapidly explore multiple elements of the data from multiple angles in a visual way. We can give our users the ability to instantly change all of the views based on a single Quick Filter, or allow them to click on one chart and have it filter the others. The result, if done well, is a data discovery gold mine.

There are three types of Dashboard Actions:

Filter

Take away all records that don't belong in a selected subset and only show those records that do apply. For example, clicking on a single country circle on the map limits the timeline to show only the line for that country.

Highlight

Make the corresponding measure show more prominently in other Sheets by fading all other measures. For example, hovering over a single country circle on the map makes it easy to spot the corresponding country in the bar chart by fading out all other countries.

URL

Open a web page either in the browser or in the Dashboard itself when the user clicks a mark that is connected to a specific URL. For example, clicking on a country circle opens a Wikipedia page of that country.

We'll consider the first two Action types in this chapter and the third in the next chapter.

There are two types of Dashboard objects that can be used to trigger actions: Sheets and Quick Filters.

Note that Parameters don't trigger Dashboard Actions, per se; they change the data that is shown based on how they were used in the Sheets that include them.

Quick Filters on Dashboards

There are currently two Quick Filters on the Dashboard: Region and Year. By default, they only control their "source" Sheet—the Sheet with which they were brought into the Dashboard. For example, the Region Quick Filter was brought in with the Map Sheet, so selecting Africa only changes what is shown in the map. As Figure 13-21 shows, the other two Sheets still show all of the Regions.

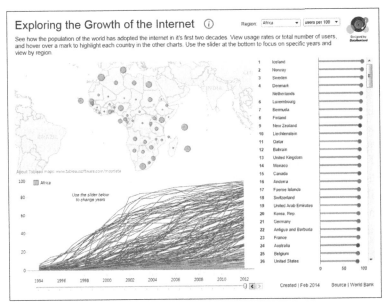

Figure 13-21. The Quick Filter in its default state, only controlling its source Sheet

If we'd like to to control all of the Sheets on the Dashboard, we can make it do so by clicking the down arrow in the upper-right corner of the Quick Filter and selecting *Apply to Worksheets → All Using This Data Source*. Now the Dashboard shows the fully filtered version shown in Figure 13-22.

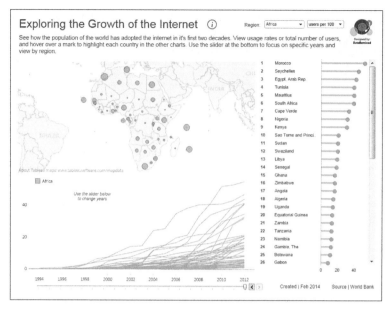

Figure 13-22. A Quick Filter configured to apply to all Sheets

Similarly, we'd like the slider at the bottom to change both the map and the bar chart, but we don't want it to filter the timeline (otherwise, the timeline would just show one year for each country in a tall column of 204 dots). To configure the year slider to behave accordingly, we'll click the down arrow in the upper-right corner of the slider Quick Filter, select *Apply to Worksheets → Selected Worksheets*, and then check the boxes for *Map* (defaulted) and *Rank*, but not for *Trend Line* (the timeline).

Now, when we change the slider to 2008, we can see from Figure 13-23 that the map and bar chart are both showing data for the year 2008.

One important thing to notice at this point is that, other than looking at the slider at the bottom, it's not very clear that the map and bar chart are showing 2008 data. A user would have to actually hover over the data point and read the tooltip to find out. This is a deficiency from the annotation step, and we really should correct it. How can we add additional signage or cues that indicate what year is shown?

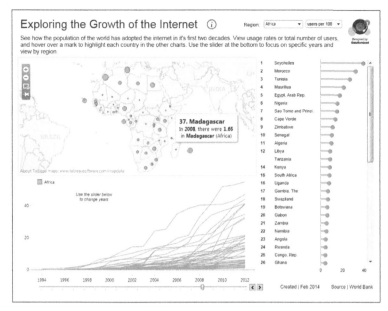

Figure 13-23. The Year slider Quick Filter affecting the map and bar chart, but not the timeline

Dynamic Labels on Dashboards

We can do two things to address this deficiency: we can add a Sheet that shows the current year, and we can add titles to the Sheets that include the current year.

To create a Sheet that will serve as a year label, do the following:

1. Add a new Sheet to the workbook.

2. Drag the Year Dimension onto the Text card.

3. Filter the text to just one year by dragging Year to the Filter shelf and selecting one year from the list.

4. Click on the Text card and format the year label to give it added prominence.

5. Right-click and remove the Row and Column dividers as we did earlier with the Info icon Sheet. The Sheet now appears as shown in Figure 13-24.

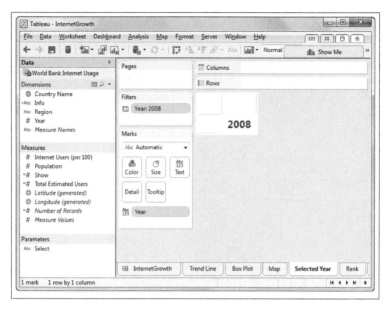

Figure 13-24. Creating a Sheet that acts as a dynamic label

Now, to add this dynamic year label Sheet (I renamed it *Selected Year*) to the Dashboard, drag it in floating fashion to a suitable location on the Dashboard, resize it and fit it to the entire width, and give it the title you want (Figure 13-25). Finally, make sure to change the year slider to check that the label updates.

We can also add a dynamic Year label to the Dashboard by adding the Year data field to Sheet titles. For example, if we edit the Title of the bar chart on the right, we can insert the Year field so that if a user moves the slider, the year in the title will change accordingly. This step is illustrated in Figure 13-26.

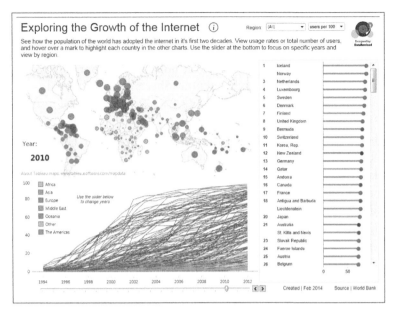

Figure 13-25. Updated Dashboard with Year label Sheet added

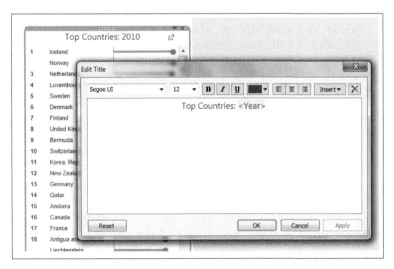

Figure 13-26. Editing Sheet titles to add references to selected Measures

So far, we've seen how we can use Quick Filters and Parameters to affect multiple Sheets on Dashboards, and we've seen how we can create Sheets that act as dynamic labels in response to changes in Quick Filter selections. Next, we'll look at how we can configure Sheets themselves to filter and highlight other Sheets on a Dashboard.

Using Sheets as Filters on Dashboards

Once a Sheet has been brought into a Dashboard, it can be used as a filter by simply clicking on the down arrow in the upper-right corner of the Sheet and selecting *Use as Filter*. Tableau generates a filter Action that we can review and edit by clicking *Dashboard → Actions* and editing *Filter 1 (generated)*, resulting in the dialog box shown in Figure 13-27.

If we take a close look at the *Edit Filter Action* dialog box in Figure 13-27, we'll notice three distinct sections.

- The top section, "Source Sheets," tells us what triggers the Action. In this case, the default Filter Action is triggered when a user selects (clicks on) a Mark in the Sheet called *Map* on Dashboard 2.

- The middle section, "Target Sheets," tells us what Sheets the Action affects, and what happens when the selection is cleared. In this case, all of the Sheets on the Dashboard are affected by this Action, and clearing the filter will show all values.

- The bottom section, "Target Filters," tells us what fields of the selected Mark(s) on the Source Sheet are used to affect the other Target Sheets. In this case, it has defaulted to all fields, meaning that when a country Mark (circle) on the Map is selected, all of the fields associated with that Mark (Country Name, Year, etc.) are used as filters for the other Sheets.

The default settings for this Filter Action will give us some problems. We don't really want the bar chart on the left to only show one country, and showing all years at the same time on the map and bar chart will be very confusing. Let's change the default settings to look like what's shown in Figure 13-28, which allows us to show the timeline for only the selected country, whether we click on the country in the map or the Rank bar chart.

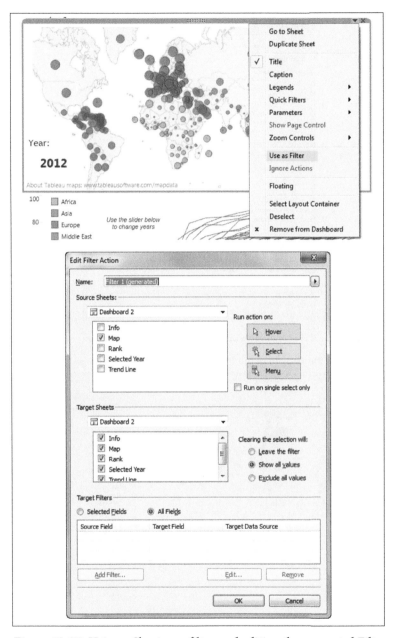

Figure 13-27. Using a Sheet as a filter and editing the generated Filter Action

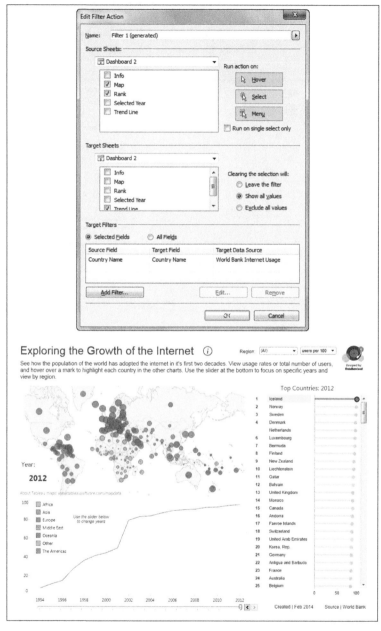

Figure 13-28. Modified Filter Action and resulting Dashboard behavior

Note that you might need to move the Year slider at the bottom back to 2012 to get the map to show only one year.

We can use all Sheets in this way to filter other sheets. Instead of using the *Use as Filter* shortcut, we can also just go to *Dashboard →Actions* and create a new action.

If we want to highlight marks so that the other marks fade instead of getting filtered out, we can do that with Highlight Actions, as we'll explore next.

Highlighting Sheets

At first glance, the bottom timeline is very difficult to read. There are 204 lines of seven different colors, so it's not easy to see any one line. We can filter out the lines to only show one color by using the *Region Quick Filter*, but it would be nice to just highlight all of the lines from one of the Regions so that the other lines could still be seen in the background to provide additional context.

One way to do this is to use the color legend to highlight all of the Sheets on the Dashboard. If we click on the down arrow in the upper-right corner of the Legend and select *Highlight Selected Items*, then we'll get the behavior shown in Figure 13-29. All of the Marks in the selected Region are now showing prominently, and the Marks associated with the other Regions are faded.

Legends aren't the only thing we can use to highlight Marks on a Dashboard. Just as we can use Sheets as Filters, we can also use them to highlight Marks on other Sheets.

Using Sheets to Highlight

To make the Dashboard feel more responsive and "alive," we can create a new Dashboard Action to highlight marks on hover (just by placing the mouse cursor over a Mark). Let's make it so that if we just hover over a country Mark on the map or the bar chart, the corresponding timeline is highlighted. To do so, we'll select *Dashboard → Actions → Add Action → Highlight* and fill out the resulting dialog box, as shown in Figure 13-30.

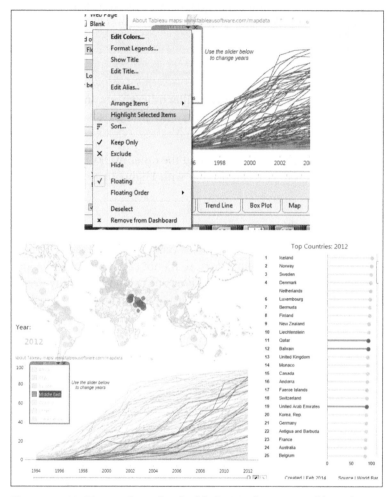

Figure 13-29. Using a legend to highlight Marks on a Dashboard

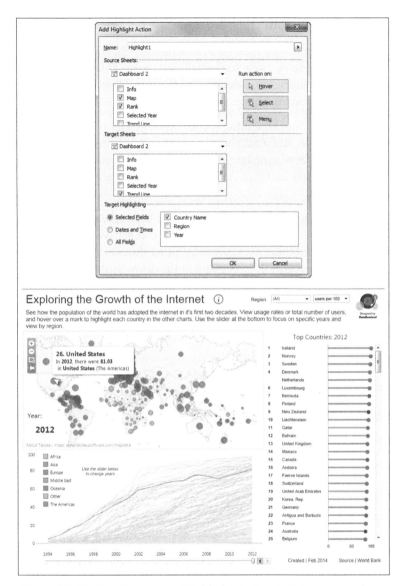

Figure 13-30. Creating a new Highlight Action to trigger upon hover and resulting Dashboard behavior

We've seen how Quick Filters, Parameters, Sheets, and even Legends can be put to good use on a Dashboard to create an intuitive and richly interactive data discovery experience. The next step often takes the most time: the fit-and-finish.

Step 6: Formatting

The Dashboard is very useful and functional as is, and often we will need to stop there and skip to the delivery phase. This may be due to time pressures, or because details like fonts and line weights simply don't matter to our audience.

However, many times the difference between a dashboard that accepts all of the defaults and a fully formatted and "pixel perfect" one is the difference between being ignored and achieving your objective. Data journalists understand this. As humans, we appreciate good design.

A number of the default formats have already been changed. Sheet borders have been removed, grid lines have been taken away, the font has been changed to Segoe UI, and the font colors have been softened. We can edit all of these parameters by either double-clicking and editing the rich text editor, or clicking in the down arrow and selecting *Format*.

Compare the fully formatted version in Figure 13-31 with a version of the same Dashboard that results from accepting all of the defaults shown in Figure 13-32.

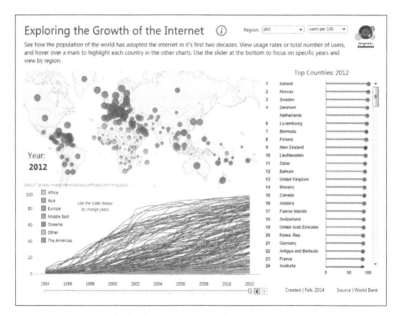

Figure 13-31. The fully formatted Dashboard

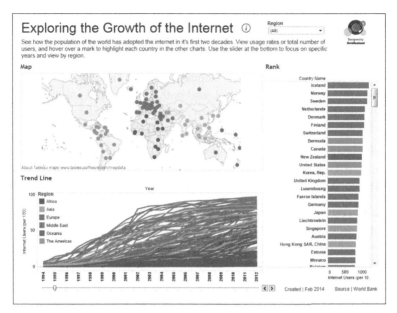

Figure 13-32. A version of the same Dashboard with all of the defaults accepted

Does it make a difference? It depends on the circumstances, and that's why it's critical to know your audience and understand what will help you achieve your object versus what will be a waste of your time. Focus on the things that really matter.

Steps 7 and 8: Delivery and Results

What remains is the most critical part: actually communicating your data to your audience. Before doing so, I highly recommend showing what you've made to multiple people. You've just spent hours poring over the data, and you're likely head over heels in love with the result of your beautiful creation.

But the simple fact is that your baby may be ugly—or worse, confusing —and it's better to know now than after the bright lights are on. Ask an expert. Ask a nonexpert. Don't tell them what to do with your dashboard, just let them play with it, and see where they trip up. It's nothing to take personally; it's for your learning.

In this case, communicating the dashboard involved saving it to Tableau Public (the data is publicly available), copying and pasting the embed code into my WordPress.org blog, and socializing it. In your case, you may instead want to switch to presentation mode, turn on the projector, and begin your eloquent speech. These two modes of delivery are extremely different, and both require up-front planning and superb execution. In either case, best of luck, and be sure to seek out feedback and make improvements for next time.

Finally, check your results. Did your presentation have the desired impact? Did your audience understand the points you wanted them to understand, and did they take the action you wanted them to take?

I can't really tell you how to gather this information, because it's highly dependent on the context of your situation. Polling or surveying your audience, tracking measurable activities afterward, or just plain asking them what they thought are all potential methods. Use your imagination, but absolutely be diligent about this step. How else are you going to improve?

Next, let's consider how Dashboards created from this exact same data would be different if, rather than seeking to empower an audience to ask and answer their own questions in an exploratory mode, we instead wanted to make two very specific points and explain something key to our audience.

Building an Explanatory Dashboard

There are many, many insights that could be drawn from the Internet usage data we've been exploring so far in this chapter. The emergence of the Internet has been one of the most significant developments of our time, and has forever changed the face of life on our planet.

Let's consider two different stories we could relate in an interactive Dashboard.

A Key Point to Explain: Nordic Countries in the Lead

One remarkable insight is that a relatively small cluster of countries in Europe known as the Nordic countries have been at the forefront of Internet usage rates since the earliest days of the Internet. Figure 13-33 is a dashboard that was created to illustrate this fact alone.

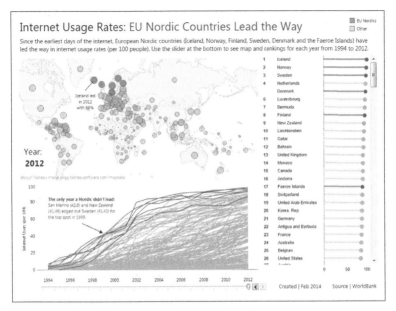

Figure 13-33. An explanatory dashboard showing the leadership of the EU Nordic in terms of usage rate

What has changed between this version and the exploratory version in Figure 13-31?

- There's a new title and lead in paragraph.
- There are only two groups of countries now: EU Nordics and all other countries.
- The color scheme has been simplified to show only these two groups, and the legend is now in a more prominent position of the dashboard: the upper-right corner.
- The Region Quick Filter has been removed.
- The Parameter has been removed so the dashboard only shows Internet users per 100. That's the story, so we're sticking to it.
- The Info icon has been removed, because the dashboard is largely self-explanatory.
- Two annotations have been added: one in the map showing Iceland and the other in the timeline showing the only year since 1994 that a Nordic country didn't lead in usage rates.

As you can see, there are fewer controls and fewer things to do in this dashboard. Many aspects have been simplified, and many elements removed in order to maintain a clear focus on the message. The goal is to illustrate a single point.

 There is another type of Dashboard called a storytelling dashboard (that we won't explore in this chapter), in which users must make a series of specific interactions in order to explain a multifaceted and sequential message, or "story."

Another Key Point to Explain: The Emergence of China

There's yet another fascinating story that we may have missed in the exploratory version: China has recently surged past the United States as the country with the highest total number of Internet users. To illustrate this fact to an audience, we could create an explanatory dashboard like the one in Figure 13-34.

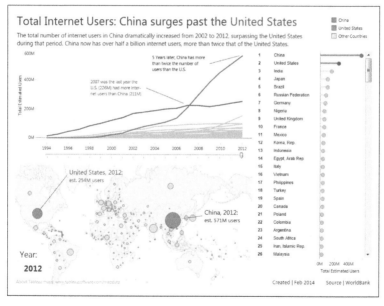

Figure 13-34. An explanatory dashboard showing the emergence of China in terms of total users

Let's list the things that have changed in this version:

- There's another new title and lead-in paragraph explaining the most salient points.
- There are now three groups of countries (and therefore three colors in the legend): China, the United States, and all other countries.
- Again, we've removed the Region Quick Filter, as it's beside the point.
- Again, there's no Parameter to change from users per 100 to total users; only this time, the total number of users is the only Measure shown on the Dashboard.
- The timeline has been moved to the top of the Dashboard. It's a message about the surge, not a geography lesson, so the timeline is more important than the map and deserves a more prominent seat at the table.
- New annotations appear that are color-coded (blue for the United States and red for China).

Again, everything else has been stripped away or made to fade into the background so that nothing gets in the way of the main message, which is that China has vaulted to the top. Perhaps a similar Dashboard will be created in a couple years' time showing how India did the same.

There are probably dozens more explanatory dashboards that could be created with this data set. I wouldn't have found these insights unless I had created the exploratory dashboard in the first place. In that sense, Tableau is not only a great data presentation tool, it's also a great data discovery tool. You have to find the story before you can tell it, and I just can't imagine finding many stories with a spreadsheet.

Summary

We've seen in this chapter how to combine multiple Sheets onto Dashboards in Tableau, and how to configure them to create a richly interactive experience for our audience. We've used functions like Dashboard Actions (filters and highlights) and we've seen how to annotate and format to create the kind of experience that we want to create. We've seen how to do this for both exploratory dashboards as well as explanatory dashboards.

In the next chapter, we'll consider some more advanced use cases in Dashboard building, like adding web pages and embedding video, among others. Returning to this chapter's analogy, if a Dashboard is a building, then these features are the high-tech appliances we install into them once they've been built.

CHAPTER 14

Advanced Dashboard Features

"Communication works for those who work at it."

—John Powell

There are many ways to take a basic, functional dashboard to the next level, and we'll consider some of these features in this chapter.

 A word of caution: basic, functional dashboards don't necessarily *need* to be taken to any other level. You shouldn't add "bells and whistles" if the only reason for doing so is because you know how to add them or you want to show that you know how to add them.

Bells (churches) and whistles (soccer coaches) can really be useful, but they just distract if they're present but not useful (toasters). Of course the trick is that one person's "useful" is another person's "distracting." You, as the communicator, get to choose. Have fun with it, but be your own toughest critic and be crystal clear about what you're trying to accomplish, and let that be your guide.

That being said, let's consider how to do the following to provide a new and useful dimension to our dashboards, when appropriate:

- Using the Pages shelf to "animate" dashboards
- Showing multiple tabs
- Adding navigation between tabs via filters

- Adding custom header images
- Embedding web pages like Google Maps and YouTube videos

Once we've decided that one of these features will serve our purposes, we can decide how to best implement it, and make use of the tutorials in this chapter to do so.

Animating Dashboards

If we return to our Internet usage study from Chapter 13, we can make a pretty good case that the real story is how fast the Internet has taken root in many countries over the past two decades. The story, then, has to do with change over time. Our timeline conveys that change over time at a glance, but perhaps there would be some value in allowing our audience to watch the growth unfold.

What value could there be in animating data? Well, we're certainly wired to be very attentive to objects in motion, and we tend to have a much more visceral or emotional reaction to events in motion as opposed to static images. I don't mean to say, by the way, that we should *always* make pixels dance around on the screen. But if the emergence of some relationship over time is at the core of our message, we might want to consider actually showing the change take place, as Rosling did in the quintessential example of communicating data from Chapter 1.

We can make use of the Pages shelf in Tableau to bring the Dashboard to life.

First, we'll need to drag the Year Dimension to the Pages shelf on all four of the Sheets on the Dashboard (the map, the bar chart, the timeline, and the selected year label), and remove the blue Year pill from the Filters shelves on each Sheet. Figure 14-1 shows what this change looks like on the map.

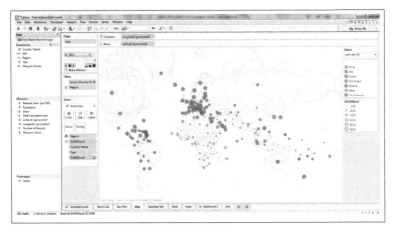

Figure 14-1. Adding the Year Dimension to the Pages shelf

When we add Year to the Pages shelf in the Trend Line Sheet, the lines change to columns of disconnected dots, so we need to change the Marks from Line (or Automatic) to Circles, and then show historical marks with trails as shown in Figure 14-2.

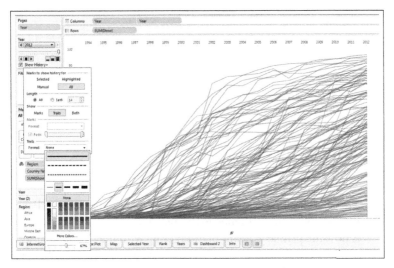

Figure 14-2. Updating the Trend Line Sheet to add Year to Pages and add historical data with trails

Next, we can add the Pages Playback Controls to the Dashboard by removing one of the Sheets (I removed the Map) and then bringing it back into the Dashboard by dragging it into place from the left panel. Along with it comes the Pages Playback Controls, and we can make sure the controls are set to "Synchronized" by clicking in the down arrow in the upper-right corner of the *Pages Playback Controls*.

I re-added the Map with the Pages shelf and made a number of design and layout changes, as shown in Figure 14-3.

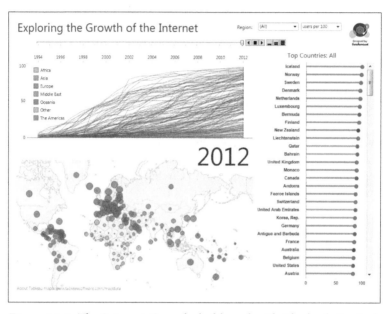

Figure 14-3. The Internet Growth dashboard with Playback Controls added via the Pages shelf

Here's what changed about the Dashboard since we last saw it in Figure 13-31:

- The map is now at the bottom of the Dashboard and the Pages Playback Control is aligned to the Year axis at the top. This control is now the primary means of interacting with the Dashboard, and placing it at the top gives it more prominence and indicates that it applies to all of the Sheets.

- The lead-in paragraph and Info hover icon have been removed, as the purpose of the Dashboard is fairly straightforward now.

- The size of the Selected Year font is much larger, and it resides in the middle of the Dashboard so that it will act as a counter as we play through the years.

- The Rank column in the table no longer appears, as using the Pages shelf would display each country's rank for each year.

Now that the Dashboard has been turned into a tool to show data in motion, we need to decide how we will communicate to our audience. We have a few options at our disposal:

- If we are going to present the data to our audience live, then we can simply turn on Presentation Mode by pressing *F7*, clicking on the *Presentation Mode* icon in the top toolbar, or clicking *Window → Presentation Mode*. We will need to determine our talking points, and how much time we will need to say what we'd like to say. We can set the Playback to *Slow, Normal,* or *Fast*: ▬▬▬.

- If we would like to send the Dashboard via email, then recipients can open the Workbook using Tableau Desktop or Tableau Reader and make use of the Playback Controls on their own.

- If we want to broadcast this message over the Internet, then saving to Tableau Public won't give readers the ability to use the Playback Controls. Instead, the control panel will turn into a simple Year slider that takes up the entire space of the Playback Control, as shown in Figure 14-4.

  The alternative is to create a video of the animation using screen capture software like Camtasia and then embed the video in a website. I did so, and uploaded the videos to YouTube:

  — 1:01 video of Internet users per 100 (*http://bit.ly/growth-internet*)

  — 1:01 video of Total Est. Internet Users (*http://bit.ly/growth-total-internet*)

Showing how the changes have played out over time in this way can have a dramatic impact if designed, built, and delivered well. The potential is high, and the effort required to achieve that potential is also fairly high.

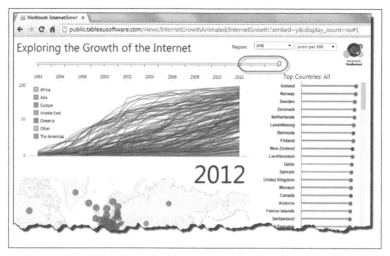

Figure 14-4. How the Playback Control bar functions when you save to Tableau Public

Showing Multiple Tabs

The two explanatory dashboards of Internet usage from Chapter 13—the one showing the leadership of the Nordics (Figure 13-33) and the other showing the emergence of China (Figure 13-34)—exist as two totally different Workbooks. If we want to give our audience the ability to switch between these two Workbooks without leaving a single environment, we can put them into one Workbook and use the *Show Sheets as Tabs* function in Tableau when saving to Tableau Server or Tableau Public.

To start, we need to add both Dashboards to a single Workbook. Luckily, versions of Tableau Desktop starting at 8.2 allow us to copy and paste Sheets and Dashboards from one Workbook to another, along with all of the associated Sheets and underlying data. I went ahead and copied the version showing the expansion of China to the version showing the leadership of the Nordics. The two Workbooks had identically named Sheets, so Tableau appended a (2) to all of the Sheets from the Workbook we brought over, as shown highlighted in yellow in Figure 14-5.

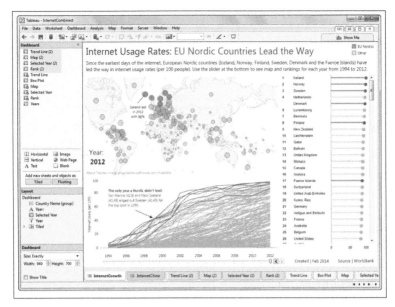

Figure 14-5. Copying and pasting from one Workbook to another

We can now publish this combined Workbook and share it with our audience such that anyone interacting with the Workbook can navigate from one Dashboard to another using tabs above the Dashboards.

1. First, though, we need to decide which Dashboards and Sheets should be included as tabs for users to interact with. All other Sheets and Dashboards will need to be hidden (or deleted). Right-click on the tabs that you don't want to let users access directly (in this case all of the individual Sheets) and select *Hide*.

2. It would also be helpful to give the Dashboards descriptive tab names that help users understand what they'll get by clicking on the tab. In this case, I changed the first Dashboard title from `InternetGrowth` to `1. Nordics: most users per 100` and the second from `InternetChina` to `2. China: most total users`.

3. Now, we can publish the Workbook and share it with our audience. To do this, click *Server → Publish Workbook* (or *Server → Tableau Public* for data we want to share on the Web) and check the *Show Sheets as Tabs* box, as shown in Figure 14-6.

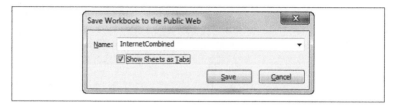

Figure 14-6. Publishing Workbooks showing Sheets as Tabs

The final version of the Workbook with the Tabs at the top is shown in Figure 14-7.

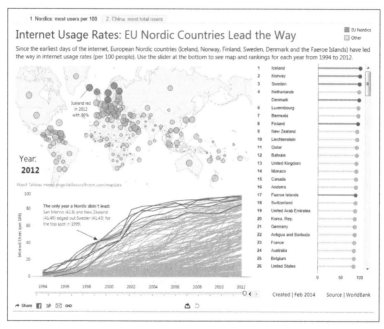

Figure 14-7. Two explanatory dashboards with top navigation Tabs

The fact of the matter is, though, that these tabs can be hard to notice. Next, let's look at a way to add additional navigational affordances to the Dashboards so that we can be sure our audience will notice that there's more to the Dashboard than first meets the eye.

Adding Navigation with Filters

We can effectively use Tableau as a presentation tool to provide a guided experience through a specific data set by adding Sheets that act as navigation aids. We'll start by adding a new Sheet and creating two "dummy" calculated fields, called Left and Right, as shown in Figure 14-8.

These fields do nothing more than add two new Dimensions that we can use to create functional arrows. To create the actual arrows, we'll do the following (starting with the Left arrow):

1. Add a new Sheet and change the Marks type from *Automatic* to *Shape.*

2. Drag the Left Dimension to the Shape card.

3. Edit the shape by clicking into the legend and choosing a left arrow icon (from the *Arrows* shape palette, or from another you add to your My Tableau Repository Shapes folder).

4. Format the icon by increasing its size, eliminating Row and Column borders, and adding a Tooltip that says Go to Previous Slide. I also dragged the Left Dimension to Color and changed it to gray.

5. Rename the Sheet tab Left and repeat steps 1–5 similarly with another new Sheet to create a right arrow. The finished gray Left arrow Sheet is shown in Figure 14-9.

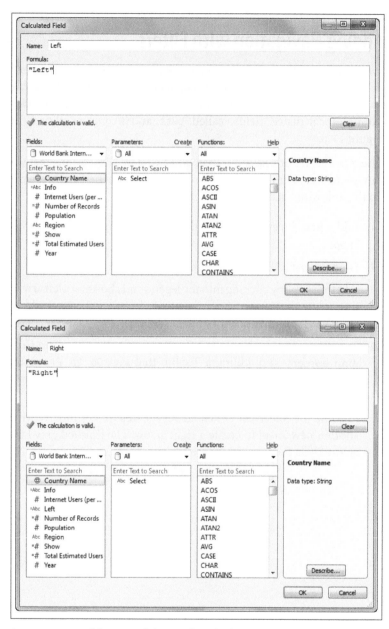

Figure 14-8. Adding two "dummy" Calculated Fields for arrows

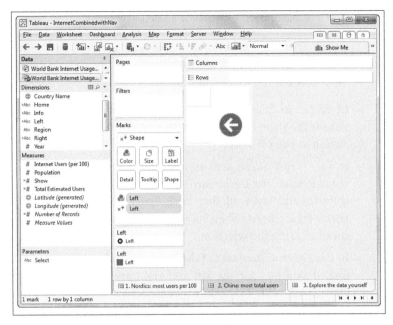

Figure 14-9. The completed Left arrow Sheet

It's possible to create more types of navigation icons, such as a Home icon, using this same method. It's also possible to create a Table of Contents Dashboard with shapes that take the user to various places in the Workbook. It all depends on what we want the Dashboard user to be able to do, and how that action can best be represented.

Now that we have these Left and Right icons created, we'll need to add them to each of the Dashboards in the Workbook. Note that I used the same copy-and-paste method to bring the exploratory Dashboard we created in the previous chapter into the Workbook, and I named that tab 3. Explore the data yourself.

To add the icons and make them function the way we want them to, we'll do the following for each of the three Dashboards:

1. Drag the Left and/or Right arrow Sheets onto the Dashboard and place them wherever we want them.

   - The first Dashboard only needs a Right arrow (*Go to Next Slide* Filter).

   - The middle Dashboard needs both a Left (Previous) and a Right (Next) arrow Sheet.

- The last Dashboard only needs a Left (Previous) arrow Sheet.

2. For each arrow Sheet on each Dashboard, create a new Filter Dashboard Action by clicking *Dashboard → Actions → Add Action → Filter* that has the following properties:

- In the *Source Sheets* area at the top of the dialog box, check the box for the Sheet (Left or Right) that you're configuring. Set the Action to run on Select.

- In the *Target Sheets* area in the middle, use the drop-down menu to select the Dashboard you want the arrow Sheet to navigate to, and leave all the check boxes blank in the *Target Sheets* area. Choose *Show all values* in the section to the right about clearing the selection.

- In the *Target Filters* area at the bottom, choose *All Fields*. The final dialog box for the left and right arrow on the middle Dashboard (Slide #2) is shown in Figure 14-10.

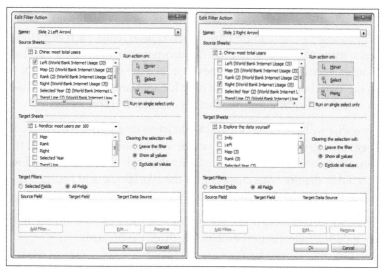

Figure 14-10. Adding Dashboard Filters as navigation controls

Go ahead and perform a similar set of steps for each of the three Dashboards. Doing so results in a Workbook with additional navigation controls, shown in Figure 14-11.

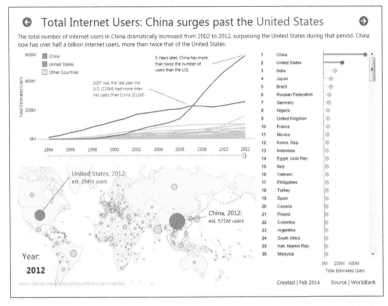

Figure 14-11. The middle Dashboard with navigation arrows added

We can now publish the Dashboard and show sheets as tabs, making sure to hide all of the Sheets with which we don't want the users to directly interact.

This was a relatively simple case of adding a few arrows, but this technique can be used to create more elaborate interconnected presentations, such as the one shown in Figure 14-12, which I presented at the first Tapestry Conference in Nashville in 2013.

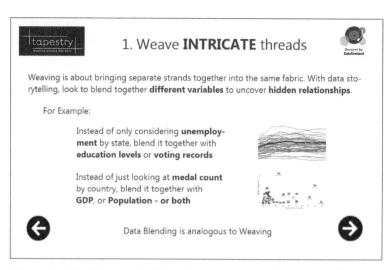

Figure 14-12. The second slide of a presentation built in Tableau using Sheets as navigation aids

Adding Custom Header Images

Adding custom graphics to a Tableau dashboard can help us achieve our overall objective, especially when our audience is less "captive," such as in the blogging and journalism scenarios. When done well, graphics can increase the visual appeal and aesthetic of the final product. We respond emotionally to pictures, and we appreciate thoughtful and tasteful design. From a functional perspective, adding graphics can serve to introduce the subject or even add to an emotional effect we are attempting to create.

Custom graphics can help or hinder our cause, depending on how they're implemented. Before considering how to add custom graphics, it's important to lay down a few rules of thumb to help us avoid making a mess of the endeavor:

1. Exercise restraint. Don't overdo it, and never add cheesy clip art.
2. Never, ever occlude the data. Blocking marks on a Dashboard is a big no-no.
3. Don't steal the spotlight from the data. The data should still take center stage and be the focal point of the dashboard.

With those rules of thumb in mind, let's consider two similar dashboards shown in Figure 14-13 that show CCTV (closed-circuit television) camera locations as provided by the city of Glasgow's Open Data site (*http://data.glasgow.gov.uk/*).

Figure 14-13. A Dashboard with and without a custom header image

The basic text box header on the left does the job, but it certainly doesn't draw in any readers. In contrast, let's consider the Dashboard with the custom header image on the right:

- The custom header image on the right is created using a custom "spy" font to convey the sense of surveillance, and it includes an image of a security camera to add additional context.

- For readers who are unfamiliar with the acronym "CCTV," the camera image provides useful information about the topic of the Dashboard at a glance.

- The camera doesn't occlude (cover or block) any data points, and it actually points directly at the data, such that the eye bounces from the camera to the map itself.

Is the custom header image useless, wasteful, and distracting? Not at all, and on the contrary it both increases the visual appeal and augments the message of the Dashboard. It's a *communication aid*.

This type of custom header image can be created with any vector graphics editor. I like to use software programs like Inkscape and GIMP 2, which are free and open source. Other programs include Adobe Photoshop or Illustrator, and even PowerPoint can be used to create simple graphics like this.

It's helpful to learn how to make image backgrounds transparent, as Tableau now supports transparency for Dashboard image objects, and a simple Google search on the topic will yield helpful tutorials.

The image itself is shown in Figure 14-14. Once it's created using your editor of choice, you can easily add it to your dashboard by dragging an Image object onto your Dashboard and opening the file. You can give it a URL as we did in Chapter 13.

Figure 14-14. The custom header image file

Next, we'll consider how to embed a dynamic Google Maps window, the part of the Dashboard in Figure 14-11 that is shown in the bottom half.

Adding Google Maps to Dashboards

In general, it's possible to embed a live website in a Dashboard by dragging the Web Page Dashboard object onto the canvas. We can have the web page itself be either static or dynamic. If we simply enter a URL in the dialog box that appears when dropping the Web Page object on the Dashboard, then that website will always appear, as shown in Figures 14-15 and 14-16.

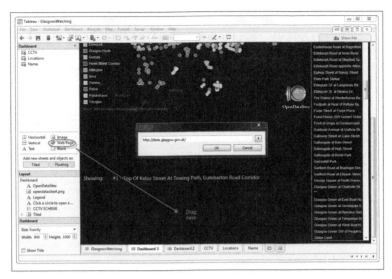

Figure 14-15. Adding a static Web Page object to a Dashboard

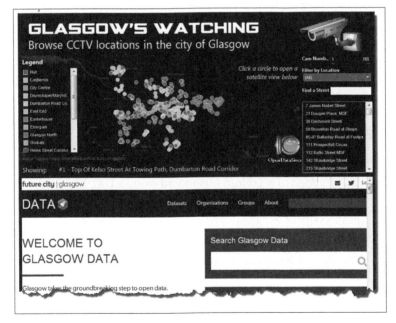

Figure 14-16. The resulting Dashboard, with the Web Page showing in the view

We can take it a step further and make the Web Page object pull up a Google Maps satellite view of each of the 399 CCTV locations, based on which circle is selected in the Map at the top. To do this, we'll make use of the fact that the data we are using includes Latitude and Longitude fields, as shown in Figure 14-17.

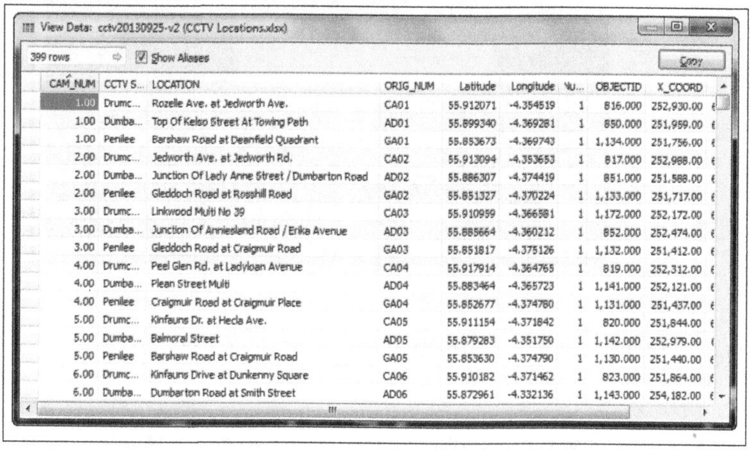
View Data: cctv20130925-v2 (CCTV Locations.xlsx)

399 rows | Show Aliases | Copy

CAM_NUM	CCTV S...	LOCATION	ORIG_NUM	Latitude	Longitude	Nu...	OBJECTID	X_COORD
1.00	Drumc...	Rozelle Ave. at Jedworth Ave.	CA01	55.912071	-4.354519	1	816.000	252,930.00
1.00	Dumba...	Top Of Kelso Street At Towing Path	AD01	55.899340	-4.369281	1	850.000	251,959.00
1.00	Penilee	Barshaw Road at Deanfield Quadrant	GA01	55.853673	-4.369743	1	1,134.000	251,756.00
2.00	Drumc...	Jedworth Ave. at Jedworth Rd.	CA02	55.913094	-4.353653	1	817.000	252,988.00
2.00	Dumba...	Junction Of Lady Anne Street / Dumbarton Road	AD02	55.886307	-4.374419	1	851.000	251,588.00
2.00	Penilee	Gleddoch Road at Rosshill Road	GA02	55.851327	-4.370224	1	1,133.000	251,717.00
3.00	Drumc...	Linkwood Multi No 39	CA03	55.910959	-4.366581	1	1,172.000	252,172.00
3.00	Dumba...	Junction Of Anniesland Road / Erika Avenue	AD03	55.885664	-4.360212	1	852.000	252,474.00
3.00	Penilee	Gleddoch Road at Craigmuir Road	GA03	55.851817	-4.375126	1	1,132.000	251,412.00
4.00	Drumc...	Peel Glen Rd. at Ladyloan Avenue	CA04	55.917914	-4.364765	1	819.000	252,312.00
4.00	Dumba...	Plean Street Multi	AD04	55.883464	-4.365723	1	1,141.000	252,121.00
4.00	Penilee	Craigmuir Road at Craigmuir Place	GA04	55.852677	-4.374780	1	1,131.000	251,437.00
5.00	Drumc...	Kinfauns Dr. at Hecla Ave.	CA05	55.911154	-4.371842	1	820.000	251,844.00
5.00	Dumba...	Balmoral Street	AD05	55.879283	-4.351750	1	1,142.000	252,979.00
5.00	Penilee	Barshaw Road at Craigmuir Road	GA05	55.853630	-4.374790	1	1,130.000	251,440.00
6.00	Drumc...	Kinfauns Drive at Dunkenny Square	CA06	55.910182	-4.371462	1	823.000	251,864.00
6.00	Dumba...	Dumbarton Road at Smith Street	AD06	55.872961	-4.332136	1	1,143.000	254,182.00

Figure 14-17. The underlying data for the Glasgow CCTV Dashboard

The first group of three steps shows you how to create a URL for each bridge, and the second group of five steps shows you how to add a box to your dashboard to pull up the bridges.

Create the URLs

1. A particular latitude and longitude (say, 55.85608 and –4.25732) can be added to a Tableau Dashboard using a URL like this:

   https://maps.google.com/maps?q=55.85608,-4.25732&z=17&t=h&output=svembed

2. Breaking down the elements of the URL, we can see that after the latitude and longitude, there are four distinct parameters in the URL:

   q=55.85608,-4.25732

   These are our coordinates for a single CCTV location. Note that if we have an address field instead of Lat/Long, we can use a street address after "q=" as well.

&z=17

This specifies the zoom level. Higher numbers zoom in, lower numbers zoom out.

&t=h

This specifies the type of map (t=m is a map, t=h is a satellite view).

&output=embed

This is a key parameter that makes sure the website we embed in our Dashboard doesn't include the entire site, just the map itself.

3. We could then generalize the URL to:

   https://maps.google.com/maps?q=<Latitude>,<Longitude>&z=17&t=h&output=svembed

   Notice that the actual numbers for Latitude and Longitude have been replaced with field names <Latitude> and <Longitude>.

Alternately, we could embed Google Static Maps using the Static Maps API, which is documented here (*http://bit.ly/staticmapsAPI*). In that case, the generic URL would be similar to:

https://maps.googleapis.com/maps/api/staticmap?center=<Latitude>, +<Longitude>&zoom=17&size=460x340&maptype=satellite&markers=color:blue%7C<Latitude>,<Longitude>

Adding Dynamic Google Maps Satellite Images to Our Dashboard

The next group of steps shows how to edit the Web Page object such that when a user clicks on a particular circle in the top map, the embedded satellite image changes to show the location selected:

1. First, in the Dashboard tab, drag a new Web Page object (or edit the one we added in Figure 14-14) onto the Dashboard from the left-center panel (just leave the *Edit URL* dialog box blank and click *OK* for now).

2. From the *Dashboard* file menu, click *Actions*, then click the *Add Action* button and choose *URL....*

3. In the *Add URL Action* dialog box, select the Sheet or Sheets that you want to use as the source for the action, and choose which event you'd like to trigger navigation to the new image (*Hover,*

Select, or *Menu*). In this case, I've selected CCTV and Locations as my Source Sheets and Select as my trigger event, but you could trigger the action from a table or other type of sheet.

4. Finally, copy and paste the generalized URL to the *URL* field of the dialog box, making sure to include the `<Latitude>` and `<Longitude>` fields, as shown in Figure 14-18.

5. That's it! Test it out by clicking on the map circles and see the satellite image change accordingly.

Figure 14-18. The Edit URL Action dialog box for adding Google Maps

We now have a Dashboard that lets users get a satellite view of each of the CCTV locations in Glasgow, and we didn't have to upload 399 images, nor did we have to key in all 399 URLs. We allowed Tableau to generate each individual website address by including field names in the Web Page object URL.

For another example of this same technique, see Figure 14-19, which shows 2,489 bridges in the state of Washington and allows users to click on each one to see a satellite image of the bridge.

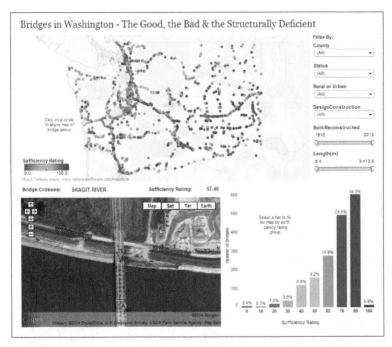

Figure 14-19. Another example of a Dashboard with embedded and dynamic Google Maps

We can do something very similar with YouTube videos, although the complete URL will need to be included in the data set itself.

Adding YouTube Videos to Dashboards

My son Aaron is a Lego pro. He also likes movies and his iPod. Put those three things together and you get stop-motion Lego movies made with an iPod! He started uploading his videos recently to his new YouTube channel, so I thought I'd make a fun little Dashboard for him to play with. The finished version is shown in Figure 14-20. Let's consider how it was made.

Figure 14-20. Aaron's LegoTube: a Dashboard with embedded You-Tube videos

We'll need to start by building a spreadsheet of all of the videos we want to add to our Dashboard (in this case, Aaron has created seven videos, so we'll need a spreadsheet with a row for each of the seven):

1. In YouTube, click *Share*, then *Embed*, and then copy the embed code. We need only the URL between quotes. It should be in the form of *http://www.youtube.com/embed/....* See Figure 14-21.

2. Next, let's create a spreadsheet with the information we want to include about each video across the columns (including the embed link URL), as shown in Figure 14-22.

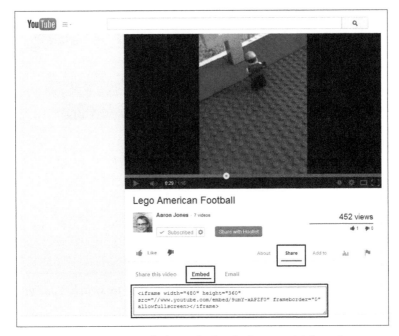

Figure 14-21. How to grab the embed code for a YouTube video

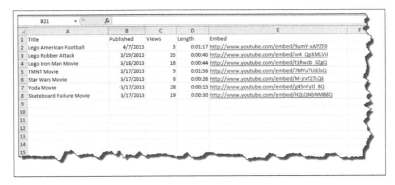

Figure 14-22. A simple spreadsheet containing information about each video

3. In Tableau, we can connect to this spreadsheet, make the chart we want to use to change the video link (in this case, I made a simple bar chart showing the views of each video), making sure we drag the *Embed* dimension field into Detail, as shown in Figure 14-23.

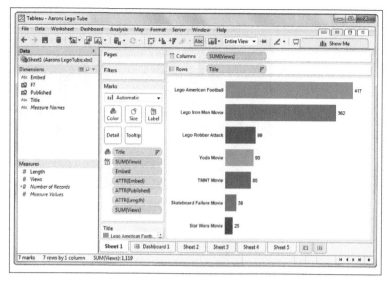

Figure 14-23. The bar chart that will be used to switch YouTube videos

4. Next, we can make a new dashboard, add the bar chart, and drag a Web Page object where we would like to place it (either *Tiled* or *Floating*, whichever works best). When the *Edit URL* dialog box pops up, just leave it blank and click *OK* for now, as shown in Figure 14-24.

5. Lastly, we'll add a Dashboard Action by selecting *Dashboard → Actions → Add Action → URL*, and fill out the resulting dialog box, as shown in Figure 14-25.

Click one of the bars, and you should see the video load in the Web Page object box.

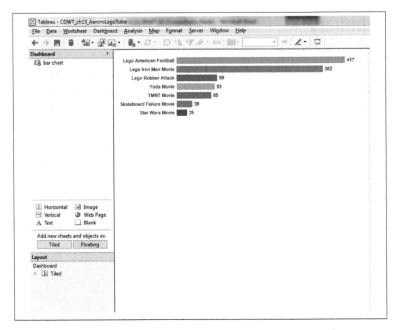

Figure 14-24. Adding the Web Page object to the Dashboard

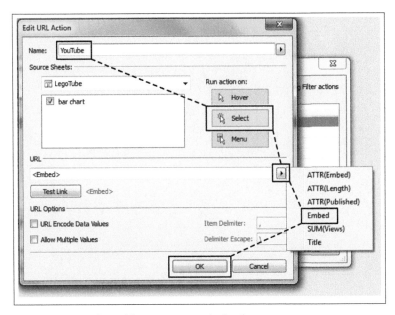

Figure 14-25. The Add URL Action dialog box

Summary

Any one of these advanced Dashboard elements can make a big difference, and it's up to you to know when to use them, and when to leave them out. Stay focused on your objective, respect and honor the data above all else, and show good design sense. Ask yourself what you *should* do, not what you *could* do.

These features can make it fun to communicate data, and they can engage and delight your audience. They can also mislead and distract, so be sure to test them out on some willing guinea pigs and gauge the impact.

Resources

All of the examples in this book can be accessed as an interactive (Tableau Public), a Tableau workbook (.twbx that requires Tableau 8.1 or later to open), and the raw data file (.xlsx) at *http://dataremixed.com/books/cdwt*.

Training

- Tableau Software training resources (*http://www.tableausoftware.com/support/training*)
- Tableau Public training resources (*http://www.tableausoftware.com/public/training*)

Examples

- Tableau Public Viz of the Day (*http://www.tableausoftware.com/public/community/viz-of-the-day*)
- Tableau Software Visual Gallery (*http://www.tableausoftware.com/learn/gallery*)

Blogs

- DataRemixed, the author's blog (*http://dataremixed.com*)
- Tableau Software blog (*http://www.tableausoftware.com/about/blog*)
- Tableau Public blog (*http://www.tableausoftware.com/public/blog*)
- Tableau Data Blog Finder (*http://www.tableausoftware.com/public/tableau-data-blogs*)
- Andy Kriebel's "Cool Data Viz Blogs" page (*http://vizwiz.blogspot.com/p/cool-data-viz-blogs.html*)
- Andy Kirk's Visualising Data blog (*http://www.visualisingdata.com*)

Other Resources

- Tableau Knowledge Base (*http://kb.tableausoftware.com*)
- Tableau Community Forums (*http://community.tableausoftware.com/community/forums*)
- Ramon Martinez's "Data and Visualization sites" page (*http://healthintelligence.drupalgardens.com/content/resources/data-and-visualization-sites*)
- Jonathan Drummey's Tableau wiki (*http://drawingwithnumbers.artisart.org/wiki/tableau*)

Index

We'd like to hear your suggestions for improving our indexes. Send email to index@oreilly.com.

basketball player statistics, 230
Baumgartner, Felix, 233
Bell Laboratories model, 3
bell-shaped curve (see normal distribution)
Berra, Yogi, 69
Bing Maps, 181
binomial probability distribution, 119
binomial proportion confidence intervals, 117
Bloomberg, Michael, 51
borders
    adding to circle maps, 189
    formatting for icon Sheet, 256
Bowman, Scotty, 101
box-and-whisker plots
    dual-axis, 94–95
    non-normal distribution and, 98
    normal distribution and, 90–95, 102
    visualizing variation with, 102, 105
Brinton, Willard Cope, 1, 9
bullet graphs
    about, 82–84
    adding reference lines, 84–85

C

Calculated Field dialog box
    adding navigation with filters, 285
    earthquakes example, 111
    garbage collection example, 53, 60
    hockey players example, 138
    Internet usage example, 191, 196, 241, 243
    population density example, 27
    presidential election example, 218
    soccer points scored example, 173, 175–178
calculated fields
    about, 26
    adding line coloring and thickness, 175–178
    adding navigation with filters, 285
    adding rank, 60–63
    determining control limits, 112
    generating error bars, 118
    hockey players example, 138

Internet usage example, 191, 196, 241, 243
    mapping to parameters, 172
    population density example, 185
    presidential election example, 218
    ratios and, 52
causation, correlation and, 125, 157, 217
CCTV (closed-circuit television), 291
central limit theorem, 117
channel for communicating data, 11–13
chess club example, 115–123
Child, Julia, 225
chloropleths (see filled maps)
circle maps
    about, 183–185
    adding second encoding, 185
    dual-encoded, 199–201
    filtering data, 188–189
    Internet usage example, 186–190, 199–201
    multiple markings, 186–190
    population density example, 183–186
circle views
    quantitative comparisons in, 35
    resolving overlapping circles, 39
closed-circuit television (CCTV), 291
coefficient of determination, 141, 145
color palette
    filled maps, 192–196
    football teams example, 207
Color shelf, 27, 39
column graphs, 11, 27
Columns shelf
    about, 19
    creating visualizations, 27
    how many comparison, 45
    how much comparison, 36, 39
    recycling example, 56
The Commercial and Political Atlas (Playfair), 150
communicating data, 31
    (see also comparisons; dashboards)
    about, 31
    Bell Laboratories model, 3

Format panel, 40

G

Gantt chart type
  baseball statistics example, 79–81
  presidential milestones example, 166–170
GapMinder scatterplot, 12
garbage collection example
  how much comparison, 33–42
  ratios and, 52–63
Gaussian distribution (see normal distribution)
generated fields, 23, 43–46, 47
global measure of dispersion, 107
goal of communicating data, 6–7
Google Maps, 181, 292–297
grid lines, adding, 40
Group control, 21

H

heat maps, 35
highlight actions, 258, 267–269
highlight tables
  quantitative comparisons in, 35
  ratios and, 57–58
hiking trail example, 215
histograms
  how many comparison, 46–50
  non-normal distribution and, 96, 103
  normal distribution and, 89, 103
  visualizing variation with, 103, 105
hockey players example
  in scatterplots, 126–137, 142–148
  in stacked bar charts, 137–140
horizontal bar charts
  fine-tuning the default, 36
  quantitative comparisons in, 35
  rates example, 65
  ratio example, 59, 61–63
  sorting, 37–39, 54
  suggesting as option, 34
Hover for More Info icons, 254–258
how many comparison
  about, 32, 42
  counting dimensions, 43–46

data at aggregate level, 43
data at incident level, 43
histograms for, 46–50
how much comparison
  about, 32–33
  comparing comparisons, 35–36
  dot charts, 39–42
  example of, 33
  fine-tuning the default, 36
  garbage collection example, 33–42
  sorting, 37–39
hurricane data example, 211–214
hyperlinks, adding to dashboards, 254

I

IBTrACS dataset, 211
images
  background, 136–137
  custom header, 290–292
impact (RUI), 13
independent variables, 46, 141
INDEX formula, 60
infographics, 233
information source (in communication systems), 3
Internet usage example
  circle maps, 186–190, 199–201
  dashboards, 240–276
  dual-encoded maps, 196–201
  filled maps, 190–196, 197–199
interquartile range, 94, 101

J

Jennings, Ken, 181

K

Key Process Indicators (KPIs), 227, 235
Kirk, Andy, 171
Korzybski, Alfred, 203
KPIs (Key Process Indicators), 227, 235

L

Label shelf, 56

non-normal distributions, 98
rates, 65
recognizing patterns in, 127
selecting suitable, 8–9, 34
Tableau user interface and, 25, 27–28
using the right data, 7
for variation, 101–105
VizQL (visual query language), 15, 17
Voltaire, 149

W

waterfall charts, 79–81

Weaver, Warren, 3, 7
Web Mercator projection, 181
Web Page objects, 292–297, 300
Western Electric Company, 106
word clouds, 35
workbooks
    adding data sources to, 64
    Show Sheets as Tabs function, 282
World Bank Indicators, 19, 187, 191

Y

YEAR formula, 108, 163
YouTube videos, 297–300

About the Author

Ben Jones is an award-winning Tableau Public author, and is also the Tableau Public product marketing manager at Tableau Software in Seattle, WA. With over 12 years of experience as an engineer, Lean Six Sigma Master Black Belt, and Business Analytics manager for a Fortune 500 company, Ben has worked on data-driven projects for every department, from facilities to finance.

Colophon

The animal on the cover of *Communicating Data with Tableau* is the turquoise parrot (*Neophema pulchella*), more specifically a male of the species, which are more brightly colored than the females. While both sexes have yellow bellies and green plumage on their back, males also have a bright blue head and red patches on their wings.

These birds are native to Australia and belong to a class of parrots called "grass parrots." Their preferred habitat is grassland and open woodland, where they nest in and forage near gum trees. The turquoise parrot primarily looks for food on the ground—while seeds make up most of its diet, it also eats leaves, flowers, nectar, insects, and fruit. They are small parrots, averaging around 8 inches long and weighing around 1.4 ounces.

Turquoise parrots flock and forage together in family groups of 30–50 in the winter, but only 6–8 in warmer months. As the breeding season nears in spring/summer, the monogamous pairs separate from the rest of the flock to mate and nest. Each clutch contains 2–5 eggs. Once they hatch, the female feeds the young for a few days before her mate begins helping.

The cover image is from the *Braukhaus Lexicon*. The cover fonts are URW Typewriter and Guardian Sans. The text font is Adobe Minion Pro; the heading font is Adobe Myriad Condensed; and the code font is Dalton Maag's Ubuntu Mono.

Get even more for your money.

Join the O'Reilly Community, and register the O'Reilly books you own. It's free, and you'll get:

- $4.99 ebook upgrade offer
- 40% upgrade offer on O'Reilly print books
- Membership discounts on books and events
- Free lifetime updates to ebooks and videos
- Multiple ebook formats, DRM FREE
- Participation in the O'Reilly community
- Newsletters
- Account management
- 100% Satisfaction Guarantee

Signing up is easy:

1. Go to: oreilly.com/go/register
2. Create an O'Reilly login.
3. Provide your address.
4. Register your books.

Note: English-language books only

To order books online:
oreilly.com/store

For questions about products or an order:
orders@oreilly.com

To sign up to get topic-specific email announcements and/or news about upcoming books, conferences, special offers, and new technologies:
elists@oreilly.com

For technical questions about book content:
booktech@oreilly.com

To submit new book proposals to our editors:
proposals@oreilly.com

O'Reilly books are available in multiple DRM-free ebook formats. For more information:
oreilly.com/ebooks

O'REILLY®

CPSIA information can be obtained at www.ICGtesting.com
Printed in the USA
BVOW11s0323170714

359457BV00002B/4/P